PATRICK CONERY

Also By Patrick Conery

SALVATION Lost
How Todays View of Faith has
Threatened your Destin

There's Something About Mary
Uncovering the Mary who Walked
Amongst the Apostles

The Chair of Peter
The Chair from Abaraham to Today

PATRICK CONERY

THE CHURCH THAT EMERGED

The Hunt for the Church that grew out of a Judean Band of Twelve

By Patrick Conery

BOTH BARRELS MEDIA

P.O. BOX 2174
Palm City, Florida 34991
www.bothbarrelsmedia.com

"I sought to hear the voice of God And climbed the topmost steeple, But God declared: "Go down again… I dwell among the people."

John Henry Cardinal Newman

To order wholesale quantities of the paperback version of
The Church That Emerged, send us an e-mail inquiry with
'BOOK ORDERS' in the subject line:

bookorders@bothbarrelsmedia.com

First Printing, 2019
Includes Bibliographical References e-book
ISBN 978-1-7343875-1-3
1. Religion. 2. Biblical Commentary. 3. Book Title

First Printing, 2019
Includes Bibliographical References and Index Paperback
ISBN: 978-1-7343875-0-6
1. Religion. 2. Biblical Commentary. 3. Book Title

Published by:
Both Barrels Media
P. O. Box 2174
Palm City, Florida 34991

www.bothbarrelsmedia.com

www.TheChurchThatEmerged.com

Printed in the United States of America
Acid-free paper for permanence and durability
Cover Design By: Patrick Conery

For those whose heart bleed…
Whose soul yearns…
Who forever seek…
The…One…
True…Church

The Church That Emerged Out Of
Judea

One. Holy. Catholic. & Apostolic Church

Table of Contents

Introduction 1

Chapter 1: The Dueling of Banjos 5

    Sheila, Sheila..9

    Bellah's Civil Religion.. 12

    Subsidiarity, Solidarity, and Social Justice.................... 12

    The Holy Commonwealth.. 14

    Bringing it together... 17

Chapter 2: Recapturing God's Plan 20

    The …isms 21

        Relativism... 22

        Skepticism... 23

        Pluralism... 24

        Modernism.. 25

        Deconstructionism 26

    Zeal... 27

    God's Four-Step Plan of Redemption 28

    Bringing It Together.. 32

Chapter 3: Judges: I'll do it my way! 35

    The Journey... 35

    The Pilgrimage Festivals 37

        Passover.. 37

        Pentecost.. 37

        Feast of Tabernacles 38

    From Joshua to Judges: The dichotomy 38

    Joshua: The Good Commonwealth.................................. 40

        Affirming Joshua's Authority 40

        The Cairn, the Rock, and the Stone Memorials........... 41

        The Fall of Jericho 42

Shiloh 43

Dealing with Secession 44

Joshua's Farewell 45

Judges: The Regime fragments 46

Gideon 47

Bringing it together 48

Chapter 4: Eved Adonai- Servant of the Lord 50

The Different Ages 51

Abraham.. 52

Eliezer.. 53

Joseph 54

Egypt... 55

Joseph's assent.. 57

Moses 59

Joshua 62

Bringing it together 62

Chapter 5: The Three Ketarim (Crowns) 65

Melchizedek.. 65

The Three-fold offices under Moses............... 66

Three Ketarim (Crowns) 67

Ordination Ceremony 71

The Second Temple Period............................ 72

At First Glance 72

Christianity.. 73

Post-Reformation.. 74

The Offices of Christ 75

Christ the King... 75

Christ the Prophet....................................... 76

Christ Our High Priest 77

Bringing it together..................................... 77

Chapter 6: Samuel: The Prophet led Regime 80

They were in charge! 82

Eli's fall, Samuel's rise 83

They demand an earthly king 86

Crossroads 87

Monarchy movement grows 87

Dealing with Saul 89

Bringing it together 91

Chapter 7: The Earthly Kingdom 94

David's Rise 97

David's Reign 99

David's Fall 100

Solomon follows that all too familiar Path 102

Chief (High) Servant in the House of David 103

Obadiah 105

Chief Servant Verses 105

Bringing it together 106

Chapter 8: Gebirah: Queen Mother of the Kingdom 109

The Beginning: The New Eve 109

Israel's Matriarch's 111

Sarah 111

Rebekah 112

Rachel 112

Leah 113

Jochebed 113

Ruth 114

Esther: A Jewish Queen Mother among the pagans? 115

Gebirah: Queen mother 116

All the king's Mothers 119

The Queen Mothers of Israel (table) 119

Wedding at Cana 122

The Ark of the New Covenant 122

Ark Comparison (table) 124

Bringing it together.. 126

Chapter 9: Passover: The Beginning of Life 128

The Passover Seder.. 129

Haggadah... 130

The Four Cups 131

The Three Pilgrimages 135

Our Journey Revealed 138

The Last Supper 139

Our Redemption Plan 139

Salvation History Repeats 140

Tabernacles 141

Old Tabernacle Sacrifices 141

Our Tabernacle.. 142

Chapter 10: The Mass: Enter into the Holy of Holies 144

Hebrews: Do We Neglect So Great A Salvation? 145

The Sole Mediator 147

A Nation or Church of Priests: 148

The Ordained (ministerial) Priesthood 149

The Bishop:... 150

Christ, Our High Priest: 150

The Bread of Life.. 150

Sacramentarian-ism.. 154

The Mass 156

What's Happening during Mass 156

Chapter 11: In Christ: Our God reigns...again 160

Musical Thrones... 161

Kingship of God 162

Christ's office of Chief Servant 164

The Seventy... 168

Call no man Father 168

House of Israel.. 169

The Transfiguration 172

The Ascension.. 173

Paul.. 174

Bringing it Together 175

Chapter 12: The Church that Emerged..................................... 177

#1) This is Tabernacles' Time! 178

#2)This is God's Time 179

#3) The Throne is in Heaven 179

#4) The Church would be One 180

#5) There is a Chief Servant... 180

#6) There is a Council of Seventy................................. 181

#7) There is a Queen Mother 182

#7) There is an Altar... 182

#8) There are Bishops and Priests 183

#9) Priests need something to Sacrifice 184

#10) Unified Hymns of praise and supplication. 185

The Church Emerged.. 186

Didache on the Bread of Life... 187

The Early Church Fathers... 187

References 191

Chapter 1... 191

Chapter 2... 192

Chapter 3... 192

Chapter 4... 193

Chapter 5... 193

Chapter 6... 194

Chapter 7... 196

Chapter 8... 196

Chapter 9... 197

Chapter 10 197

Chapter 11 198
Chapter 12 198
Index 200

PATRICK CONERY

Introduction

" What exactly does "Full Gospel" mean?" I knew his answer, but I wanted to hear his response. "It means we follow the whole bible! We believe in the whole Gospel" He proudly replied. I guess he honestly believed that they were the only ones who did.

It begged the question, "Are the rest deceived by demons? Or Satan?" I guess most people come to this unconscious but predominate assumption...i.e. belief...the ties that bind.

The "Full Gospel" congregation was on the menu in this small town. It was one of many choices. People had the choice of about 30 different Christian bodies to "fellowship" with. Everyone is free to "church" shop on Sundays until they find one of their liking or one that preaches according to their beliefs. It is universally believed that each person, each pastor, and each body is led by the spirit, yet they don't agree. People ignore that fact but find unity in their distaste

1

for the Catholics down the street. This across the board disunity always disheartened me. This REALLY bothered me.

The church growth movement over the last 40 years, sought to make Jesus relevant to people today; to make Christianity applicable and current. For over a decade, I was involved in the church growth movement. I was a part of an Evangelical start-up church that met in a school auditorium and grew from there.

We attended church leadership conferences at Willow Creek Community Church; one of the first Mega-churches that has grown a worldwide membership. We set up our services to be 'relevant' to 'seekers' who didn't attend church. Every. Single. Aspect…of Sunday was planned to cater to this crowd. We held small groups in our homes to grow intimate relationships to aid discipleship as people grew in Christ.

The idea was to be an Acts Chapter 2 church. It was to model the "day after" Pentecost. But, to me, there was more. I would have long conversations with the pastor about my concerns and my yearnings. He felt his 'calling' was to be the welcoming committee. Then, a 'believer' was free to explore all the varied different traditions. Another pastor friend of mine confirmed this thought…all the different 'flavors' was to give people different options.

I just don't see the Holy Spirit as schizophrenic. That's not the Holy Spirit, that's the author of confusion. It leads us to pride and strife. And, eventually a church of one, ourselves, we are a god of our own making

Our Lord told to us stay unified and hold to the tradition or deposit of faith that was left to us. Every assembly or every TV pastor has a different opinion. And, they warn against investigating other traditions. So, what was/is the answer? We know they're not all right with the old axiom being…" Both, and in this case, all, can't possibly be true".

Many people feel called to rediscover the first church. I know this firsthand. It was then, and still is now, a constant yearning of countless Christians. But what exactly is the first church? What does that look like? I needed to find out. I was hounded by my desire.

I prayed to find the real God and the real first church. Did it still exist? What were my options? I pressed in and set my sails to discover the first church. I studied the Church fathers diligently. Hoping to throw my biases to the wind, I constantly asked God to lead me to the truth…wherever that led. I wanted to "study to show myself approved" …to be a Berean if you will.

I wasn't ready for the result. I checked and rechecked. I stalled and stalled again. I began checking all the other fashionable movements and charismatic pastors. I was looking for the real Acts 2 church with a lot of stumbling along the way.

This book is a result of this journey. It is more than 10 years in the making. Having left my preconceived notions behind, I kept digging and the first church began to emerge from Judea at the time of Christ, and also from the ashes of the Israelite nation. Once you see it, a brilliantly cohesive picture develops of God's continuing Redemptive Plan.

This plan was, and is, the same from the beginning. It's renewed. And, it's superior. But, the Church, and you, are living out the same plan for salvation. The Old was the *"shadow of things to come."* There were models for us today. Pre-figurements of the past and the journeys of God's people are for us to recognize our voyage. The Church is amazingly on this same road as each of us individually... from Passover to the Land of Milk and Honey.

After several years of absorbing study, I went back to the Church I grew up in. My wife went from, "I'll never step foot in that church" to being received, along with my teenage son, into the real Full Gospel AND real first Church. You'll discover that the Gospel message has been transformed, or better yet just misunderstood. Lost in translation.

I grew to realize that even those within the Church, don't understand her. They don't understand the first Church, or the Gospel, or their relationship with their God. What is it that is to be believed?... Who do we have faith in? And, why? We think we know. But, do we? Christ was speaking into Judea and their culture. We were called out of that culture.

Some two thousand years in the future, we like to think He speaks to us, and our culture. HE DOES! God created us. His message and His wisdom are timeless. But, what exactly did He teach? This book is about rediscovering the Church that emerged...to learn the truth about Christ's Gospel and His ongoing relationship with us through His bride. Use this book as a beginning...the beginning of your seeing the glorious first Church; the Church of Acts; the Church that the Apostles built as they spread the Gospel across the globe.

My wife once said, "I see the bible with new eyes...it never ceases to amaze me!" You will too. This opens the door that brings peace as it fills in the pieces...that Ah-Ha! that you finally get it. The book is easy to follow and understand. You won't be left scratching your head wondering how it all fits.

If you're like me, deep theological debate, more times than not, makes me sleepy. And, it's difficult to understand. This book is not that. I felt compelled that God was asking me to just tell the story and illuminate the cast of characters.

Not too deep, the big picture if you will. There is no scriptural calisthenics that seems to reach where…well, you get the idea.

I discovered the many narratives and stories of the Israelites were "shadows of things to come", as the Apostle Paul said. You will discover how this fits. The summaries of biblical events, the festivals, and the ceremonies are the stories you all know. When simply laid on top of each other, it offers a complete background to Christ's Gospel, and His Church.

This is of which the Apostles spoke. They brought this message to the world. Without a shadow of a doubt, you will see how this foreshadows the events of the first Church, and the Church today. You will see how their lives fit. You'll also see how your lives fit. You'll discover how you almost missed…ah…salvation.

I encourage you to dig deeper. It will only help you see the big picture more clearly. And, as they say, once you see it…you will never be able to UNSEE it again. On the night that Christ was betrayed, He held up a cup. It was the third cup. He said, "Do this…" Do the third cup. Do you 'do' the third cup? Many do! You will soon understand the Gospel. There will be no doubt. You will have eyes to see... Let's discover the Church that emerged, once delivered. Enjoy!

Chapter 1: The Dueling of Banjos

"I sought to hear the voice of God And climbed the topmost steeple, But God declared: "Go down again - I dwell among the people."
John Henry Cardinal Newman

The sign read "Full Gospel" church as I passed it to meet the pastor. I was working for the city and he wanted to add a temporary stage. During our meeting, I couldn't resist asking the young pastor what the term "full gospel" meant. "It means we believe in the WHOLE bible!" he quickly responded. He began to elaborate while he walked me back outside, but my mind wandered with my eyes rolling backward in my sockets.

The familiar *"Dueling Banjos"* playing in my head, drowning out his words. Was it that I was hardening my heart to the message of the gospel? Or, was I simply full to the brim and unable, or more likely unwilling, to connect *his* dots?

My journey seemed very long, and I wasn't currently attending church. I could readily understand how Christians got to the point of quitting "Church" and going it alone. I came to believe that there was **no sure** word, or at least not one you could put your trust in. You see, I worked in a city of about 7800 people. There were about 30 listed Churches or religious affiliations.

They all had land and/or real estate holdings, finance committees, different leadership groups and/or affiliations, and separate evangelizing efforts. It seems like a waste to me, and there's one dirty little secret. They all disagree with one another on some level! That is apparently just dandy, as long as they all agree, that the Roman Catholic Church has gone astray.

I was raised a Catholic and I was completely ignorant of the Protestant landscape. I thought there were two lineages, Protestant and Catholic. That was it. If I could go to any Catholic Church and have the same beliefs and services, then, of course, I could go to any Protestant church and it too would be the same. I was soon to find out how wrong I was.

In my journey, I have found that the basic Christian is quite oblivious to it or ignores it somehow. It is rooted in, what I soon realized, unfounded trust and it is common to hear "Blossom where you're planted" across the Protestant landscape.

Each parish, or church leadership body, implore their parishioner to blossom where they are. At the same time, they organize membership drives, witnessing for personal salvation and other evangelistic efforts to take people away from other churches to follow *their, yes their,* tradition or interpretation of the written word of God. It always seemed immersed in pride to me. And, for many Christians, this pride is called faith, and/or the leading of the Holy Spirit.

There are supposedly over 30,000 Protestant denominations worldwide all having various forms and degrees of disagreement. You can turn on one of the numbers of Protestant television stations and watch show after show, pastor after pastor, with various interpretations of bible passages, parts of verses or chapters, all compiled in such a way to give the message from the Lord.

Context and/or who the letter, or "scriptural words", were directed to at the time is of no consequence. The message is packaged by pulling parts from all over the Old and New Testament to give the 'up to date' message to those in attendance. Plays and skits are planned to move the 'unchurched' to Jesus and the gospel.

The whole service, or experience, is planned from the time people arrive in the parking lot to the time they leave. All of this is to elicit an emotional response from the attendee, "to *feel*". Now, I'm not saying that all of this is bad, and I am sure that I have raised the ire of some readers so far. (Just as my family has been at times on this journey) But, take a deep breath. There are many on the same journey, both clergy, and laity. Your zeal is welcome.

There was a time in my life that I watched Protestant TV several hours a week. Many Christians will take offense saying that they aren't Protestant, they're evangelical, or they're non- denominational. I have heard it asked many times by well-meaning new Christians, "Are we Protestant?"

The term "Protestant" came from the Latin term "protestari" which means to publicly declare or protest. It began with Luther protesting some of the beliefs and practices of the Church. After disagreements and debates, formal decrees and documents, the protesters, if you will, issued a "Letter of Protestation" at Speyer in 1529.

While talking with one of my Lutheran friends, her son interrupted and asked,

"Mom, why don't we have a Pope?" It quickly became apparent that she didn't know how to respond or didn't want to respond as she glanced my direction. I tried to make light of it, but I did try to get a point across when I responded with a smile, "You do!". I said, "There's only one, it's just that the church you go to is really mad at him." I laughed hoping that she would see that I was trying to make light of it. But history does tell us that's pretty much the case.

From the beginning of the protest, the different reforming theological leaders had trouble agreeing amongst themselves but that's a deep subject itself. Today, you can surf the internet trying to advance your studies, your understanding of Christianity, all with a good and loving heart, only to find a sea of conflicting opinions. The truth is in there somewhere, but it can deflate your bubble. We must call it as it really is and admit that people just don't know.

The media is awash with well-meaning souls ardently defending their version of the gospel. Christians believing, they have been called to apologetics and ecumenical discussions, defending the faith and gospel of their Lord. They believe they are led by the Holy Spirit to ward off the demonic forces of deceived souls trying to convert people into Cults like Catholicism, or Pentecostalism, and vice versa.

We also must admit that the Holy Spirit of God is probably not schizophrenic and **NOT** leading more than 40,000 interpretations, in thousands of different directions, and causing the strife and splits within the Christian community. In fact, through Scripture itself, we'd all agree that this is not the case.

This is the world to which I became increasingly numb. One day I was paging through my wife's Bible and I noticed that many, if not most, bible verses had never been highlighted. She had used the same bible for probably a decade and highlighted or underlined all the time. Many verses had been underlined, highlighted, and boxed in several times. On different occasions, it was only a part of a verse.

I noticed that many of the verses that I had questions about were never highlighted. I asked other Christians who didn't know or would defer to their pastors (which is a good thing I guess). I've also had pastors laugh when I asked about concerns that I had about different verses. I learned that many are called problematic. But I didn't believe it. I wanted an answer. I wanted to know the real God.

I think all Christians can identify with how people close you off when you are *"witnessing to them"* AND *"proclaiming* the good news". You can watch their eyes roll back in their heads just as mine would soon do. Even when discussing the Gospel, or different verses between Christians you'll hear "interesting" or "I'll put that up on the shelf".

It is the drone of the drumbeat of the "faith" of someone else pressing in on us. I watched *SO much* of it, studied *SO much* of it, attended *SO much* of it, read *SO much* of it, and defended *SO much* of it. I have those I've alienated and those that I would rather not talk to about it anymore either. The sea of verse after verse, after BLESSED verse in proclamation and defense of one's interpretation, tradition, and belief is desensitizing. And in the end, we still might not agree.

If you have been a Christian for very long, then you probably have encountered some of this. But with my ferocious zeal, I burned out. I got "to the end of the internet" as one might say. I couldn't stomach even one more book or article of verse after verse after blessed verse. I was done. You could stick a fork in it.

And for several years when I encountered any kind of Christian expression, all I heard was the back and forth banter of the banjos in *"DUELING BANJOS"* as my eyes rolled back in my head. Or, as someone recently said, "It makes blood shoot out of my eyeballs".[1]

More than a decade later, this hit home again when I was having a conversation with a business colleague over wine. Diverse opinions were somewhat out of control in her business and this carried over into personal life. I'm not sure if it was because she had a bone to pick with me, but the conversation soon turned to religion. She knew that I had become Catholic again, as she would have put it.

Like most of us in today's world, she has enormous cognitive dissonance about religion…tossed to and fro. She was about to get emotional over it. Her male friend and business partner was a lax Jew. Her store manager was a former protestant who was now deeply involved in the Hebrew Roots Movement; to the point that the manager "believed" to be of Jewish heritage, *and* the divinity of Christ was now in question.

Here was the issue at hand that evening. She had been dabbling her way through these ideas searching for religion. Perhaps, even unbeknownst to her. She was angry. At family gatherings, people didn't talk to each other. Some were Catholic. Some were Protestant. She claimed it was an enormous emotional roller. It still brought tears to her eyes.

She gave up and wanted no part of it. But something still obviously propelled her. The reformation did nothing positive in her life, or in the lives of most. More than a decade before, I was right with her. I had checked out. And, I like her, began searching.

So how did this start, I mean, I can't imagine the Holy Spirit leading the church in so many directions. Where was the real church, or Christianity, both rhythmically and historically? What was the story of the people of God? I began studying the Church Fathers and the Old Testament. It was necessary for me to overcome anger and spiritual pride.

To understand the Church today as opposed to the early Church, we need to define the normative views that influence Christianity today. The early Church was influenced by a completely different set of beliefs that were based on the people of God as a nation. Let's quickly look at some of these contemporary influencers as we set the stage

.

Sheila, Sheila

The real God was in this kaleidoscope somewhere, or so I hoped. I knew that the Holy Spirit was not leading conflicting groups in opposite directions in such a way as a sink sprayer diverting water in an almost infinite number of directions. Then I met Sheila.

While I studied on my own, I met many new and fascinating people. They weren't television evangelists and teachers. And, they weren't trying to get my money. These people simply shared their insights, developed studies, and researched the ancient past. Professor Robert Bellah is one of those people. So is Sheila Larson.

Robert Bellah, along with a number of associates, wrote *Habits of the Heart* in the **1980s.** The highly acclaimed and widely studied book was a sociological study of contemporary religion in America. "Sheila Larson" was a registered nurse who was interviewed in the study.

"I believe in God," she said, "I'm not a religious fanatic. I can't remember the last time I went to church. My faith has carried me a long way. It's Sheilaism. Just my own little voice... It's just to try to love yourself and be gentle with yourself." *(Bellah 1984) Habits of the Heart* became widely studied in social science academia and Sheila was quite famous. Over a decade later, Bellah described Sheilaism as "a perfectly natural expression of current American religious life..." *(Bellah 1996)* [2]

Across American religion, across the denominational landscape, Sheila caused quite a stir. Her religious belief was a reality that American Churches have needed to face for quite some time, and in the decades since Sheila expressed her view. Now they had a name to it. A face, if you will. Many non-denominational churches sprang up over the last couple of decades to provide her and those like her, services and to introduce her to Jesus.

She became the target market in the many of the Evangelical "seeker" churches that are so common today. She obviously has a heart. And, there are more who share her view. Perhaps, they may be seeking more from a church. Yet, she seemed satisfied just where she was and didn't need anything beyond herself.

That is really the logical outcome of the Reformation movement. Where does it end up? When extrapolated, it logically ends with the individual and a church of oneself. The individual is free to take the bible, or not, and create a God to the individual's liking. Bellah described this "radical individualism" as the way of American life, but within Christianity, it just doesn't work.

He described Americans as being so self-absorbed that they saw everything in terms of satisfying their individual needs-spiritual, physical, and emotional. Or, the "imperial republic of self" "It's Sheilaism, just her own little voice".

Charles Colson and Ellen Vaughn described the "identity crisis that is confronting the American Church" in the book *The Body* as *"a failure to understand what the Church really is: its biblical purpose, mission, and authority"*. They explained:

> *For many Christians, church means the buildings where we meet on Sunday. Building a church means constructing an edifice. When we think of church, we think of it as a place to go -- that's our first mistake -- to satisfy our spiritual needs -- that's our second mistake. This confusion limits our ability to impact the culture and to spread the Gospel. Focusing on our needs is simply a manifestation of a philosophy that has gripped American life -- what sociologists call "radical individualism." (Bellah)* [3]

American and perhaps all contemporary, denominations have privatized the faith of the followers far beyond a balance point between the individual and the community, or body of the Church at large. It is as Bellah described "radical" in its form. The "Evangelical" form of Christianity, with its post- Protestant stance, is very susceptible to the individual's focus on oneself. Ultimately, this undermines the very concept of the need for a church and for its authority. There is no need to attend any church or be submitted to the authority in any of them. It has become hard for the church leaders to expect followers to submit to their teaching and leadership, when the entire enterprise may have been built on division and strife, and arguments of doctrine in the first place.

Bellah further describes this recently developed church doctrine as the *"near-exclusive focus on the relationship between Jesus and the individual."* Accepting Jesus, he says, *"is one's personal Lord and Saviour [has been] almost the whole of piety."* When we are "alright with Jesus" then we don't have the need for a church. One would have to ask then, why are we to be stewards? and what would be our purpose on earth? Are we not to be in relationship with one another? Why then, with this personal relationship, are we not immediately transported to be in Heaven?

In *The Body,* Colson and Vaughn suggested that seeing Christianity as *an "exclusively, or even primarily, a personal relationship with Jesus falls woefully short of historic Christianity."* Contemporary Evangelical Christians are completely blind to the fact that this is untethered from history. Reformers like Luther, Zwingli, and Calvin certainly did not view the Christian life this way. None of them would recognize the brand of Evangelical, post- Protestant Christianity that is so prevalent today.

The early reformers would not have tolerated this doctrine. It would have been so foreign that these groups would have been punished and/or excommunicated. Calvin was notorious for punishing aberrant people and groups. They would have been "traitors" and considered heretics. Calvin himself would have believed these groups placed themselves outside of the Church.

Whether we look to the Catholic Theologians of the 2000-year-old Church, or the Reformation Theologians of Luther and Melanchthon, or Zwingli and Calvin, they understood what many contemporary Christians do not:

> *There is a social and communal dimension to real Christianity -- a dimension that is not optional. This dimension includes matters of discipline and doctrine. Being part of the Church means that you don't have the final say in what you should believe or how you should live."* [3]

Robert Bellah describes these longstanding tenets of Christianity as "fighting words" for many of today's Christians. Whether cafeteria Catholics, Protestants, or post- Protestant Evangelicals, the final authority in matters of morality, practices, and doctrines has been usurped and appropriated for themselves.

As Catholic Theologian Saint Augustine taught, *"He who would have God as his Father must have the Church as his mother."* Charles Colson and Robert Bellah laid down the Gauntlet more than 2 decades ago, *"The Church has no room for "Sheilaism".* Do we want to know the real God and his people, or invent one to our liking? As Charles Colson wrote, *"Christian identity is not a matter of me, but of we.*

Bellah's Civil Religion

Is Sheila a product of secular culture with their generic god? Or, did culture adopt the narcissistic/individualistic views of Sheila? Prior to *Habits of the Heart,* both Robert Bellah and Lutheran professor Martin Marty centered much of their work on the cultural phenomenon called, *"Civil Religion".*

In the context of American life, it is a national, somewhat structured 'folk' religion. Religion, in general, is accepted by most Americans and by many, it is expected. The tenets of American civil religion are only slightly more elaborate than the set of beliefs that Jean- Jacques Rousseau elaborated on in his 1762 treatise called *The Social Contract.* His theory was popular during the era of the American nation's birth. Rousseau believed that Civil religion was a set of beliefs that were universal, and the nation had a right to uphold such beliefs as, belief in a deity, belief in an afterlife where good and evil will receive justice, and of religious tolerance.[4][5]

Contemporary secularized governments needed a secularized religion. JJ Rousseau's Freemasonic theories allowed countries to overthrow the historic Church and replace it with this "Civil religion. His ideas were a major contributor to the French Revolution and the development of governmental structures such as Socialism.

In America, we see this played out in our expectation that our leaders believe in God. We can talk about praying in the public arena. We can invoke the name God in the public sphere, speak about the morals of past leaders, and generate national myths and lore. It engenders a national patriotism, under God of course. This is less than the establishment of a national religion that requires the participation of citizens. But Americans still require a national belief in God.

Subsidiarity, Solidarity, and Social Justice

This quick overview of Solidarity and Subsidiarity, and how it relates to the Holy Commonwealth, will help you as we continue forward trying to uncover God's will for His people *Israel* and God's will for His people; *the Church.*

The issue of social justice is very prevalent in American society today. First, there is no such thing as "social" justice. That should be your first clue that it's just a political device. There is only *Justice.* Right and wrong…Truth. That is why the scales of justice is blindfolded. We are to treat others the way we want to be treated.

This contemporary secular idea is split between individualism and communalism in many Christian circles. In other words, self-reliance versus reliance on community. Individualism bad, communalism good. The problem in putting together a secular nation with its civil religion has always been the Catholic Church and Her views.

The ancient Israelites had their own struggles with individualism versus communalism. They both tried confederalism and federalism. Were they to be a loosely connected group of tribes or a group of tribes with a federal government and division of powers? To understand the early Church, we'll have to investigate their decisions a little further.

In the coming chapter, we'll explore Israel's desire to create the Holy Commonwealth. Historically, a Commonwealth is a political community formed for the common good. The Israelite community was under covenants made with God and the "common good" was seen as limits to national governance where most issues were settled in the tribe and family. There were no large national social programs in Ancient Israel. [6]

Solidarity and Subsidiarity are terms that are used in Catholic social teaching on justice. Both concepts were gleaned from the history of the Church and the Ancient Israelites before the Church age.

Solidarity, you may remember, gained worldwide recognition in Poland when Lech Walesa worked to unite people [and workers] against a large and overreaching government in Poland's shipyards. It is essentially when people unify and work together for the common good or common interests of the group. They seek the common good through uniting to form a larger community to seek freedom from some injustice.

Subsidiarity is a companion term used in Catholic social teaching and it seems to have been completely ignored as 'social' justice is debated today. You can't take one without the other, however. It doesn't work. You'll lose the equilibrium necessary within a 'balanced' Commonwealth or Church. Subsidiarity is the principle of social doctrine that states that any problem should be handled by the smallest unit, furthest away from any central authority as possible.

This could be an individual, or family. The matter should always be looked to be settled locally without interference from an overarching government. So, people were taught the responsibility to help each other on a local level. This enables tasks to be performed efficiently and effectively; they are handled before they get out of hand.

We will ponder these thoughts as we grow in understanding of the once-delivered Church that emerged from the struggles in Judea...

"The new (testament) is in the old (testament) concealed...
The old (testament) is in the new (testament) revealed."
-Saint Augustine

The Holy Commonwealth

While hunting for the First Church, I began to discover the Old Testament had a treasure trove of socio-political aspects needed to see the first Church and soon realized just how important the social and political dialogue is in these books. The biblical story of the ancient Israelites endeavoring to build, and rebuild, a good and holy commonwealth was such an important story. What did it mean to us today?

The bible is historical, and concurrent stories can be overlaid. Salvation history tends to repeat itself. The bible is both a political and a social document. It is both individualistic and communal. There are spiritual components for healthy souls, bodies, families, and societies. And, there are the natural aspects of living in a natural world with the regulation of fairness, freedom, and justice in society. Jesus summed it up in its entirety.

"To love the Lord God with all your heart, mind, and soul, and your neighbor as yourself".

I didn't realize how much of Jesus' teaching about the Old Testament and the Israelite people. He addressed Rabbinical thought and the history of the people of God. They understood more than we give them credit for. They weren't a culture that just wandered the desert with flip-flops on.

The Israelites of Jesus' time understood the intimate details of the Old Testament and their ancestry more than any of us could. The Old Testament records an intimate and comprehensive story of a people, their relationship with each other, and with their God. Israel's God would be the ultimate overseer, or that was their vision.

The Ancient Israelites were a people built on the covenant and on kinship; on loving-kindness, and on desire and commitment. The Old Testament reveals the successes and failures. We also have the commentators, the fixers, and the prognosticators who attempted to expand people's understanding.

This book is an exploration of the big picture, piecing together the story of the descendants of Abraham and Jacob from a natural perspective. They lived in the real world and needed to relate to each other just as we do. Their society had earthly socio-political aspects and these features are there for us to plainly see.

Granted, using the term 'socio-political' is scantly too simplistic. They were theo-social, theo-political, and theo-cultural people. The Torah can be seen as a covenantal constitution that was ratified by the entire congregation (*Adat Bnai Yisrael*). It could be said that their sojourn in a complex Egyptian society helped them develop a societal structure.

God's called them out of bondage in Egypt, banded them together, and sanctified them in the sea as they headed for Sinai. This was expressed and codified in the Mosaic constitution. They sought to achieve this 'good life' both individually, then communally, that would lead to a good and "holy" commonwealth. The nation of the children of the covenant with God could then be known as the proverbial *"City on a Hill"*.

This effort was ultimately not without hierarchy, but it was without human tyranny and despotism. Their common practices as a "set-apart" nation, was unique among the societies in the era in which it grew. The Israelites began as a hereditary group, but they allowed those who would be grafted in; those committed to the covenant of the nation that was set apart onto God.

To sum it up, the family of tribes descended from the 12 sons of Jacob, who consented to and ratified a covenant with God and each other, became a nation… *"out of which flow the principles and practices of religious life and political organization that have animated the Jews as a corporate entity ever since"*[6][8]

Professor Stuart A. Cohen has summarized this experience quite distinctly in *The Three Crowns*:

> *Structures of Communal Politics in Early Rabbinic Jewry, "Jewish political traditions, it has been argued, constitutes an integral facet of Jewish civilization in its entirety. They reflect a constant — albeit often implicit — understanding that the validity of Jewish teaching can best find expression in a political setting. They also embody Judaism's commitment to the establishment of the perfect polity. As implemented through the process of covenant (brit), and as buttressed by the attribute of loving-kindness (hesed), political traditions in effect comprise the vehicles whereby the Congregation of Israel attempts to transpose the kingdom of heaven* **(Malchut shamayim —"the good commonwealth")** *to earth. [6][9]*

We can also say that Theo-political phenomenon that began in the Canaan wilderness, arguably fought some post- Egypt pluralistic tendencies. However, one thing is for sure, it was not pluralistic in its covenant with the One God. It wasn't pluralistic in religious rituals or in the interpretation of God's word. Leaders taught and maintained the tradition; the rituals and the culture that surrounded the servanthood of the Lord.

The understanding of the ancient office that maintained the authority for interpretation of God's word has been lost today. The Mosaic office had God's authority and was granted God's charisma that was necessary to keep constant the Word of God and maintain the reality of the Sinai covenant.

As we will soon see as we dig in, God gave us a warning through the biblical account of the period of Judges. Namely, what would happen without the restoration of the Mosaic office through Samuel? The loose-knit confederation of the Judges period turned into, what has been termed by contemporary Jewish scholars, "confederal anarchy". This coalition could not keep the Israelites from falling away from their covenantal traditions and beliefs.[6][8][9]

The Old Testament does not give us a command from God that stipulates the formulation of a specific political structure, but it does allow us insight into what has worked and what has not. Whereby, there needed to be the solidarity of the people (*Adat Bnai Yisrael*) to a central teaching authority entrusted to "bring the will of God to the people" and to interpret the covenantal constitution.

This combined with the concepts of subsidiarity to leave decisions as local as possible; for individual identity; for the responsibility of the individual in the family and tribe, and within the community. Still, the people wandered off. They had lost the Mosaic office. They began to call for an earthly king with what would be catastrophic results.

The Israelites hadn't had an earthly king before, but there had been "Servants of the Lord ", or "*Eved Adonai*" in Hebrew. These leaders had always acted as God's servant, making God the center and the decision-maker, but these servants were not a king. The people of Israel wandered off to their own devices, their own idols and in many directions.

We're hunting for the first Church, so we'll have to learn how they saw it. It had structure. There was the Jerusalem Council almost immediately. So, let's develop some of these standardized traditions and structures. In chapter 4, we will dive into the ancient Mosaic office and how that would impact the Church today.

And, in chapter 5, we will look into the offices of Christ. We will elaborate on the concepts of civil functions of the (King) *Keter Malkut*, the prophetic functions of the (Prophet) *Keter Torah*, and the priestly functions of the (Priest) *Keter Kehunah* within Israel's society, and how this assimilates within the body of Christ, or God's Kingdom.

It will be important to see how the *Household of God* became the *Kingdom of God,* and how the office of the *"Eved Adonai"* and the *Ketaric* domains matter in the early Church. And, how this applies to us today. Both Bellah and Marty separated the religious functions of the prophetic and the priestly in their study of Civil Religion from the role of civil governance and the secularism that our civil religion demands.

They attempted to distinguish or ignore the teaching (prophetic) and priestly roles within America's civil religion. Bellah defined the priestly role as *"an institutionalized [independent] collection of sacred beliefs about the American nation."* He also addressed the prophetic role in the American experience *"national self-worship"* and called for *"the subordination of the nation to ethical principles that transcend it in terms of which it should be judged.
"*

Bringing it together

So, there is the landscape as I saw it. I lived within it for more than a decade. With my political and social science background, I began by applying that point of view to the problem of finding the Church that emerged. We quickly delineated some distinctions between the old and the new. We began outlining the division between the contemporary democratic view of Christianity and the Israelites desire to create a Holy Commonwealth. It is where we start to discover the Church that Emerged some 2000 years ago.

From the beginning of the protest, different theological leaders had trouble agreeing amongst themselves. Germans such as Luther and Melanchthon and Swiss Theologian Zwingli worked semi-independently to develop doctrine to "Reform the Faith". The Holy Spirit, however, apparently had a hard time getting through clearly, and theological splits separated them.

Each claimed to have the "truth" of doctrine and scriptural interpretation. And, the debates were sometimes not all that friendly. Calvin came along and tried to mediate between opposing doctrines. His attempts **to mend these** views have left theologians wanting more while calling his views on the Eucharist "opaque" and less definitive.[7] Imagine that!

Reforming, or the "Reformation", has never really amended nor did it improve the tenets of the 2000-year-old Church in any lasting and unified manner. Reformation theologians and those that followed had their own set of followers and taught their own "oral tradition"; or interpretation of scripture. Rather than just read biblical text from the pulpit, they spoke orally, developing a new oral tradition based on the text.

Sermons were immediately "extra-biblical" expanding on the Bible. Eventually, like the 'phone game', there were "first-cousin, once-removed" Reformation churches that grew independently following the teachings of enigmatic theologians who were versed in Holy Scripture.

One has to realize, however, that none of the first cousin-once-removed denominations were receptive to individual members reading Scripture while being led by the Holy Spirit to understand it. A better way to say it would be that Luther, Zwingli, or Calvin each believed they had properly interpreted Scripture, and their followers needed to submit to their teaching and doctrine.

It was common to receive severe punishment for not adhering to their doctrines. One could say that, immediately, they replaced the Pope, or Bishop of Rome, with themselves. And, they took on this authority with zeal, believing that it was their mission to maintain the 'unity' of **their** 'true doctrine'.

New second and third cousins- once-removed churches "reformed again" from the first and second reformations, changing and amending rituals, practices, and doctrines in new and progressive ways. Soon, these new generations of breaks and splits found it unappealing identifying with Protestantism and sought to sever any of the connections and stand alone. So, the term "Protestantism" got replaced with "Evangelicalism".

They aren't protesting the Church anymore. They stand on their own merits. Now, with the tens of thousands of splits, it has been pleasing to identify yourself and your church as *non-denominational*. This common contemporary emotion casts off any connection with historical ancestry by circumventing it to claim an early church identity. They are merely New Testament Christians who are very sad that so many have been led astray over the centuries. But, is that really the case, an apostate Church from the earliest of times?

There is a deep desire that permeates throughout evangelical Christendom. It is the desire to return to 'biblical Christianity'. This hope is generally expressed as a desire to return to Early Christianity; the "Book of Acts" brand of Christianity.

The reality of the early Church existing today has become inconceivable, I had a chance to discuss the desire to return to this early Church with a Catholic parish priest. His response was one that I wasn't expecting. He replied that it didn't exist anymore. I was taken back. I think this priest's answer about the early church was Providentially wrong.

I increasingly adopted the theory that the tenets of the Church could be identified right from the start, just as they could be today. There was also undoubtedly more structure in the early Church than we normally give it credit for. Each of us is on the same spiritual journey to find the truth; the truth of the first Church Yet, it seems common that we fail to hear or see.

This steady drumbeat reverberated through my spirit. It was that I had difficulty seeing the big picture. I felt that seeing the big picture was a common problem. To get a clear picture from among the sea of conflicting denominations and interpretations, it's necessary to step back to see the big picture. An overview. Or, to see the forest for the trees.

It is to know that they are trees, and what a forest is. Not just in spirit, but in the natural too. It can be so easy to get sidetracked and quickly travel down rabbit trails. It can also be easy to only see and then debate and discuss, the trees.

It reminds me of what a great Caribbean philosopher Captain Barbossa once said, "There are a lot of long words in there, Miss; we're naught but humble pirates. What is it that you want? ......: I'm disinclined to acquiesce to your request....... Means "no".
(*Pirates of the Caribbean: The Curse of the Black Pearl*)

Chapter 2: Recapturing God's Plan

"...I am the LORD, and I will bring you out from under the burdens of the Egyptians, and I will deliver you from their bondage. I will also redeem you with an outstretched arm and with great judgments. 7 'Then I will take you for My people, and I will be your God, and you shall know that I am the LORD your God..." Ezekiel 6:6-7

The first chapter got deep into state Christianity today. They say that if you want to fix something, you first need to see the problem. They're the same people that claim 'denial' is a river in Egypt. My heart grieved with this division, and I agree most people don't see it, or it's beyond their ability to feel compelled for change. What change?

Therefore, so many who sought the true Church of the first century. Entire movements have sought it. Bear with me. You'll finally find it. It won't be what you expected. We'll dig deep, but it will be in a 'big-picture' form. It will become easy to see. You'll get it.

So, how do we recapture God's plan for our redemption? The difficulty is that many of us think we have already found it. We've arrived and there's no need to search any longer. It's what we've been taught. However, I REALLY needed to find that first Church. There would be no peace until I did.

We tend to have Christ and church as part of our lives, yet when asked to identify what makes you, you, that may not be the first thing out of our mouths. We're teachers. We're homemakers. We like to fish. And, so on. Seldom will the first thing be...we're of Christ because?... We're just us.

We act as if we are each helium balloons, un-tethered, floating around with complete independence especially as far as Christianity goes. Our governments have become secular. Many times, governments replace the church. They take on many of the traits and responsibilities of church in our lives. It has co-opted the ideals that lead us to call them 'church-like', but without those cumbersome affiliations. As we quit going to church, we ask them to take its place... We have no place else to go.

In this light, it is easy to understand Sheila-ism and cafeteria-ism (picking and choosing our favorites, a smorgasbord). Like we discovered in chapter one, the ultimate culmination of "Reform" ends up being a "church of one"; our own little church with our own little [g]od of our liking, created for our own purpose.

Necessarily, Relativism, political correctness, and tolerance are necessary components that end just shy of knowing the "glory of the Lord". We end up with a contemporary Christian pantheon strikingly like that of Ancient Egypt.

From our perch some 2000 years in the future, it's easy to assimilate the view that the society in Judea was backward. They were so technologically deficient that we are far superior to them culturally. Really? That's a stretch, but I get it. Been there. Done that. Did technology usurp wisdom? Let's look at it another way. Contemporary culture has killed wisdom for the sake of self-righteousness.

This view sees Judea as a bunch of wanderers wearing flip-flops in the desert sand. So, this untethering of the past, and of wisdom, leads to independent charismatic pastors who shepherd their flock. These flip-flopping desert sheepherders lead the flock that they convinced to follow them. And, this is not without consequences.

The **quest hunt** to discover the first Church begins with understanding the contemporary landscape. At least for me, it did. I spent so much time buried in it. Christianity as it is today, and where it lives. Before we dig into God's plan of redemption, let's identify some of the biases, or thought systems, that cloud our search. I call them the -isms. Let's spend a little time outlining the players. Then, it's headlong into the quest for the Acts 2 Church…the Church that Emerged.

The …isms

We've all been reminded that in the end days, God will send a powerful delusion to those who don't love the truth…so they will believe a lie. (*2 Thessalonians 2:11)* Or,

"For the time will come when people will not put up with sound doctrine. Instead, to suit their own desires, they **will** *gather around them a great number of* **teachers** *to say what* **their** *itching ears want to hear." (1 Timothy 4:3)*

Our Lady of Fatima's warned of the coming *"Diabolical Disorientation"* that would affect those in the Church. However, it's become evident that this disorientation has long been taking place outside the Church also.

21

Somewhere in time, there came the following "...*isms*". It's a matter of what came first, the chicken or the egg. Did culture create Sheila? Or, did the following "...*isms*" come first? Each is types of *"wolves in sheep's clothing"* that creep in as pseudo-thought unannounced. The *"...isms"* are Relativism, Skepticism, Pluralism, Modernism, and deconstructionism. To this, we need to add unrestrained zeal.

Relativism

Relativism is just that. Everything is relative. There is no objective truth. There is only subjectivity. We've all heard it countless times. What's true for you isn't true for me. That's your truth. And, I have mine. As opposed to logic and reason, everything is a matter of our subjective selves and our feelings. It's based on emotions and personal likes and dislikes.

> *"We all do no end of feeling, and we mistake it for thinking"*
> *Mark Twain*

Subjective truth depends on whether it conforms to the preferences, opinions, and beliefs of the person making the claim. My favorite color is green. Well, mine is red. That's all subjective. I like short hair, and you like long. We apply this subjectivity to all things objective, especially as far as religion is concerned.

It's also all my view...my opinion. This 'church of one' can then be coerced unbeknownst in one direction or another...influenced to accept and adopt different 'truths' by groupthink. It's 'go-along', to get-along. Or, just don't cause a stir.

In short, (moral) relativism is the idea that moral values are based on your society or culture, group thinking, and therefore subject to individual choice. It can be your peer group, a cult, or where you and work. I can be based on age, education, wealth. A moral relativist tends to believe there are no rules governing right and wrong.

This led to Cardinal Ratzinger's call upon the Church to:

> wield Jesus Christ as a shield against a "dictatorship of relativism." He depicted the church as a "little boat of Christian thought" tossed by waves of "extreme" schools of modern thought, identified as Marxism, liberalism, libertinism, collectivism and "radical individualism.[2]

22

Cultural Relativism is the "groupthink" of a culture. It is inter-subjective as in the customs of a culture. It may be manners such as opening doors for a woman or burping at the table. However, it could also be infanticide, polygamy, bestiality, or same-sex marriage.

> **Side Note:** *Overton's Window*- Imagine a large television screen. The entire range of ideas, customs, and policies that the public (culture) is willing to consider or accept appear on that screen. Just off the screen is all of the intolerable ideas. Politicians and special interests attempt to either co-opt these ideas, or erase them altogether, or make an intolerable tolerable and screen worthy- to get you to buy into it. Think *The Truman Show*.

Objective truth is NOT based on conformity to the beliefs or customs of the individual or the group. An example of this would be…all life on earth would die without the sun. No matter what we believe, it true. Objective truth is always under assault. We like to bring all things into submission to ourselves, or our group.

The belief in Christ, the Gospel, the Church, and Scripture have all been under this assault. Everything gets questioned as NOT objective, but subject. It's only relevant to certain individuals or groups. The idea is that if there is absolute truth, we can't possibly know it. So, the truth of Christ is subjective. God's Providence is subjective. There is no sin. There is no need for a savior.

Skepticism

Skepticism is an even stranger breast. It is what it says it is. Skepticism rejects all truth. All truth claims are invalid, or at least they are skeptical of all truth claims. This would mean that any supernatural claims could not be proven. To the Skeptics, all morality is questionable. Any evidence would have to be in the natural world.

There just isn't any knowledge that can be known for sure. So, in other words, this person is Agnostic. An Agnostic is a person who believes that nothing is known beyond material phenomena. Nothing can be known about the existence or nature of God, so they claim neither faith nor disbelief in God.

Pluralism

Pluralism is what we have been seeing through the entirety of the Reformation era. I'm ok, You're ok. All roads lead to heaven, within Christianity that is. Once saved, always saved. All religions are the same. They are equal. They all lead us to the same place Instinctively, we know that's not true. At least, they are completely different [g]ods.

Through *Ecumenism* over the fifty years, there has been a watering down of the faith, and of the truth, so we all can be saved. Oh, except the apostate Church and the cult down the street. When we don't find unity, we make do and change the rules. No one wants to say someone else is wrong, at least to their face.

Evangelicals have sought to fight Relativism by focusing on avoiding the evils and immoralities of the world. But Pope Benedict saw this fight as something much deeper. He saw all relativistic ideas as a product of Pluralism- the idea that any congregation, any profession of faith, any religious gathering, or region itself were all valid forms of searching for meaning in life. [1][2]

William Portier, a professor who specializes in Catholic intellectual thought at the University of Dayton stated, "He thinks relativism is something that happens when people live in pluralism…it's as an occupational hazard- you begin to think this way because you live with all these different people." [1]

This has had a profound effect in the years since Pope Benedict. Through some sort of theological and ecumenical extension, a couple of things have happened.

The Emergent Church- groups claim that there is a new emergent church that the spirit is drawing out of an old and stuffy Christianity. The spirit is moving in new ways, in a new age…to surprise us all.

Universalism is being revisited. Everyone is saved and no one goes to hell. It is completely empty. Just tumbleweeds…oh, wait, they would burn up, that is if hell existed. At least, the claim dictates there's hope. It's an emotional invention that makes us feel better.

One world religion- pluralism maintains that all religions are the same. They are all valid expressions of salvation. All men are saved. Now, that's ecumenism. All under one umbrella religion that takes parts of them all.

You've undoubtedly seen these ideas bandied about in recent years, and yes, all the way to the Vatican. It is really all around us. Let's hold onto that Cross. The boat is tossed to and fro in heightened seas. The importance to find and hold tight to the first Church is ever-increasing.

Modernism

Modernism essentially casts the precepts of morality and virtues of past societies and cultures as inferior to those of today. Pope Pius X called this the *"synthesis of all heresies"*. Modernism murders all concepts of Lady Wisdom, especially in a Christian and biblical sense. The concept of learning from history, or our past successes and failures are completely laid to waste.

This too is a product of Relativism. At its core, the theory needs to oppose any supernatural elements including God's Providence. Once again, the view is completely naturalistic. It is only what they see, or feel, or touch today that matters. In a nutshell, the Modernist's system of thought freely teaches that what is considered moral or just today may have been something that was condemned in a prior age or culture.

It becomes a systematic and calculated walking away of truth. The past was for the people of the past. We decide for ourselves. We know better today. They weren't as well informed as we are. We have Oprah…and *The View*…and blogging. They didn't. What did they know about us?

Modernists infiltrated the Church long ago, slowly trying to move our views of morality from within. They believe that the Israelite's views of truth and morality right for their era, but not for today. Whether the ancient age, the middle age, or contemporary age, each gets to age and culture decide for themselves. All right and wrong is adopted by the culture and time period, and not words of wisdom from an ancient book.

The bible would never be infallible. It would never be God's Providence given to mankind as unchanging truth. Here is an example of Modernism that I personally encountered. He is hiding in plain view and has no fear of reprisal.

A former priest who had rescinded his vows and went on to get married taught an RCIA class at a local parish. I attended with my family while they were going through the class. The priest had great difficulty following both the RCIA guides, the Tradition of the Church, and any biblical concepts that would support it.

Calmly, I rose several objections throughout the winters' long class. Perhaps because of my challenges, one of the other attendees ended up quitting the class. Before he did, he stated that I read the bible too much. What? Well, I certainly didn't want to cause a commotion, but I wanted my family to be taught correctly. Both this priest and the parish deacon stopped to talk to me after class one evening.

I was told that each culture and era got to decide what was right or wrong.

He said, for instance, that the bible made no mention of same-sex marriage. What? I was bewildered. Of course, I was once an Evangelical. I can rattle of verses in response with the best of them. We talked for quite a while. Both the Priest and then the Deacon kept trying to convince me that the Israelites or the culture of Jesus' time were just that...of their time.

Again, they pushed the idea that we could decide our own morality without any concerns to what was the prior norm. This was my first encounter with anything like this. I let them know that in my entire time in Evangelical Christianity was much more biblically conservative than the views they espoused.

I finally blurted, "The Church isn't a democracy." They looked at me bewildered for a few moments before asking, "What is it then?" I responded that it was a kingdom, and Christ was king. That Sunday, during the Homily, the pastor informed the congregation that the Church was, in fact...*Not* a democracy. I wonder why that came out.

That's Modernism, truth is gleaned by our experiencing life today...and not some stuffy unrelatable past. Modernism has been repeatedly been condemned as a heresy. And, any biblical Christian can undoubtedly see why.

Deconstructionism

We also need to take a quick look at religious Deconstructionism. I kind of made up the term. I borrowed Deconstructionism from both literary and philosophical critiquing and analyzing. It was because I noticed myself doing it. So many others were doing it as well.

We've seen how *Relativism* attacks our traditional moral fabric, and also Christianity itself. The, *"what's good for you, might not be good for me"* or, *"whatever floats your boat"* so, *"who am I to judge"* deal. Deconstructionism is the tool that people use to arrive at a relativistic view.

Deconstructionism, Religious Deconstructionism is, essentially:

> I will listen to you until I can find one little thing that I believe doesn't fit with what I believe is the truth, my truth. Then, when I find it, I can reject everything else you had to say... Or,
> If I can find a Bible verse or even a part of a verse, that, in my opinion, disproves what you have said, then I don't have to listen to anything else you had to say."

26

Ah-ha, you say. Yep, I've done it. Maybe, you say something like, "Interesting", or "I'll pray about it." You have no intention and have already discarded it. We're just too busy. The world is too fast-paced. "Oh hide, here he/she comes again." You got it. They can't possibly have anything to offer me. It would never be a "God thing".

Ecumenism and cross dialogue has gotten lost in this religious Deconstructionism. We compartmentalize. We don't want our apple cart turned over. There will be NO cognitive dissonance here. No anxiety…Quick hide. You get it.

The other side of the Religious Deconstructionism coin is that we just don't want to receive it. We don't want to hear it. No. Matter What. You can't make me. You can't make me. We fear we may be wrong…so we run away seeking justification and support where we can find it. We're too busy. Then, phew, we won't have to change my view.

Deconstructionism is generally defined as a philosophical theory of criticism that seeks to both expose and solve deep-seated [and long lasting] contradictions by looking beneath the surface, tearing it apart [deconstructing] it. It is an effort to find its problems.

In our fast-paced world, people seem to spend just long enough on a specific subject, deconstructing in a rapid critical thinking exercise, only to throw it away as something not valid in their lives. Whether it conflicts with past experiences or creates the possibility of future dilemmas, it may well be rejected as valuable in their lives for good.

"Don't throw the baby out with the bathwater"
(Appeal to Fools) Thomas Murner

Zeal

Finally, zeal, and I know something about zeal. Personally. We race off. At least I do. All we need is the bible. But zeal can be harmful. It can be all over the place. Zeal may need guard rails. The bible, the Holy Spirit, and me. That's all I need. That can be a train wreck. I know so.

We end up making all the mistakes we needn't make. We get in the ditch. I did. Then we try to fight our way out. God may certainly be asking you to explore the unexplored. And, without zeal, you won't get there. Zeal doesn't feel delicate, but it is. Zeal can cause us to run headlong into a brick wall.

Zeal can cause pride and self-righteousness as we race headlong into the wilderness. An elder once said to me, "That way will cause you great trouble, many times you will be all by yourself." Was this a prophetic utterance? Don't know, but it turned out to be true. I didn't heed the advice and I still don't know if I should have.

"Son, in thirty-five years of religious study, I've come up with only two hard, incontrovertible facts; there is a God, and, I'm not Him." Father Cavanaugh to Rudy (Rudy 1993)

People need spiritual mentors; I've been one and I've had one. This time I was going it alone. I got in a lot of pickles. I learned a lot. Ran away a lot. Someone told me it was all of God. I was ravenous for peace amid what was hounding me. There was unity and I wanted to find it. Catholics, and Lutherans, and Evangelical were SO different. I unconsciously compared everything to my past.

What made sense? I asked God to show me the true Church. Repeatedly. That's what made me uncomfortable. What I read, and what the pastor preached about at my local Evangelical church or on Protestant television didn't always sync up. It wasn't copasetic. Though more than a decade in the making, zeal helped me find the Church I was looking for.

It took a long time to get this playing field, set, and to understand the rules of our game today. But, it will be worth it. Step by step we'll hunt the Church that grew out of the 12 disciples in Judea. We'll unpeel the glory of the Gospel and of SALVATION *Lost*. Let's go find this Church. The one that emerged once delivered.

God's Four-Step Plan of Redemption

"if we are to have an impact today, we need to recapture God's vision for His people"
Robert Bellah

As we've seen so far, most have gone on to serve Sheila. They left the Gospel behind. Salvation…*Lost*.

So, what was, and is God's plan? What did the Old Testament teach? How did Jesus see this? Christ was born into a people, a culture, and a history. He spoke into that life. He spoke into Judea. The 12 were of the nation too. They were of Judea…they were the relics of their past; the nation of Israel.

There are Four steps that define the Redemptive Purposes in God's Plan. One, two, three, four. In the coming **chapter**, we will see how the four redemptive steps match the four cups of the Passover Seder. The four proclamations in Exodus 6: 6-7 are "… *I will bring you out…I will deliver you…I will redeem you…and, I will take you as my people."*

The climactic ending is revealed in the next verse. *"I will bring you into the land that I swore to give to Abraham, Isaac, and Jacob; I will give it to you for a possession. I am the Lord" (verse 8).* That is God's redemptive plan; His end game for them, and as a *"shadow of things to come"* for us, our lives and journey. Here it is…

> *I will bring you out*
> *I will deliver you*
> *I will redeem you*
> *I will take you as my people*
> *I will bring you into the land*

The 4 steps of the Redemptive Work of God are found in the spaces between the proclamations. They bleed together and overlap as the work continues. The end game of this process is the Promised Land. They will, we will possess this land. If we bring this forward, what is your end game? What is your "Promised" possession? Where is your Jordan? Begin to think about this as we move forward. It will become more apparent.

Salvation history tends to repeat itself. It provides a mirror for us to look at our journey today. Thankfully, we won't need to be scholars to see it clearly. His Redemptive Plan is continually repeated, in the cups of the Passover Seder, and the Pilgrimage Festivals. He was to deposit them in the Land of His Promise, and they would remember through the rituals and ceremonies. Ultimately, we will land where…in Heaven with God.

Let's look at the 4 redemptive purposes of God, both in Israel and for those in Christ. A comprehensive online biblical commentary called Theology of Work Project has a great paper on the Redemptive work of God. I encourage you to read it. It's not that long and is easy to read. I included the link at the end of the book. It is called, God's Work of Redemption for Israel (Exodus 5:1-6:28).

Let's summarize the key points the commentary makes about God's work of redemption. It completely centers on the verses that encompass Exodus 6 and focus on Exodus 6:6-7. We'll learn to see the same redemptive plan as it relates to us. His plan hasn't changed. As the Apostle Paul stated, Christ, our Passover, began our new journey with Christ. We have embarked on this same journey. God's redemptive plan allows us to see the Gospel. "Thy Kingdom come, on earth as it is in Heaven".

God begins His plan through Moses with the proclamation "Let my people go!" in conjunction with the plagues that afflicted Egypt. You know the rest of the story. God lays out His plan in Exodus chapter 6. We discover that He intends to make Himself known to His people in a more direct and intimate way. He remembers the covenant He made with Abraham, Isaac, and Jacob.

His plan unfolds through Moses… *"He speaks to who He is"*, then God assures them that He is the same "covenant making-promise keeping" God of their forefathers.

> *"The New (Testament) is in the Old (Testament) concealed…*
> *The Old (Testament) is in the New (Testament) revealed"*
> *Saint Augustine*

Just as God clarified His design of redemption to the Israelites, He revealed His plan to us. This becomes the framework of Christ and the Gospel throughout the bible. The biblical thesis effectively draws the four parts of God's plan of redemption for the Israelites. We will increasingly draw on the parallels of God's plan as we move forward.

It remains the same through His Son, Jesus Christ. The four parts of God's Redemptive plan are repeatedly revealed throughout both the Old and New Testaments in various ways. Christ used different parables and analogies to describe God's plan and man's relationship with *"The Lord"* as was described in Exodus 6. We have God's work of Redemption.

First, I will bring you out. God called them out and delivered them from bondage. He reclaimed Israel from captivity. He set them apart and fulfilled His promise to Abraham. He began to band them together as a nation. They believed and began their pilgrimage to the new land.

God's redemptive work through Christ, His Son, who conquered Satan, called people out of Judea to a new world delivered and freed from sin. From Law to grace.

Second, I will deliver you. They grew in knowledge of the Covenant-making Promise-keeping God of Abraham. The "Lord's" desire…a Godly nation. Through the cleansing baptism of the sea, they were physically delivered from their past. They set their course toward Sinai.

Through Christ, God called people out of Judaism first, and eventually offered this relationship to all of mankind. Out of the center of Judea, they landed in the center of the known world. They landed in the center of the known world, Rome. This became the Church (nation), a new bride, of both Jew and Gentile. It was delivered from the bondage of the Law. Neither Jew nor Gentile, just one Church set apart to God. What was one recognizable nation became one recognizable Church with disciples from all nations.

Third, I will redeem you This is God's desire for Relationship. They arrived at Mt. Sinai. They ratified their marital Covenant with God. They went on to have an ongoing relationship with Him and they *confirmed* their obedience to God's Law and commands. God would dwell amongst them, and they would live in faithfulness to the Covenant. They have now grown in knowledge and intimacy of God in a new way.

The disciples of Christ ratified and confirmed the Gospel, the New Covenant, at Pentecost. They affirmed faithful adherence to the Gospel and committed to spreading the good news.

Fourth, I will take you as my people" YOU shall know that I am the 'Lord' your God... His people will experience a relationship with the God of Deliverance and Redemption. They travel on with God's sovereign leadership towards the final destination. He dwelt amongst them. He was faithful. God provided for them in the wilderness...through Tabernacle sacrifices, the three Pilgrimages, and the Manna. Look what the 'Lord' has done for them. *"He will be their God...they will be His People."*

Now, through His Son, Christians can "know" God in a way never before possible. God provides in our wilderness journey. This is an even more personal and intimate way than the covenant of Old. "...He abides in us, and we abide in Him...". The exchange is both physical and spiritual; both tangible and intangible. The word for "to know" has such an intimate connotation that the Jews use the word for sexual intimacy. It makes sense...the bride in communion with the bridegroom.

Finally, they landed at their destination. We, too, will land at our final destination.

So, first, you have God's deliverance from bondage. (Passover). Second, we see the nation fitted together as a people, a bride, at Mt. Sinai. They will be his people. (Pentecost) Third, we have thanksgiving for God's faithful Providence and provision. They have an ongoing relationship with their God. (Tabernacles) And fourth, the last part of God's redemptive plan is that of a Good and Abundant Life. Then, we arrive at the Promised Land.

We grow in our relationship in much the same way. It is with and through Christ It is through the Church with the sacraments to assist us in our relationship. We give ourselves as Ambassadors of the Ministry of Reconciliation.

We are sent, with abundant life, on a mission for the Kingdom of God, both in its present state and in the Kingdom to come.

> *From now on, therefore, we regard no one from a human point of view; even though we once knew Christ from a human point of view, we know him no longer in that way. So, if anyone is in Christ, there is a new creation: everything old has passed away; see, everything has become new! All this is from God, who reconciled us to himself through Christ, and has given us the ministry of reconciliation; that is, in Christ God was reconciling the world to himself, not counting their trespasses against them, and entrusting the message of reconciliation to us. So, we are ambassadors for Christ, since God is making his appeal through us; we entreat you on behalf of Christ, be reconciled to God. 2 Cor 5:16-20*

The visible Church and its people settle amongst people and nations of the world just as Israel once did. We are called to be a holy people and a light in their midst.

The Sabbath rest was given to the Israelites because of their transgressions, our "rest" is in Christ. This freedom offers a "good' life now. We are to promote this participation in God's kingdom…Christ the King…as we await the fullness of the Kingdom; a new heaven and a new earth. We live amongst the world as they lived in Canaan, *"The shining light in the transformed lives in the Church as a holy people."*

Bringing It Together

I kept studying. I kept reading. They say when you pray for God to show you something, He will. If you ask for knowledge or wisdom. He will give it. If you get out of line, He'll straighten you out. You know what I mean. Whew. It's a bumpy ride. Pray. Wait. Get in trouble…get straightened out. I was challenged from the pulpit one Sunday," *Make your calling and election sure…"*

Ok. That was unnerving. The same preacher began talking about *Judges* continually when we talked, repeatedly. It was a God thing I kept hearing *'Judges'* all the time. My biggest burden, the thing that bothered me the most, was the disunity. I prayed about that all the time. I would soon find out what 'Judges' was about.

I finally decided to quiet the noise. I was going to simplify things. The pursuit was to search for the nuggets of truth in the early Church. If possible, I was going to find God. Find Christ. Find the Gospel. Find the forest that was entangled in all the underbrush. Stop looking at all the trees. The bark. We hear about the view from 40,000 feet but that's not the view from 40,000 denominations.

We all know 'denominations' is not biblical. It is a word that is made up to describe pride, divorce, strife, quarreling, or quest for power, within the context of "following" Christ. But it is extra-biblical, and it can also be described as anti-biblical. The word is not in the bible. Christ and His Disciples warned against it…as wolves who would come to tear apart the body; the sheep.

So, let's impose. Occam's Razor. Let's use his principle. We'll search for the simplest answer and navigate outward from there. Let's remove as many assumptions as we can. Let's tell the simplest stories and narratives. We will try to avoid theologians competing hypotheses whenever possible. Abraham married Sarah, etc. We'll look at things socially and politically. What is the simplest narrative that we can understand?

My heart had screamed for the answer. Why there was so much disagreement in Protestantism? In Church? I opened my bible one day. It opened to the book of Judges. I knew Judges was the answer. This verse popped out.

"For in the days there were no kings in Israel, so everyone did what was right in their own eyes."

I had been challenged to study the book of Judges and to be honest, I didn't want to. There was an occasional half-hearted scanning through the book of Judges on several occasions. Same with Joshua. The Old Testament is boring and un-useful, I thought. And, Catholicism was certainly not on my radar.

The day had finally come. I had to finally admit the need to dig in. The verse in Judges appears twice in the book. Exactly. The. Same. I opened my bible to Judges and saw the passage…twice:

"For in those days there were no kings in Israel, and everyone did what was right in their own eyes".

I was fascinated. That's exactly how I, whether right or wrong, lived as a Christian. Then, it became apparent that the vast landscape of Christianity lived that way too. Was there a problem with Christianity not having its King? Every person and church did their own thing. They did what was right in their eyes. Did. What. Was. Right. In. Their. Eyes.

I attended "non-denominational, evangelical" churches for some time, attended church leadership conferences, held small group bible study in our home, and met many wonderful people and pastors. They seemed very much at peace with where they were.

To me, however, there was always that 'haunting' question. Why the divergent views? The Holy Spirit wouldn't do that. Jesus prayed for unity, community, and commonality. So, what about the King? I knew Jesus was king, and the kingdom of God had come near; so also, the household of God.

This was the answer. The theme of the Book of Judges was about a people who loved God, but where segments and groups continually wandered astray. This was the first time that a central "servant" of the Lord was not there. There was no central earthly figure to point to God as the King. The people wandered off.

The Israelites hadn't had an earthly king before, but there had been "Servants of the Lord ", or *"Eved Adonai"* in Hebrew. These leaders had always acted as God's servant, making God the center and the decision-maker, but these servants were not a king. The people of Israel wandered off to their own devices, their own idols and in many directions. Finally, they wanted a King. I began to see the Old Testament with different eyes.

Chapter 3: Judges: I'll do it my way!

"Where there is no vision, the people cast off restraint;
but blessed is he who keeps the law." Prov. 29:18

I began to investigate just what this Judges period was all about. My background is in social science, political science, and history. So, I decided to attempt to erect simple historical narratives and not get lost in what I feared would be a deep theological mess. In fact, I really didn't want to be theological. I felt compelled to simplify and find the basic historical stories and try to construct them to see their desire for a king.

How did they get there?...in the land of milk and honey? Could I discover some of the contrasts? And, who were the players? And, remembering the ever-present verse that had sent me here...looking for the throne. I went hunting:

"In those days there was no king in Israel; everyone did what was right in his own eyes."

The Journey

Let's define the Exodus a little deeper than the last chapter. The Israelites needed deliverance from the oppression and slavery of Egyptian captivity. Their nation began with the families of the brothers of Joseph who offered them shelter in Egypt. They grew to over 2 million strong and had become increasingly oppressed.

Finally, under God's guidance, Moses led the Israelites out of this bondage and toward their own promised land. The following timeline marks the milestones on this journey. Here is a quick summary of the high points that help us begin to put together a cohesive story.

The evening before, they were to take an unblemished lamb, roast it, and the family was to eat it with unleavened bread. The lamb was to be completely consumed. And should be shared amongst families if it couldn't eat it entirely. The thresholds of their dwellings were to be marked with the blood of the lamb.

Angel(s) would come and kill the Egyptian's firstborn but the Israelite's firstborn were safe. While still dark, they escaped across the desert. All 2 million+ Israelites followed Moses out across the desert. This was the first Passover. They were identified as set apart to God.

The Red Sea parted before them, and they crossed before the pursuing Egyptians could overtake them. The Egyptian armies, the oppression of their past was swallowed in the cleansing baptismal waters of the Red Sea. They were at once physically free from their past.

Within 2 weeks, God began providing Manna each morning to teach the Israelites to rely on God. They needed to abstain from all work and God would provide extra on Friday…It was the only day he would.

During the counting of Omer, the 7 weeks beyond Passover, they grew in the knowledge of the "Lord". They grew to see that He was the promise-keeping, covenant-making God of their ancestry.

Seven weeks after the Passover, God gave the Torah to the nation of Israel that was gathered at Mt. Sinai through Moses. There was a ratification ceremony that bound them in the covenant. The nation committed to serving God. This was the Pentecost. The fiftieth day. The marital covenant was sealed with the sprinkling of blood.

For 40 years, they lived in temporary structures, received supernatural manna from God, water from a rock, and necessarily relied on God for their entire existence. With gratitude and thankfulness, this became the Feast of Tabernacles.

During this time, some longed to return to Egypt, there were many struggles, and some never made it to the land that God promised them. They labored to overcome their transgressions and to be continually reconciled to God. It was an enormous undertaking, and needed rest because of it.The Sabbath was given to Israel because of their predicament.

They labored within the Tabernacle, continually. It kept both the nation of Israel and the individual Israelite reconciled to God. This was their ministry of reconciliation. The Tabernacle provided to place to address the needs of the people and to present themselves to God.

God provided the supernatural manna until the final day. The day, they crossed the Jordan and entered the promised land. They received a final spiritual cleansing as they crossed through the waters of the Jordan and entered in.

8

The Pilgrimage Festivals

Out of all the feasts and festivals of the Israelite Commonwealth, God wanted the nation of Israel to remember three specific festivals as milestones in their relationship. They were the Passover, Pentecost, and the Feast of Tabernacles. God required the entire nation to come in pilgrimage to the Tabernacle every year for these three festivals. Each represented a significant landmark that would forever seal their memory of what God had done for them.

Passover

Passover was the beginning of the 7-day Feast of the Unleavened Bread. It commemorates their liberation by God and memorializes the Exodus story of the Israelites flight from captivity and slavery in Egypt. The evening Passover Seder meal, a meal that mirrors the first Passover meal, is the vigil that begins the feast. It features the telling of the Exodus story, and always includes this prayer, *"You shall tell your child on that day, saying,"It is because of what the LORD did for me when I came out of Egypt."*

So, in this memorial, each person is commanded to view themselves as having been delivered by God from this captivity. So, perhaps it makes sense that it became a spring festival and grew connected to the first fruits of the grain harvest.

Pentecost

"All that the Lord has spoken we will do!" The fiftieth day. God made a conditional covenant with the nation of Israel at Mt. Sinai through His chosen leader Moses. The Law was a comprehensive set of requirements; a constitution, that had requirements on both sides. It was a bilateral agreement.

God had made an unconditional covenant with Abraham based on grace. Yet, now God reminded his descendants of their required obedience, and they agreed to the conditional covenant: a marital covenant. Moses recited the contents of the agreement and the entire nation ratified it at the base of the mountain.

The confirmed nation now had the constitution that would guide them to the establishment of a Holy Commonwealth that would be 'set apart' and a light to the world around them. Eventually, this necessarily ended the 7 weeks of the grain harvest that began at Passover. It also marked the first fruits of the fruit harvest.

Feast of Tabernacles

This is a festival of thanksgiving; one of gratefulness for God's provision. During the entire 40 years of the Israelite nation's journey in the wilderness, God provided for them. He also provided for every individual along the way. They lived in temporary structures and they received supernatural manna from heaven. While there was only one tabernacle in the wilderness, they were continually reconciled to God through the priestly ministry. They were completely dependent and had no one else to turn to.

Over time this festival has been referred to as the Gathering or the Ingathering. It also became associated with the harvesting of fruit. Christ chose this time to reveal Himself to the Apostles at the Transfiguration. Representatives of the Law (Moses) and the Prophets (Elijah) appeared. God made it clear to the Apostles to listen to Christ as opposed to the Law and the Prophets when their figureheads were present.

These simple storylines were the beginning of what was to become a discovery. I was going to discover the clearest and most uncomplicated path to the Church that would have emerged, otherwise, I would get lost and/or lose interest. Yes, these were simplistic explanations of the Exodus to the Promised Land and then the three Pilgrimage Festivals, but you'll see they end up being profound.

The Israelites found themselves in the era of Judges. So, how does that relate to us today; maybe just as important to us was the issue of kings. I discovered how important these little summaries are in the big scheme of things and we'll get more into it as we discover what that first Church would look like. But now, into the land of Judges.

From Joshua to Judges: The dichotomy

By contrasting the biblical account of the period of Joshua and Judges, we learn what worked and what didn't. Did God allow the time of Judges and the exasperating attempts at nation-building by the ancient Israelites as a teaching-tool for successive generations to learn from? Was the regime of Joshua a model for successive generations to shoot for in efforts to recapture a national, and unifying, identity?

The biblical account of Samuel certainly points to His desire to restore nationalism, with God as Sovereign leader, through the re-institution of a Joshua-like regime. The discourse at the end of the book of Judges and the first part of Samuel reveals that it would have also been God's will. Ultimately, God told Samuel that it was God Himself who had been rejected.

Joshua is a straightforward (some say idealized) telling of a time when God ruled His people. It is presented as a period when the nation worked and was singularly focused. There was a balance between national leadership and local governance.

An *Eved Adonai*, (See Ch.4) chief steward, preserved a singular vision for the nation on one hand and conveyed and taught God's will on the other. This kept the doctrine unified, gave the nation a common vision and code, and most importantly allowed God's reign. And, in contrast, the nation continually unraveled whenever it lost the unifying earthly presence.

Judges is presented differently. Somewhat discombobulated. It is a group of narratives that may or may not overlap, and are for the most part, local. There is a repeated "straying" from a unified national center, or essentially God. We most commonly have called it 'idolatry'. Personal, and local, self-sufficiency became more important than unity under God.

Before long, the Congregation of Israel unilaterally repented and yet held the leadership (God) somewhat accountable. And, the drumbeat for an earthly king continued to gain momentum. What developed in the absence of an *Eved Adonai* was for all intents and purposes, an 'anarchical' mood of a national proportion. "... *Everyone did what was right in their own eyes.*" *(Judges 17:6 and 21:25)*

There is a distinct dichotomy between the two periods of early Israelite life in the land of Canaan. The societal, political, and spiritual aspects of life in the two eras are noticeably polarized opposites. The lessons to be learned by these two opposing narratives are commonly spoken of by the Minor Prophets and relevant for us today, in our Post-Reformation world.

The books of Joshua and Judges deal intrinsically with an oft-repeated theme in the biblical record: the decline and fall of civilizations both from the outside but also from decay on the inside. The biblical narrative of the conquest of Canaan makes it clear that the Israelites sweep of the land was accomplished because the indigenous inhabitants had been greatly weakened from within.

The idea of civilizations collapsing from within before they are conquered from the outside is a common theme in the Bible. It becomes a vital part of the Prophetic message. The prophetic books illuminate similarities between the Canaanite cities and the Israelite kingdom(s) where the many symptoms of decline weakened morale and unity.

Joshua: The Good Commonwealth

Contemporary Jewish political scholars such as Stuart Cohen and Daniel Elazar, among others, believe that the book of Joshua reveals an ideal regime that promotes an almost perfect society. The covenantal society was sought by God through both Moses and Joshua and was confirmed by the whole nation.

It was a Holy Commonwealth. One led by an *Eved Adonai*, and with a separation of powers. There was a council of 70. And, it was one that left the power of daily governance to the 12 local tribes. Elazar put it this way,

> *The Book of Joshua, an idealized version of the conquest and settlement of Canaan by the Israelites, can properly be viewed as an expression of what the ideal Israelite polity should be, describing as it does in some detail what the polity was conceived to have been at the time of Joshua, that is to say, at the time of its greatest achievements in Canaan.*
>
> **If this biblical utopia looks to a great past situation for its inspiration, Ezekiel's utopia looks to a great future situation; yet, the description that emerges is quite similar to that found in the Book of Joshua. Finally, Isaiah's messianic vision implicitly assumes conditions such as those described in Joshua and Ezekiel"** [1]

Affirming Joshua's Authority

The book opens with Joshua's ascension in leadership and his affirmation from the entire body politic. In the first verse, we see the introduction of the term *Eved Adonai* or, "Servant of the Lord". It is the highest political title in the tribal federation. It is clear contextually that wherever the term is used in the Bible it means more than just "Servant of the Lord". It is the highest office and moral leader in the Israelite federation; a leader who serves the "King" of Israel. The *Eved Adonai* was the Chief Steward for the Lord, the Prime Minister; God's Prime Minister. We devote the entire next chapter to the biblical roots of this office with its roots deep in the Abrahamic Covenant.

In the first chapter of Joshua, the terms of God's covenant with Israel are restated, He repeats its promises and its conditions, and Joshua receives God's mandate and vision for the Trans-Jordan crossing and the settlement of the tribes in the nation of Israel. Joshua also needed to receive his authority from the *Edah*, or the entire nation, who then ratified God's appointment. *(Joshua 1:12)*.

Once the series of covenants is completed, God could deliver the mandates that included the conquest of the land directly to His chief steward, who was *Servant of the Lord*.

"Be strong and of good courage". This is a classical statement of strength that was necessary for this new *republic* and yet God continually reminds them that they are bound by covenant and the Torah constitution. They are also reminded that they sit under His judgment. Finally, God concludes with a blessing and a warning about living to the dictates of the Torah's constitution. This offers us a Prophetic vision about the failure of Israel to see the full promise of God; Israel's sin was the abandonment of the Torah: Idolatry…Adultery.

Beyond a Chief Steward, the regime was diverse with the degree of both national and local offices of administration and republican by the degree of elective representatives and appointments. There were special commissions such as the 12 spies to scout out the land, the commission to carry the Ark of the Covenant, and the commission to work with Joshua and the High Priest for the allocation of the lands.

The Cairn, the Rock, and the Stone Memorials

The "portable seat of government" was also the "Tent of Meeting" where God had established His earthly throne so He could dwell amongst His people. The focal point of the "seat" of government was the Ark of the Covenant. The Ark was also referred to as *(Aron HaEdut)* the Ark of the Testimony, or the Ark of Witnessing. *(Joshua 4:15)*

It contained the focal point of the *Edah*; the holiest possession; the tables of the covenant; *(Aron HaBrit)* or the Ten Commandments. This holiest possession testified to the central role of covenant in the nation of Israel.

As the Israelites assembled on the banks of the Jordan, they were commanded by Joshua, as the Lord had required, to sanctify themselves prior to the assault on the land that was promised them by God. Here, God is addressed as the *"Lord of all the Earth"*.

The priests that were carrying the Ark were ordered to stop in the middle of the Jordan and the waters of the Jordan were held back to enable the tribes to cross over into the land. Each tribe sends an elected representative, an indication of the federal character of this national undertaking, to participate in the crossing.

The elected representatives from each tribe are ordered to take a stone from the dry bed of the Jordan, at the feet of the priests holding the Ark, and erect a stone cairn at the site as a memorial of the event. This was the first "national historic site" of the *Edah* turned republic.

The actual site marker was designed to make this event vivid in the eyes of all future generations who would make pilgrimages to the site in remembrance of the day they crossed into the land promised them by God. The day that, *"Israel crossed this Jordan on dry ground"(4:22)* solidified Joshua's grip as Eved Adonai by showing the people that, God was with him just like He was with Moses,

"For the Lord, your God dried up the waters of the Jordan before you until you had crossed, just as the Lord your God had done to the Red Sea…" (4:23)

We are told that this national historical marker, the stone cairn, *"still stands there to this day." (4:9)* So,

> *"Let this serve as a sign among you. In the future, when your children ask you, 'What do these stones mean?' Tell them that the flow of the Jordan was cut off before the ark of the covenant of the* LORD. *When it crossed the Jordan, the waters of the Jordan were cut off. These stones are to be a memorial to the people of Israel forever."(4:6-7)*

We see that this memorial is considered highly significant to the nation, historically bonding them to their heritage. The act of commemoration of events through the use of a stone or rock memorial was commonplace for the Ancient Israelites and its importance was certainly understood even centuries later when Jesus' ministry confronted the status quo.

The Fall of Jericho

The conquest of Jericho was a stunning initial victory for the Israelites. The victory served to demoralize the already fearful indigenous civilizations. The Bible indicates that it was God who had greatly weakened them. The psychological preparation of the Canaanites was undoubtedly essential for the quick victory.

While it is clear that it is God's might that causes the fall of Jericho, there is also evidence of the necessity of the covenantal workings between God and the *Edah:* Joshua transmitting God's commands, the Ark of the Covenant, the priests as manifestations of God's presence, and the people all led to the fall of Jericho. *(6:6-24)*

In contrast, the Israelites suffer an unexpected defeat soon after the victory at Jericho. Some had looted and took the spoils of the earlier victory, against orders, and as a result, they can't even beat a pile of ruins *"Ai"* just east of Beth El. The results made it clear; the Israelites must remain holy and follow the commands of the Lord. Actions of a few could cause serious consequences for everyone and increased personal awareness as to how an individual's actions affect others.

This is another illustration of the Prophetic viewpoint of the book. It shows what happens when the covenant is broken. It also illustrates how civilizations can collapse from within before being destroyed by some outside force, sometimes without any shots fired.

The Bible implies the similarities between the collapse of the Canaanite cities and the many symptoms of the decline of the Israelite regimes. The holiness, the morality, and the unity of the Israelites were required if they were going to accomplish, or more accurately receive, the blessings in store for them from God. *(Joshua chapter 6-8) [4]*

Shiloh

"The whole assembly of the Israelites gathered at Shiloh and set up the Tent of Meeting there. The country was brought under their control," (Joshua 18:1)

The seat of the government came to rest at Shiloh. Shiloh was established as the place of the national assembly. It was the seat of the republic and the tribal federation. For the first time in Israelite history, Shiloh became a concrete place. By placing the Tent of Meeting at Shiloh, the place became all those things.

The *Adat Bnei Yisrael*, *"the whole congregation"* assembled and set up the *"tabernacle of the congregation"*. In this, God's earthly throne was set up at Shiloh and it remained there until the end of the period of Judges when it was captured by the Philistines.

But through all this, Shiloh is referred to as a 'camp' *(Joshua 18:9)* and not a permanent settlement staying consistent with the tradition that they carried out of the desert wilderness. The tradition was that the Lord's dwelling place could not be part of a fixed settlement.

The Israelites appeared before the Lord there. It was a place where the tribal delegates convened on national issues. The *Edah* assembled, *"three times a year you are to appear before the Lord",* at Shiloh; they assembled for all the mandatory feasts

43

and sacrifices at the Tent of Meeting. It was the religious center; the center of Israelite worship.

It was also the center of Ancient Israel's identity as a body politic. The place was the site of the throne, where God was afforded opportunities in the decision-making for His people. But it was also the last place that God dwelt amongst His people in the capacity as[direct] Sovereign ruler.

Dealing with Secession

With the campaign for the settlement over, though not complete, Joshua gives what was, arguably, the first of a long tradition of republican farewells. He urges them to go home and pick up the shattered pieces of their lives as he demobilizes the troops. He commends them for their commitments to the Lord's commandments and to Moses' injunction.

Joshua charges them to remain true to the covenant in all their endeavors and exhorts them to:

> ...*keep the commandment and the law, which Moses, Servant of the Lord* **[Eved Adonai]***, commanded you, to love the Lord your God and to walk in His ways, and to keep His commandments and to cleave unto Him and to serve Him with all your heart and with all your soul (verse 5).* And with that, Joshua blessed them and sent them home.

The two and a half tribes that originally settled on the east bank of the Jordan went home and built a new altar. This new altar was apparently at an important point along the banks of the Jordan. Though couched in the terms of religious observance for the people of those living east of the Jordan, this new center of worship appeared to be a secessionist activity to the rest of the nation. The establishment of the new center of worship could have ultimately ended in the shifting of political allegiance away from the remainder of the nation.

Short of civil war, the *Edah,* acting as a federal body, warns them of the consequences of straying from the covenant before they take any action against the tribes. They are given an opportunity to repent.

A delegation is formed under the terms of the constitution and is sent to meet with the leaders of the east bank tribes. The delegation included the High Priest's son, known to mediate between the tribes, and many high-ranking officials and military leaders, sent to impress upon them the gravity of the situation. They are asked directly if this was an act of rebellion and they are reminded that this could cause a backlash from God against the entire *Edah.*

The leaders of the east bank settlement deny that they have any interest in rebelling against the national authority and insist that they are not secessionists. They state that they were only trying to find a way to communicate national unity on both sides of the river to their descendants. They affirm their belief in the Lord of Israel and deny that their altar was to be used for sacrifice. They insist that it was to be a historical monument to remind descendants of the unity of the people on both banks of the Jordan. Their statement was convincing:

> *In time to come your children might speak unto our children saying, what have ye to do with the Lord, the God of Israel, the Lord hath made the Jordan a border between us and you; you children of Reuben and you children of Gad, you have no portion of the Lord, so might your children make our children cease from fearing the Lord." (Joshua 22:28)*

Finally, the east bank tribes confirm their loyalty to the Tabernacle at Shiloh and the local altar would only serve as a witness that the east bank tribes accept the Lord of Israel as their God. The delegation is pleased, and the son of the High Priest of Israel says, *"This day we know the Lord is in the midst of us because you have not committed treachery against the Lord."(22:31)*. With that, the *Edah* is satisfied and the threat of civil war has been averted.

Joshua's Farewell

The entire *Congregation of Israel* was assembled at the Tent of Meeting in Shiloh for Joshua's final address to the nation. As a witness to the complexity of governance in the tribal federation, Joshua's message is directed at the multitude of tribal and national officeholders, all of which were apparently in attendance.

Joshua explicitly mentions several categories of leaders in attendance, there were: the heads of families and clans, the heads of tribes, judges, and the national civil servants. The assembled leaders are reminded of the rewards that God has bestowed upon Israel through His direct involvement in Israel's affairs *(24:3)*.

Constitutional issues such as the Canaanite remnants, isolationism, and intermarriage are addressed. Joshua finishes his charge by reminding the leaders that just as the good things of the Lord have come to pass, so to can the bad things if the people depart from the terms of the covenant. In doing so, he exhorts them to be committed to the maintenance of the covenant, and the constitution of the Israelite nation.

After Joshua recites the historical lineage of the Israelites, even beginning from pre-Israelite times in Mesopotamia, the general Congregation was re-presented the covenant. They were also presented with constitutional changes. The changes made necessary by the settlement of the Land. The entire body politic was required to reaffirm their commitment to both.

Joshua urged them to be sure of their vow and to understand its consequences. The vote was taken three times considering the seriousness of this event and the *Congregation* affirmed it each time confirming their decision. A large rock (stone) is erected in the shadow of the Lord, and the Tent of meeting to bear witness to the covenant-making, a witness to all those that heard the words of the Lord that day. The words as presented by Joshua, the Servant of the Lord, and that they had affirmed the covenant; affirmed the Lord's constitution.

The large rock would also continue to stand as a witness to the descendants, the future generations of those in covenant with the Lord. *(Joshua 24:2-29)*

> *The people of Israel served the LORD throughout the lifetime of Joshua and of the elders who outlived him--those who had personally experienced all that the LORD had done for Israel." (Joshua 24:31) "And it came to pass after these things, that Joshua the son of Nun, the (Eved Adonai) servant of the LORD, died, being a hundred and ten years old." (Joshua 24:29)KJV*

Judges: The Regime fragments

The book of Judges represents a time of considerable transformation on many levels. There is a biblical shift in its focus from the tribes closely aligned with Joseph to the tribe of Judah and her sister tribes. The tribes become more tied to the land for their needs; hence there is less dependency on any of their needs outside of their local environment.

They slowly begin a walk away from their covenantal promises that are only arrested during the periods in which a charismatic *Judge* can pull them back. These characteristics are presented at the beginning of the book of Judges as having begun almost immediately after Joshua's death.

Their dilemma is quite clear; if they want to be successful, they will remain faithful to the commitment they made, through the covenant, to God. On the other hand, they see the idolatrous/ adulterous consequences of the constant temptation of the local customs of the Canaanites.

The remainder of Judges generally replays the same historical pattern repeatedly. The Lord had resolved not to drive out the remaining temptations from the lives of His people. They would be free to make choices for and against the Covenant. The people repeatedly fall and lapse into idolatry and sin against God and His Covenant. Their self-sufficiency and their reliance on the land lessened their 'need' of the Covenant promises.

This increased their tendency to just ignore it. God would eventually intervene and deliver them from their predicament by sending a Judge to redeem them and bring them back into communion with the Covenant.

Unfortunately, this would only last during the life of the Judge and the people would quickly lapse back into sin leading to a repeat of this pattern. The names, dates, and specific issues of rebellion, sin, and idolatry may have changed as the account unfolds, but the pattern is the same.

Gideon

Gideon is a perfect example of God's modus operandi as a Judge, chosen from a poor and insignificant family. He was to become a leader of significance to the Israelite nation. His rise begins with a test from a messenger of God in which Gideon destroys *Baal* altars and reaches its peak with him gaining national distinction through military victories against the Midianites.

The victories confirmed Gideon's favor with the Lord, who employed tactics that were directed by God down to the last detail. Through these experiences, Gideon demonstrated the characteristics of a true charismatic national leader. His public stand against idolatry, his belief in God's promises through divine dreams, and his use of unconventional God-directed tactics secured victory in war.

Israel asked Gideon to be their king, but also a hereditary kingship. The offer is immediately rejected by Gideon.

"Rule over us--you, your son and your grandson--because you have saved us out of the hand of Midian." But Gideon told them, "I will not rule over you, nor will my son rule over you. The LORD will rule over you."(8:22-23)

In his finest hour, he rejects the idea of a king for the nation of Israel. He rejected the monarchy as being consistent with the covenant *"...the Lord will rule over you"*. This didn't end Israel's infatuation with an earthly king, but Gideon lived out the rest of his life as a Judge. And, we're looking for the king.

Bringing it together

As Christians, we hear of prefigurement(s) until we're blue in the face, but maybe it's just me. There are certain stories, journeys, and models that we uncover and that are, yes…prefigurement; a shadow of things to come. Add to that the realization is that Salvation history has a tendency to repeat itself; and that all history has a tendency to repeat itself…We tend to ignore it.

"Those that forsake history are doomed to repeat it."

Paul called this *"the shadow of things to come"*. So, we are to look at many of these narratives as mirrors for us today. If we don't know them, we won't know what the Church looks like, or our own path. The Church and each Christian throughout time partake of the journey trans the Mosaic Law in their relationship with Christ. We'll soon put together more of the narratives of the Old Testament that help us illuminate the Church that emerged.

The Holy Commonwealth, the Wilderness Tabernacle, the Manna, the Three Pilgrimage Festivals, the entire journey out of bondage is lived out once again in our lives; and much more.

Gods Sovereign leadership was unquestioned in their journey out of Egypt and into their own land under God's recognized Chief Servants, *Eved Adonai*, with a goal of establishing a Holy Commonwealth that was set apart onto God. But, without the Chief Servant, the Holy Commonwealth became increasingly confederal and almost anarchical and adulterous in nature.

This led to the Israelites flirtation with the monarchy. *(For in those days there were no kings in Israel)* The ideal regime of Joshua disintegrated into a loosely held confederation. *(Everyone did what was right in their own eyes)*. The book of Judges ultimately pushed a pro-monarchal viewpoint and an earthly throne sans God as Sovereign.

Though the concept of a monarchy was consistently rejected as a regime that was compatible with the covenant, the condition of the nation would eventually lead to an earthly king. This debate became paramount throughout the rest of the Old Testament and majored in the Prophets. Eventually, the Congregation of Israelites settled on the kingdom idea.

Israel recognized their failures repeatedly throughout the book of Judges, they refused responsibility. They believe the answer would be the establishment of an earthly monarchy. However, Samuel tries to redefine the issue. He restates the problem as being one of the inability of the nation to hear the will of God

[Keter Torah] (we'll discuss the three crowns in ch.5) in an attempt to ward off the growing tide of demands for an earthly king.

The stark differences between the regime of the *Eved Adonai*, with God as the Sovereign Ruler and that of the disjointed almost 'anarchical' Judges period, need to be revisited today as we look at the disarray of the condition of Christianity today.

The political perspectives of the Israelite forays into the Holy Commonwealth, set apart onto God, need to be considered in association with both the early Church as well as the church today. When there was a lack of national focus, there was a 'falling away' that permeated the societal fabric.

Apparently, just as today, when left to our own interpretation, or own devices, we wander off in many different directions. And, just as with the people of Israel during the time of Judges, we know that this wandering about is not led by God. Jesus himself taught the importance of unity.

"...that they may all be one; even as Thou, Father, art in Me, and I in Thee, that they also may be in Us; that the world may believe that Thou didst send Me."(John 17:21)

Chapter 4: Eved Adonai-Servant of the Lord

"Son, in thirty-five years of religious study, I've come up with only two hard, incontrovertible facts; there is a God, and, I'm not Him." Father Cavanaugh to Rudy

Before we proceed to the pivotal time of Samuel, and the advent of an earthly king, let's look at that 'perfect' regime in Joshua. In studying the epochs of Joshua and Judges, I became aware of the title of the definitive office held by both Joshua and Moses. Contemporary Jewish scholarship has given this office a name: *"Eved Adonai"*.

This chapter will explore this office and its ramifications if any can be identified going forward. Jewish scholarship makes a compelling case for the title. We can all agree that they held an office that was ordained by God. And, that it was recognized and ratified by the entire nation.

The entire next chapter is devoted to the long-established domains, or separations, of authority. At the time of Christ, we certainly see these separations of powers operating. I wanted to introduce them here. We can ponder them as we move forward. The differing roles are *Keter Malkhut*(Civil), *Keter Torah*(prophetic), and *Keter Kehunah*(priestly).

Remember when Christ explained to those gathered that the Pharisees and scribes sat in Moses' seat. We're like…What?? Christ identified the Pharisees and scribes operating in the domain of the *Keter Torah*. They conveyed and taught the will of God both by oral interpretation and by the written law. So, in that sense, both the Pharisees and the other teachers of the Law held a portion of Moses' authority. But that still doesn't say much.

At first glance, Moses operated in an office that was unique, but was that truly the case? Let's explore the Mosaic office by looking at the historical connections that led the way. Who came before Moses…and after? Christ, while addressing the Pharisees, obviously explained that the Mosaic office still existed…sort of? We may discover that Moses' office has existed from Genesis to today. So, what is this *Eved Adonai*?

God used Moses to deliver them from Egypt, and He also used Moses to deliver the Covenantal Law at Sinai. The leaders and elders of the fledgling nation didn't run him off because of false doctrine. Moses delivered, decided, and they accepted it. But God also confirmed, and the nation ratified.

This wasn't an edict by consensus, not by the individual, but by Moses himself. Moses had God's 'Charisma' chosen to lead the more than 2 million+ Israelites. He was a 'Servant of God' who freely chose to serve the Lord.

We can also see this servanthood, this love, as like of family; the family of the household of God. This was Moses' seat, an office, overseeing the entire household of God. We know this, *"that the founder of all is God"* and *"... Moses was 'faithful in all his house' as a 'servant' to testify to what would be spoken" (Hebrews 3:4-5*

Today, we like to use the term 'office' to denote a specific authority and/or function. This allows us to delineate the duties and responsibilities of each office. Moses' seat is one such office. Contemporary Jewish thesis began calling the title to the Mosaic office, *Eved Adonai*. Moses was 'Servant of the Lord'. God was directly in charge and ruled over His people.

One could say that the throne was in Heaven. God was the "father" and Moses [servant] served the Lord. He communicated God's will to the household of God. The *Eved Adonai* was always loyal to the Lord and only acted on God's behalf. He was the servant of the one who reigned.

So, where did this concept of a single political leader under God come from? Was it just ordained by God for the first time with Moses? Where and how far back, do we look? We find that Moses created several offices with divisions of authority in the initial confederation of the tribes of Israel.

The council of 70 [Sanhedrin] and the ratification of the office of *Eved Adonai* was sanctioned. Let's go back and see if we can find any prior biblical evidence of the office. Can we clearly lay out the development of the office of *Eved Adonai*? We discover the "Servant of the Lord" has roots from the very moment the first covenant was made with Abraham.

The Different Ages

Many divide the span between the start of the Abrahamic Covenant to the first constitutional epoch that began with the Exodus out of Egypt consists of two ages [epochs]. The biblical record suggests a patriarchal age and an age of the Egyptian sojourn. Joseph is the transitional figure that that somewhat muddies the waters between the patriarchs and the establishment of the nation.

> **Side Note:** Christ debated with the Pharisees and scribes all the time. They repeatedly stated that Abraham was their father, and Moses was their teacher. They defended their positions of authority. Christ responded *"call no man father, and call no man teacher"* [*call no man father*]

The patriarchal age began with God's covenant with Abraham [*call no man father*] and ends sometime in the land of Goshen under the umbrella of the Egyptian pharaoh and his vizier Joseph. The second proto- national age encompasses the entire time of the Egyptian sojourn. And, finally the Mosaic [*call no man teacher*] age with the development of the Holy Commonwealth.

Abraham

There is no debate that God's desire has always been an intimate relationship with humankind. He has long desired to live and dwell amongst his greatest creation. We failed twice before God made his covenant with Abraham. We were cast from the garden, and God flooded the Earth to begin again. It was our disobedience.

At one point, we decided that we could get there ourselves, so we built a large tower to reach Him. God promised that He would never again flood the Earth and destroy His Creation, so this time He made a covenant with a man, Abraham, who would be a father of a great nation.

Daniel Elazar, in his article *The Polity of Ancient Israel,* summarized the patriarchal period this way:

> *During the first epoch* ***[age]*** *the patriarch was the sole repository of governmental powers. He was governor and military leader and he conducted foreign relations. He also received instructions from God and made the covenants with Him which constituted the constitutional framework for the emergent Jewish people. In that context, he prayed, sacrificed, built altars and monuments, and offered blessings.* [1][2]

The patriarchal age consisted of God's covenant with Abraham and his family; his son Isaac, and his grandson Jacob. Jewish sages have always taught that the forefathers (patriarchs) kept the 'precepts' of the Torah They 'fulfilled' the teaching of the Torah even prior to Sinai. It illustrates for us how far humility goes with God. There is an oft-repeated rabbinical phrase about Abraham, *"God looked into the Torah and created the world, Abraham looked into the world and discovered God".*[3]

Eliezer

Within the story of Abraham's family, there is a little-known figure named Eliezer. Christian theologians have completely overlooked him. However, rabbinical Judaism, as well as contemporary Jewish scholars, has certainly found him to be an enigma. Arguably, he may be one of the most important characters to a Christian who is looking for the authentic Church.

We find the roots of the office of *"Eved Adonai"* in the first covenant. Actually, it dovetails exactly. The person was Abraham's chief servant (steward) Eliezer. He is most commonly referred to as the 'servant' or the 'Servant of his Master'. Eliezer was the wisest [oldest] of Abraham's servants. There were 318 servants of Abraham, but Eliezer was numero uno.

He provided oversight and was responsible for all that Abraham had. He was in charge of everything the master owned. He was Abraham's chief servant. *(Genesis 15, 24)* It was obvious that Abraham trusted Eliezer completely, so he must have been quite an impressive figure. He became the first *Chief Steward* or *Prime Minister* in the Abrahamic covenant, the first "Household of God", and remained in that office after Abraham's death.

Jewish tradition gets confounded by Eliezer. *"And the servant told Isaac all the things he had done". (Genesis 24:66)* The Midrash comments on this statement, as there could have been more written: *"There is more general statement in the Torah than detailed statement, for had he wished, he could have written two or three columns."* The Rabbis also said this: *"He disclosed to him the more welcome incidents [only, e.g.] that the earth had contracted before him."* (Midrash Rabbah - Genesis 60:15)

It was first arranged that when Abraham died, Eliezer would become the head of the household. *(Genesis 15)* However, God stepped in and gave Abraham a son. After Abraham's rightful sole heir is determined, Eliezer, the chief servant was given a special mission. He was commissioned to lead a group of servants in search of his son's bride. (See how these stories work yet?)

> ***Get this:*** *Eliezer was commissioned by his master. He was commissioned to lead a group, and go...Into the world, and gather a bride for his son.*

The Torah continued telling the story of the chief steward as he went looking for a bride for Abraham's son Isaac. Shockingly, the Torah retells the story all over again. So, we have the account of Eliezer's search for the "bride of the Covenant" repeated.

Read Rabbi Aha's comments. He is shocked that it's more important than a serpent elsewhere in scripture:

> *The mere conversation of the slaves [servants] of the Patriarchs' household is more important than the laws [Torah] of the (Patriarch's) descendants. This chapter dealing with Eliezer covers two or three columns, and his story [his conversation] is not only recorded but repeated. Whereas [the uncleanness of] a reptile is an integral part of the Torah, and yet it is only from an extending particle in Scripture that we learn that its blood defiles as its flesh.* (Midrash Rabbah - Bereishit 60:8)

One of the goals of the Torah is to teach the law. Again, the Rabbi's confusion is certainly profound, *"The mere conversation of the slaves of the Patriarchs' household is more important than the laws [Torah] of their descendants".* Hmm, they point directly at the servant's words over the law of the Torah itself, but then at the time, they didn't have the Torah.

There is also a surprise that the words of the 'servant' became recorded in Sacred Scripture. *"So much ink is spilled on the words of a servant."* These words were spoken by a chief steward and servant, who served Abraham and his master; And, a servant with trust in, and from, God.

So, in the everlasting Abrahamic Covenant, the chief servant emulated selflessness and humility and magnified his loyalty. His service transcended Abraham's death and he continued on as chief servant for Isaac. He loyally protected the family, its past and its future. The chief servant oversaw the entire household in an almost nameless fashion, trusting God and not promoting himself. His words became truth. And, he searched for and found a worthy bride for the heir of what would become the household of God.

Joseph

Historically, Jacob has been the last of the patriarchs. And, it makes perfect sense. He was the father of the 12 sons who became the 12 tribes of Israel. But they were also the sons who ended up on Joseph's doorstep. About 70 when into Egypt and more than 2 million came out. Another way to put it is that a family went in and a nation came out. God's way of protecting his young ones by hiding them out under the large umbrella of an Egyptian Pharaoh until they were strong enough to fend for themselves.

In *The Polity of Ancient Israel*, Daniel Elazar also summarized the second age:

> *At the beginning of the second epoch of Jewish history, the families of the twelve sons of Jacob were well-ensconced in Egypt, living under a foreign rule which sooner or later reduced them to slavery. There were no more patriarchs. In their place are zekenim (elders) and shotrim (maintainers of the peace), officials who administer the customary law of the tribes, perhaps recalling in a latent way the patriarchal covenants.* [1][5]

Joseph, with his coat of many colors, spent almost all of his life in Egyptian society. What were the politics and culture like? What role did he play and how high was his rise? How did this socio-political culture influence, Moses? It's important to realize that this must have had an enormous impact on the future of the Israelite nation.

First, Egyptologists and cryptologists have not been able to put together a nice, neat and cohesive Egyptian timeline, let alone dovetail it with the biblical account. But it also doesn't discount it either. We don't have an exact extra-biblical date for their Exodus.

Even in this light, there is a consensus among these experts, of a mass exodus of people out of Egypt. Joseph received them into Egypt, and Moses took them out. So, spending a little time can help us biblically, and also how Joseph and Moses relate to our hunt for the authentic Church.

Egypt
Interesting note: Egypt descended from Noah's youngest son, Ham, as did Canaan. Noah cursed Ham, presumably for Ham having "seen his nakedness"

We know that the Israelites lived for almost 500 years in Egypt. The ancient Egyptian culture was one of the longest-lasting societies to ever exist. It was one of the most peaceful and static cultures in history. It was also intensely traditional.

In *The Ancient Egyptian Culture Revealed*, Moustafa Gadalla characterizes much of the empire this way:

The essence of such traditionalism is in the Egyptians' total adherence to precedence established by their ancestors. Everything they did, every action, every movement, every decree, had to be justified in terms of their ancestral precedence--to abide by and explain their actions and deeds . [6]

The long-standing priestly caste is believed to have pre-dated the dynastic period of the pharaohs of Egypt. The priests, along with the scribes and sages, maintained the stability of the culture. The priestly caste was not only "the keeper" of the religious rituals but also the law, science and technology, and its culture.

The nation's participation in, and almost total adherence to, these religious rituals and the precedence set by their ancestors is a perfect recipe for retaining knowledge and a static social order. *"...when the ministers of religion were also the ministers of science (and knowledge)... so that they united in their own persons two of the noblest missions in which man can be invested, the worship of the Deity, and the cultivation of intelligence..."* [7]

The geography of the Egyptian kingdom also plays a significant role in the stability of Egyptian culture. It was largely isolated from other empires, so they had no need for a standing army, and it was also a nation of bountiful harvests. There was an annual flood of the Nile that virtually guaranteed an abundance of food for the growing kingdom. They were the "Gift of the Nile", who had a marvelous garden in the midst of the desert.

Because of this, there was little need to venture very far. So, they became a massively successful agricultural culture, raising animals and growing crops. They faced very little external pressure but also had few internal upheavals that would create instability in the political order.

The Egyptian pantheon was a mirror of the Egyptian culture. It was highly developed and complex, yet at times it pivoted as new gods rose to national prominence. While mostly pantheistic, there were forays into monotheism or at least recognizing a god that appeared to tower above the rest. Akhenaten was the pharaoh who became known as the, albeit heretical, "first monotheist" who made Aten, the god above all. Moustafa Gadalla explained it this way:

Amenhotep IV or Ahkenaton, ("(He who serves) the Spirit of the Aton") would rock Egyptian civilization to its core by announcing that the Aton was the one and only, single and exclusive, divinity. And of course, that Ahkenaton was his regent on earth, in the exact same way as Osiris was

Re's regent on earth. Ahkenaton, with his version of the Aton, had bootstrapped himself into godhood while still living. He had, in the sense that the Egyptians understood best, usurped the throne of Osiris. No human had ever dared such blasphemy ". [6]

Joseph's assent

It was this elaborate culture that Joseph was grafted into, and in which he excelled. Let's set aside the familiar stories of Joseph's life; the stories of his betrayal and his ascendancy. What's important is that he became well-schooled in the Egyptian school system; its law and history, and math, science, and technology. This enabled him to ascend in the highly developed political structure.

During Joseph's ordination ceremony the:

> *…Pharaoh said to Joseph, "Since God has informed you of all this, there is no one so discerning and wise as you are. "You shall be over my house, and according to your command all my people shall do homage; only in the throne I will be greater than you." Pharaoh said to Joseph, "See, I have set you over all the land of Egypt." (Genesis 41:39-41)*

This was an interesting development for me. The Pharaoh recognized that Joseph heard from God. We know that God made that possible. It's still interesting. Still, Joseph was there waiting to receive the children of the Covenant, his family, into the garden on the Nile and under the protective umbrella of the Egyptian culture.

A full body of Joseph's story is difficult to piece together. Egyptian historical evidence uses a completely different set of names than those used by the Hebrew chroniclers, and with that, we still don't have a consensus of a unified timeline. However, that should not be a consequence.

There are artifacts that show Hebrew mushroom hairstyles within the 12th dynasty, and we know there was a mass movement of Asiatic people from the Egyptian kingdom eastward. They have also found an empty tomb that could indeed be that of Joseph. (Remember, Moses, took the bones of Joseph into the new Canaanite land.) Some archeologists claim to have found an intact statue of Joseph. Photos of the statue reveal it to be an Israelite and he seems to be wearing a coat of many colors.

So, how high within Egypt's political hierarchy did Joseph climb?

And God sent me before you to preserve you a posterity in the earth, and to save your lives by a great deliverance. So now it was not you that sent me hither, but God: and he hath made me a father to Pharaoh, and lord of all his house, and a ruler throughout all the land of Egypt. (Genesis 45: 7-8)

At the end of verse 8, there are three separate descriptions of Joseph's titles:

The father of pharaoh: Egyptians would also see that as "father of god". Their kings (pharaohs) were normally considered deities. This title was common in the middle and late dynasties and generally is referred to as "god's father". In Joseph's case, it most probably meant that he was an elder statesman.

Lord of all his house: This title would normally be looked at as a palace overseer by the Egyptians. A Chief Chamberlain, the chief steward of the king, or the chief overseer of the household. Based on the biblical description, the chief steward of the [king] would best fit Joseph. This was also a common office in the middle kingdom. Many scholars seem to believe that this title is most befitting of Joseph.

Ruler throughout all the land of Egypt: This would be the office of the Egyptian Vizier and would compatible with Genesis 41:41: *"I have set you over all the land of Egypt"* While there is some debate, you will commonly see Joseph's name associated with that of the Egyptian office of Vizier. [8]

If we accept that Joseph was set over all the land of Egypt as the Bible claims, then his rise to Vizier of all of Egypt is certainly astounding. The Vizier was second only to the pharaoh, and the pharaoh was considered a sovereign deity. We could also call him the Prime Minister of Egypt.

The deputy of the pharaoh was the highest official and was usually awarded large tracks of land and became quite wealthy. This gave the Vizier enormous power in Egyptian culture. The Vizier could accumulate so much power that he could also become the chief priest. Some of the duties of the Vizier included the following list:

- He sat on the high court\

- Appointed government officials
- Adjudicated major legal disputes
- Maintained civil order
- Taxation and census
- Controlled food supply
- Oversaw archives
- Recorded rainfall for the taxation of farmers
- Occasionally oversaw the priesthood

Joseph is now the second person in the biblical record to hold an office that is considered a chief steward or a Prime Minister to the master, in charge of all the master had; the household of the master. In a sense, could we also say king? These early offices were obviously complex and were more than just precursors; they teach us how God was expanding on the concept of *Eved Adonai,* for the Israelites to see as we move forward in time. They certainly weren't flip-floppin' desert wanderers.

Moses

There will be many aspects of the "Mosaic" life of the Israelites that we will explore as we look to discover the Church that emerged out of first-century Judea, but here we just want to look at his office; his anointing as some would say. Political scholar, Professor Daniel Elazar's research has really opened a new understanding of the era.

Joshua 1:1 "After the death of Moses, the 'Eved Adonai'…".

Professor Elazar makes a compelling case for this *"Eved Adonai"* to be the title for an office in ancient Israel. The highest in the land, but faithful to God's throne, His sovereignty. Other contemporary Jewish scholars such as Stuart Cohen have also jumped on board. For those of you interested, Daniel Elazar's complete library is available at the Jerusalem Center for Public Affairs, which he founded.

Elazar reveals…

This is the highest political title in the Israelite tribal federation. From its *context wherever it is used in the Bible, it is clear, that it does not simply mean "Servant of the Lord" but is the title of the highest political and moral leader of the Israelite nation who serves **God the King**. God's "servant" is used herein in the same sense as Minister is used today in parliamentary systems of government. Hence, it is best understood as "God's Prime Minister.(see also Exodus 14:31; Numbers 12:7)*

There we go...Yes...God the King. God's throne. We have already come a long way. Moses was a man who served God; the God of the Israelites; and the God of the patriarchs. Moses was *Eved Adonai*. God spoke through the *Eved Adonai*. He was similar to the Vizier in Egypt, but the throne of Whom he served was in Heaven. Moses is called *Eved Adonai* 15 times in the Old Testament and Joshua twice.

Eved Adonai is the title used for the office of God's Chief Steward as they journeyed and settled in the Promised Land. The term *"Eved Neeman"*, God's faithful servant, appeared in describing Abraham, Eliezer, and Joseph, who were all true to God's intent and to the values that God taught, but they didn't have the Torah.

In this new epoch, the *Eved Adonai* was tied to the idea of a prophetic theocracy. Moses was responsible to convey the will of God to the people and to maintain the constitution; God's Covenant. His Sovereign remained in heaven and yet He would be able to dwell amongst His people through the Wilderness Tabernacle Elazar..." The *Eved Adonai* can be the head of the government *of the Israelites but only God can be the head of state."*

During the first two post-captivity epochs, the Israelite people were led by Moses and Joshua; a single *"Eved Adonai"* given God's charisma and granted the authority to oversee the 12 tribes of Israel. However, God was the One who directly governed his people. And, as God's representatives, the "Chief Stewards" primary function was to act as God's messenger...and to maintain the faithful teaching of the Law.

The *Eved Adonai* brought a "solidarity". God's Chief Steward kept the importance to adhere to the will of God, their common values and keep their rituals before their eyes, or before the *Edah (congregation)*. There was a common set of traditions; and maintenance of beliefs and practices. Still, there was not a 'federal' government. There weren't any large government social programs.

These programs were all expected at a local level. *All politics is local.* However, Moses did begin separating powers with the establishment of the council of 70 elders for adjudicating the law federally, and the responsibility of maintaining the service in the Tabernacle with Aaron and the Levite tribe. Then again, God completely took the Tabernacle out of Moses' hands with His separate Covenant with Aaron.

The local tribes also had own leaders' representatives; they had tribal 'gates', or government centers. Mosaic Law taught their moral responsibilities; those of the individuals, families, and clans. There was a realized need for individualism within the local community with the context of the individual's adherence to the moral law. The individual or family also needed to submit to a unified set of national beliefs, rituals, and traditions. (Catholic doctrine of subsidiarity)

Professor Elazar expands on this separation of power:

> *The Mosaic constitution laid the foundations for the first Israelite polity, which was organized federally around a loose union of tribes, traditionally twelve in number. This union, perhaps the first true federal system in history, was bound together by a common constitution and law but maintained relatively rudimentary national institutions grafted onto more fully articulated tribal ones whose origins may have antedated the Exodus.*

> *This situation prevailed, in great part, because the constitution specified that God Himself was to be considered the direct governor of the nation as a whole, assisted by a "servant" or Prime Minister (Hebrew: Eved Adonai) who would be His representative and who, in turn, would maintain a core of judges and civil servants to handle the transmission of his or, more correctly, God's instructions to the tribal and familial authorities.*

> *Depending on the importance of the issue in constitutional terms, the Prime Minister also interacted with the assembly of the children of Israel congregated as a whole -- men, women, and children -- the assembly of all men of military age, a national council representing the tribes, or ad hoc assemblies of tribal elders (zekenim) or delegates (nesi'im) for purposes of policymaking.* [1]

Professor Elazar went on to explain:

> *The Eved Adonai also shared power with the priests, particularly Aaron and his sons, who had their own covenant with God establishing them as a hereditary priesthood with certain constitutional functions, principally*

61

judicial in character, as well as cultic ones ". [1]

The fledgling assembly was not without its share of internal struggles predicated on acquiring political power. Aaron and Miriam challenged Moses' authority with marriage as its backdrop. After they were summoned to the Tent of Meeting by God, they repented and came back into communion with Moses and the assembly. *(Numbers 12)*

Korah rebelled; he was a relative of Aaron and he wanted a position of leadership. He never repented and separated himself from the congregation taking some with him. (a church split) He chose not to come back into union with the assembly and God dealt with him accordingly. That ended that. *(Numbers 16)*

God essentially had "Moses' back" and He defended Moses. Moses was greater than other prophets. "

> *When there is a prophet among you, I, the Lord, reveal myself to them in visions I speak to them in dreams. But this is not true of my servant Moses; he is faithful in all my house. With him I speak face to face, clearly and not in riddles; he sees the form of the Lord. Why then were you not afraid to speak against my servant Moses? (Numbers 12:6-8)*

The events are a stark reminder of our ability to choose, through our own free will.

Joshua

Joshua is last recognized *Eved Adonai,* the office of the chief servant of the Sovereign Lord. The Israelite nation's Holy Commonwealth under the Chief Servant is seen by scholars as to the perfect political structure. Strangely, no provisions are made for the continuance of this office. But we will see in the future of the nation, there was a struggle to return to this style of governance. Except for the chaotic period of Judges, this is the last time God directly ruled over His people as a nation up to the time of Christ.

Bringing it together

Abraham journeyed out of Sumer and settled amongst his cousins in the land of Canaan. He became a friend of God. And, through faith, God made an eternal

Covenant with Abraham. We look at this in terms of the "Household of God". Abraham's household had grown quite large and was very blessed. It is noted that in the Household of God, there was an office of the Chief Servant. This was before the Mosaic Covenant, and before the Davidic Monarchy, The Chief Servant that oversaw all the master owned.

Joseph was placed by God in Egypt before his brothers arrived "... *before you, to preserve you, a posterity in the earth, and to save your lives by a great deliverance."* Joseph was sent into the civilization of his distant cousins...the descendants of Ham. He excelled and became a great and powerful servant; a 'Prime Minister' in a foreign land. He was in charge of all that the Pharaoh owned. He is the second example of a humble and faithful servant that was placed with this responsibility.

God's plan was always to remain Sovereign Lord of His people. Through this, the rest of the world would learn to see the true God. So, essentially, His throne is in heaven. Up until Moses, the term *"Eved Neeman"*, God's faithful servant, was used in describing Abraham, Eliezer, and Joseph.

Then, Moses became His Chief Servant, or *Eved Adonai*, on earth just as Eliezer and Joseph had modeled other eras. But, the 'Master' was in Heaven. His anointing or the recognition of Moses' office would require some different tactics. The uniqueness of this arrangement required an extraordinary solution. It was the idea of a prophetic theocracy. God spoke through the *Eved Adonai*.

There is no doubt that both Moses and Joshua, who were charismatically singled out as having held this office, by God and the people, used this prophetic realm to establish and teach a Law laid down by God at Sinai.

So, we have a biblical history of Chief Servants, the Hebrew, *Eved Adonai*, from Genesis to Judges. We'll see in future chapters how this concept, the office of Chief Servant, was apparent during the Davidic kingdoms and on to the time of Christ. Watch for this office to keep reappearing as we move forward, even into the New Testament.

They held things together. However, as we saw in the last chapter, it all fell apart during Judges without this office. The important issue was they lost the glue that kept the consistent doctrine or beliefs. Without the centricity, we are shown that it falls apart quickly. When it says..." *everyone did what was right in their own eyes",* does that mean the prophetic, or teaching, fell apart? Yes, I think it does.

Today, it's common in modern Christianity to look at the prophetic realm as a bunch of fortune-tellers. And, people gravitate to it. But, that's not really it. It is first a teaching ministry. They communicate and teach the will of God. Then, yes, there is a warning for failure to do so.

In the next chapter, we'll explore the three distinctive realms of authority that Jewish thought has identified since at least the time of Christ. Yes, as I've been revealing throughout, the prophetic domain is one of those separate domains.

We're beginning to see that the authentic Church that emerged would be more advanced than we give it credit for. It isn't a bunch of independent and charismatic shepherds leading their flocks, flip-floppin' through the wilderness. Let's confirm it even further.

Acknowledgment

My search for the First Church, the Church that emerged, certainly made a dramatic shift when I found a Contemporary Jewish scholar and political science professor quite by accident. I was studying political science and as I explained in an earlier chapter, I was driven to the Book of Judges. Professor Daniel Elazar founded the *Jerusalem Center for Public Affairs*. Most of his academic papers are still available there today. I rely heavily on his socio-political insight to help us untangle the clutter.

Chapter 5: The Three Ketarim (Crowns)

Mishnah Pirkei Avot [The Ethics of the Fathers] 4:17:
R. Shimon said: There are three crowns - Keter Torah *(the crown of Torah),* Keter Kehunah *(the crown of Priesthood) and* Keter Malchut *(the crown of Royalty).*

The Three-fold ministry of Christ has its roots deep in historical revelation from Genesis with the first household of God and throughout the Israelites attempt to form a Holy Commonwealth. We're all acquainted with these offices. The threefold offices of Christ are the familiar Prophet, Priest, and King. We will examine these offices as they pertain to Christ, but first, let's dig into the historical evidence for the offices. All three offices actually appear quite early in the relationship God has with Abraham.

Melchizedek

Melchizedek *(Malkī-ṣedeq or King of Righteousness)* appeared out of nowhere to essentially deliver a blessing and a message to Abraham in Genesis chapter 14.

And Melchizedek king of Salem brought out bread and wine: and he was [is] the priest of the most high God. And he blessed him, and said, 'Blessed be Abram to the most high God, possessor of heaven and earth, And blessed be the most high God, which hath delivered thine enemies into thy hand'. And he gave him tithe from all. (Genesis 14:18–20)

Abraham won a great battle in which he rescued Lot and his family. After this, Melchizedek appeared as the King of Salem. The name "Salem" means peace and it is said to be the land in which Jerusalem sits today. He brought out bread and wine to make an offering to God. With this bread and wine offering, Melchizedek is said to be the priest of the most high God. He gives Abraham a blessing and a message from God. Finally, Abraham gives tithes to Melchizedek.

The first syllable in his name, Melchi- or Malchi-, refers to the royalty of king. He is called the *"priest of the most high God"*. And, third, he delivers a message and a blessing from God. So, we see Melchizedek operating in the realm of all three offices. Those of King, Prophet, and Priest. This is the first revelation of these offices. It is important to note that it is revealed far before the Mosaic Covenant during the Abrahamic Covenant in the Household of God.

The Three-fold offices under Moses

The most important aspect of the division of powers within the *Edah* (Assembly of Israel) is that it was always established through covenants and sets of covenants. Their journey through the wilderness reveals the Covenantal relationship between God and the people who desired a Holy Commonwealth set apart onto Him. At first, the divisions of duties, or powers, were divided between Moses, the Elders of the Assembly, and Aaron as High Priest; each of whom further delegated this power.

God covenanted with Moses as *Eved Adonai*, the Servant of the Lord, the Chief Steward. He relayed and interpreted God's Word (Torah). It was the Covenantal constitution that the nation relied upon and Moses judged the people accordingly. Almost immediately, God gave instructions for the creation of a senate that consisted of 70 elders selected from the tribes.

The group of Elders would share in the 'anointing' and take over the primary responsibility of "judging" the nation; they functioned as the *civil* branch of government. Still, Moses retained the *prophetic* responsibility for the interpretation of God's (will) teaching. That gave him, or God, the last word.

By the end of the Judges era, the idea of a monarchy was integrated into the set of covenants within the nation. And, the separation between the prophetic and the civil became somewhat institutionalized. Samuel tried to resurrect, with God's approval, a Mosaic style office of Chief Steward and a national Elder board while retaining the local civic leadership. Samuel was the last to attempt to straddle both domains.

In a separate covenant with Aaron and his sons, God instituted the priesthood. The priesthood had the authority to be the reconciling ministers between the people and God through both ritual and sacerdotal functions. The divisions of authority developed early in the account of biblical Israel and the ancillary covenants of the polity begin to describe the tripartite division of authorities between the civil, priestly, and prophetic (interpretive) functions necessary in the polity of the "City on a Hill". [1]

Three Ketarim (Crowns)

During the Egyptian captivity, they certainly learned from the complexity of the Egyptian system, yet the nation of Israel already had the beginnings of civil authority that was distinct from that of Egyptian rule. There were elders (*zekenim*) and maintainers of the peace (*shotrim*) that were necessary to administer the customs and laws (judging) of their predecessors. However, the first glimpses of order and governance came during the transition to a free-standing and independent nation. (9)

It was always God's Plan... *"I will be their God...they will be My people...I will dwell amongst them."* And, that was readily apparent. During Israel's first Commonwealth period,
"

> God is sovereign and exercises His sovereignty more or less directly, mediated only through His servants who act as national leaders and the traditional institutions of the people. Those institutions are federal and republican in character, with the federation of tribes at their base and the popular institutions growing out of that federation the major instrumentalities of governance alongside God, His chief minister, and supporting staff." [3]

We immediately see a rudimentary tri-partite separation of authority with Moses, the council of 70 national elders, and God's Covenant with Aaron.

Civil: As *Eved Adonai*, Moses was responsible for interpreting and teaching the will of God that was transmitted at Sinai. He was also responsible for judging the people. The beginning of the 'civil' government was created when the council of 70 was formed to judge civil disputes.

Prophetic: Moses retained the prophetic responsibilities of interpretation remained with Moses. He communicated and taught the will of God.

Priestly: God covenanted with Aaron to perform all of the priestly duties to communicate the needs of the (people) *Edah* to God and to handle the sacerdotal needs of the people.

> To the extent that the Eved Adonai's principal function was to serve as God's messenger, as was particularly true in the case of Moses, we already

have the embryonic division of powers which was to become classic in the Jewish polity and which a thousand years later was to be defined in terms of three Ketarim (literally, crowns or investitures of authority). Under this system, the principal task of the Eved Adonai was to bring God's word to the people. This later became the task of the prophets and the soferim ("Scribes") who developed the ketaric terminology" [3]

The three divisions of authority became recognized and defined, the *ketaric* divisions became the *Keter Malkhut*, the *Keter Torah*, and the *Keter Kehunah*. They translate as civil governance (Malkhut roughly translates as King), prophetic, and the priesthood, respectively. The domains gained their authority through a mix of the Divine and popular agreement from the *Edah* (congregation). This was done through a set of covenants between God and man, and between people. The nation or tribe would need to ratify any decision or ordination however there was almost never a challenge to a prophetic proclamation.

Politics was a means of achieving a Holy Commonwealth. It was also a means to maintain it. We see that the domains of the three Ketarim existed in practice from the earliest biblical accounts. The domains became increasingly defined throughout the history of Israel.

The emergence of a well-defined concept of a "separation of powers" in an increasingly secular sense came during the Second Temple period, but the division's significance grew from the prior Monarchal regimes of the Davidic period. Power struggles within the domains, and between them, during the Second Commonwealth, the Maccabees, and the time of Christ is well documented biblically, and through the historian Josephus.

Keter Malkhut (lit. kingship), It can be easy to assign this domain only to the time of the Davidic kings and the delegated authority within the king's household. However, it does not refer solely to the kingship, but to all civil authority and during all periods. This would have been what Jesus was referring to when He spoke of "Moses' Seat" in Matthew chapter 23. In chapter 23, the "scribes" or the "teachers of the law", and the "Pharisees" sit in the "authority" of Moses.

So, in the Pharisees and Scribes of the time of Christ, we see a strange blend of the civil and prophetic roles. When Jesus spoke to the odd blending of authority sitting in Moses' seat at the time, He pointed to the original office as having transcended the kingdom when He remerged the domains of *civil* and the *prophetic.* It must have been purposeful.

However, the historical role of Moses or Joshua as *Eved Adonai* was a step above both "those that sat on Moses seat and of the Davidic Kings in overall authority. Their offices were distinctly different. (More on that in future chapters) The authority rested in their office.

Whether that be of local magistrates and/or delegates (nesiim), elders, and/or ad hoc councils (zekenim), judges (shofetim), officials/peacekeepers (shotrim), and later various other offices of civil authority (e.g., parnassim, community leaders). They led local families, clan, and tribes, as well as the entire nation.

The domain of the *Keter Malkhut* exists by virtue of Divine authorization, although the people are, for the most part, empowered to choose their leaders within the limitations imposed by the Torah as a constitution. This authority was for the sole purpose of administering a Holy Commonwealth, their theocratic nation. And, that purpose would have necessarily been constrained by the prophetic domain of the *Keter Torah*.

The Jewish concern for the *Keter Malkhut* and the return of their own earthly king was addressed in both Mark chapter 12, and Matthew chapter 22. They were living under the umbrella of a foreign nation and had hopes of a white stallion riding deliverer that would once again sit upon the throne, aka David.

But that wasn't happening, or so it seemed. So, they changed the subject. They asked about it when they asked about taxes. Jesus replied, *"Render unto Caesar, what is Caesars"*. To those listening, His answer left them without their king, without their *Keter Malkhut*, and without their national civil leader. Little did they know, Jesus would transcend the old limits of their nationality and He would place the Throne back in Heaven where it belonged.

Keter Torah- (Lit: God's teaching to mankind) It is the domain of those who have been entrusted to communicate God's message and will to His people. Clearly, a large part of the role of *Eved Adonai* was to communicate this Divine will to His people, Israel. Let's add to that, the teachers of the Law along with the scribes and sages, taught the *Torah* "teachings of Moses" to the nation of the Israelites. Later, the Pharisees and sages of the Second Tabernacle era taught the Torah as did the Divinity and Rabbinical schools of the time of Christ and thereafter.

The prophetic domain's role has been clearly defined over the generations and has experienced the least change. It had unquestionably established itself as the authoritative keeper of the covenantal and constitutional tradition. They taught and interpreted. They embraced stories and analogies to express the essence of life emanating from the Torah.

The domain's homiletic discourse of the "Teaching of Moses" made the oral tradition and interpretation as integral to the nation as the Deuteronomic constitution itself. The people learned by rote, and by memory, reciting the traditions they learned.

The *Keter Torah*, by its Divine nature, has had the ability to control aspects of the roles and rituals of the other two Ketarim. And in contrast, while its role has been highly identifiable, it's structure, ritual, and daily tasks were the most challenging.

Their routines developed mainly as an accessory to the domains of the *Keter Malkhut* and the *Keter Kehunah* but also held power over them. And yet, when the prophetic realm communicated God's Divine Will, it would only be received when spoken by those who were recognized as authoritative by the people.

And remember, they always seemed to kill their prophets.

Keter Kehunah (lit. priesthood), The *Keter Kehunah* is authorized to communicate the people's needs and wants to God: they were namely priests, and in later times, the synagogue officials replaced the priests after the Temple was destroyed.

The Priesthood is the channel by which the people, whether *laity or Edah,* could approach Heaven. This was the opposite direction of the *Keter Torah.* The priestly domain was originated by a Divine commandment and separate covenant at Sinai. Again, it was only implemented through public action. The 'Golden Calf' incident had sealed the fate of the idea that the entire nation could operate soberly and reverently within the priesthood; intimate with God.

Initially, the responsibilities of the *Keter Kehunah* were handled by the kohanim (priests) and levi'im (Levites). They were led by the Kohen Gadol (Chief Priest). The Chief Priest was assisted in the Wilderness Tabernacle by Levites and by kohanim. Regularly, some were scattered among the Israelites to perform basic sacerdotal duties. Eventually, most if not all, of the priesthood and Levitical ministries became centered and concentrated in the Jerusalem Temple.

The channel through which the people communicated with God grew out of the Divinely instituted pilgrimages in remembrance of the first Passover. This expanded into a set of different offerings and sacrifices through the Tabernacle (Numbers) There was a defined set of offerings surrounding the idea of thankfulness and various sacrifices necessary for reconciliation.

One of the basic commonalities of the set of offerings and sacrifices was that they were almost always eaten by the priesthood. With prayer and supplication, this was the heart of the "Ministry of Reconciliation" that Paul wrote about in his epistles. *(2 Cor 5)*

Ordination Ceremony

Old Testament scholar, Professor Stuart A. Cohen has written several academic works on the divisions of authority in the three Ketarim, or Crowns. Here, we introduced a brief description of these domains enough to gain an understanding of the distinct offices.

From the appearance of Melchizedek, the growing nation was always steeped in ritual and tradition. It seemed everything was presented as before God. Any 'anointing', recognition, installation, or ordination was accompanied by a formal observance. Stuart A Cohen has described the ordination of offices, and the officeholder, in the Israelite Commonwealth:

> *As is the case in all political systems, the issue of legitimate succession poses problems of a, particularly thorny nature. These are too intricate to be detailed here. Briefly stated, the Jewish political tradition requires that prospective candidates for appointment to governmental office (minui) fulfill at least two of the following three criteria: appropriate heredity (yihus); popular approval and/or recognition (haskamah); and the enactment of a constitutionally recognized ceremony of induction into office (meshihah— "anointment"; or semikhah— "ordination").*
>
> *The point to be made here is that the "mix" between these various requirements varies from Keter to Keter, with no two ketarim demanding identical qualifications. As much is evident, to take but one example, from the Deuteronomic passage quoted above: the melekh, in that case, derives his power from a process which combines both popular selection and divine approval (in later coronation ceremonies symbolized by both acclamation and meshihah); the position of the kohanim [priest] is made principally dependent on genetic circumstances; the Navi [prophet] is "raised up from amongst his brethren" by virtue of his divinely inspired understanding of God's will (which can be given formal recognition within the Keter by a process of semikhah, as in the case of Joshua, who was thus ordained by Moses).*

A thorough analysis of this issue citing classic sources and specifically referring to the differences between the three ketarim is to be found in Moses Sofer, Responsa Hatam Sofer, Orafi tfayyim, no. 12 [10]

One can't help but notice the stark similarities between the description of the ordinations of officers in Israel, and the offices of Bishop and Presbyter described in both letters to Timothy and Titus.

The Second Temple Period

They rebuilt the Temple after the remnants returned to Israel after the captivity. There was a problem. We are told that Jeremiah had hidden the Ark of the Covenant along with additional artifacts from the First Temple. They haven't been found even though Harrison Ford spent an enormous amount of time and energy looking.

They rebuilt the Temple with nothing in the Holiest Place. It was a shadow of its former glory. This seems to have been confirmed by the Roman soldier who entered to ransack the place when the Temple was destroyed. He exclaimed, "It's empty!". The sacrifices remained in the outer court, but we have no record of God ever dwelling there. The cloud, the Shekinah, never descended to "dwell amongst His people".

Arguably, they also never ruled themselves autonomously as a nation again. It was fractured and disjointed, without most of the tribes. They were certainly a remnant of the once-great people. This had a drastic effect on the three domains. We'll examine what they warped into in chapter 11, as Christ speaks into their redefined authority. They still look for their King. And, now, they dream of their Temple.

At First Glance

At first glance, it's easy to disregard the complexity of organization and structure the nation had right from the get-go. Society and culture were well-formed. Politically, they struggled mightily as they sought to create this great Holy Commonwealth. It's a parallel narrative.

Cain kills Able, Jacob usurps the birthright, Joseph is sold into slavery, Korah revolts seeking the high priesthood, Saul feels continually threatened, and King David's dynasty is repeatedly challenged. The jealousy, envy of power, and powers quest is a dominant biblical theme that runs parallel to the forgiveness, remission of sins, storyline.

Christianity

It's important to note, the Church wasn't grown in some sort of antiseptic vacuum either. It wasn't free from historical blunders of the polity of Israel, both the failures and its successes. There is a misconception that the environment during Christ's earthly ministry and the infant Church was neither complex nor was it advanced socially and politically.

However, this same storyline, one of a dominant political and social backdrop runs concurrently with the salvation story. Jesus spent a considerable amount of time addressing these issues with the leaders of the day. So, we need to see it to find the authentic Church. That Church emerged out of this atmosphere.

We are beginning to see this playout. This will get more defined as we move on. Within the Church or kingdom, Jesus is recognized as King. He appoints a Chief Steward, Peter, as had been the custom all the way back to Abraham. There is also a Royal court or cabinet.

King: It becomes apparent that civil governance will be split between the Church and a secularized exterior. Peter takes a lead on the day of Pentecost, in the meeting(s) with Paul on doctrinal issues, and in the Jerusalem council.

Prophet: The council of Apostles yields to the teaching 'anointing' of an Orthodox James for his expertise in traditional practices. These events clearly show the importance of local governance by the Bishops and criteria is established for their selection.

Priest: The priesthood is expanded with the entire Church participating in the ministry. Yet, Paul takes a somber view of the importance of the priestly office as the Ministry of Reconciliation *(2 Corinthians chapter 5),* and in the importance of receiving the body and blood in a worthy manner (1 *Cor.* 11).

He requires a learn(ed) and certainly ordained presbytery to lead the ministry. Gone is the central Temple, Christ having rebuilt it in 3 days, with a new altar that is to last until the end of this age. The Melchizedekian Ministry of Jesus transcends time and geography, transforms bread and wine offerings into the Body and Blood, multiplying them for all those present, where and when 2 or more people gather. But I'm starting to get ahead of myself.

From the very beginning, Church structure modeled the structural dynamics in the Judaic culture at the time as well as the Ancient Israelites beforehand. The tripartite divisions of authority were well known in Jesus' time. They were dealt with directly in the Gospels as well as the Book of Acts, and these concepts were used to formulate the Church.

The existing multi-lateral covenants were reestablished in a new way within the Church and the domains of Civil governance, Prophetic (teaching God's will), and the Priesthood (reconciliation to God) are alive and well. By that time they were known as three Ketarim (crowns).

Post-Reformation

Today's average churchgoer may be surprised that the reformers of the 15th century, such as Luther, Calvin, and Zwingli, generally recognized the domains of authority and most of the liturgical ritual of the Church of the first 1500 years. They just desired to usurp that authority, claiming it was wrong. They recognized the need for both priestly and civil governance. The reformers, almost to a person, co-opted secular civil government and kept the responsibility of interpretation for themselves. This allowed the reformers to hold sway or have control over these governments.

A separated Post-reformation Christianity has traveled far from these beginnings, however. Civil governance is almost completely secular. Protestant Christianity is completely scattered, and Church discipline as described in Matthew 18 is essentially impossible.

Even though the offense has always been difficult to deal with, now people just leave the local church and find another one. What is left has seemingly grown into a form of consensus-driven pure democracy that in times of trouble will always descend into mob rule. So, unity, by any stretch of the imagination, is gone and theology of spiritual unity has developed.

The prophetic domain charged with maintaining and teaching God's will has also gradually walked away. There's nothing that ties it together. Teaching authority has ultimately come down to individual pastors, and more importantly everyone. People will receive their own interpretation or their charismatic pastor's interpretation rather than read some of the profound documents written by trusted disciples of Apostolic age.

The priestly domain, though few would admit it, is non-existent. There aren't any priestly tasks to be done in the newer Churches. They sing and then listen to oral teaching. This has become a type of Synagogue They might not realize it but would be reminiscent of the Talmudic homilies of Jewish oral tradition. This homiletic tradition is a new tradition, one of the last couple hundred years in the mostly non-denominational world.

The domains of authority, the civil, the teaching, and the priestly, are vastly different from those that have been used throughout orthodox Christianity for the past 2000 years. Modern post-Protestant, post-denominational Christianity has little grip on governance (justice, i.e. judging), the prophetic (teaching) has become personal interpretation and/or modern consensus, and there is little need for priestly sacerdotal matters even though our Chief Priest still ministers at the Heavenly Altar, and through the rent veil, on our behalf.

The Offices of Christ

There is overwhelming agreement that Christ holds the offices of King, Prophet, and High Priest. Christianity carried on the traditional concepts of the *Keter Malkhut*, the *Keter Torah*, and the *Keter Kehunah*. We can gain new insight into the early Church when we read the New Testament considering the longstanding divisions of authority.

The "separation of powers" was always more of a "sphere of authority and responsibility" within the Holy Commonwealth of the Israelites as well as the Kingdom, or Household of God. The distinction is one of power. Whether the power is invested in a human office or person, or in the Sovereignty of God.

Is it the pride in the accumulation of power by humans on one hand, or the 'fear' of the Sovereignty of God on the other? We all should realize that it is through humble servanthood. The "sphere of authority and responsibility" and the three distinct domains remain vital in the New Covenant.

As opposed to humble servanthood, *secularism* has leaned increasingly on earthly power, excluding any real heavenly dealings while offering only a token tip of the hat upward. God's providence is still usually claimed by almost any nation, but the thought of His rebuke is readily chastised, as is any messenger.

One of Christ's accomplishments was to point our eyes, whether Gentile or Jew, back heavenward. And, with the throne reestablished in Heaven, mankind's division of authority and responsibility is always one of servanthood. These days, there is a King. No one can forget that and do whatever they want.

Christ the King

Christ is currently seated at the right hand of His Father. His Throne is in Heaven.[4] We also know that *"He who overcomes, I will grant to him to sit down with*

Me on My throne, as I also overcame and sat down with My Father on His throne."(Rev.3:21) NASB The Church is repeatedly called the Kingdom of God in Sacred Scripture. She is at once, a reflection of all the Davidic house, Abrahamic 'Household of God', and the ideal Kingdom of Heaven.[5] As we wait for the fullness of the Kingdom to come; the new earth and new heaven.

The Gospel of Matthew offers the image of the Church through the prism of the Kingdom of God. It may be filled with grace, yet it is still filled with people who need moral regeneration. Kingdoms are places of courts and councils, institutions and customs, and ministers and citizens to make it work.

People enjoy the privileges of the spiritual Kingdom, but she's also a physical and visual Kingdom. She has as her Head, Jesus Christ, the Heavenly King. He will never leave her nor forsake her. *"Jesus went about all the cities and villages, teaching in their synagogues, and preaching the gospel of the kingdom," which is the good news [that the Kingdom of God] is coming" (Matthew 9:35).*

He also frequently began teaching using the words *"The Kingdom of Heaven is like..."* And, we are told that we must enter through Baptism, *"Except a man be born of water and of the Spirit, he cannot enter into the kingdom of God. That which is born of the flesh is flesh; and that which is born of the Spirit is spirit" (John 3:5-6).*

The Kingdom is a popular New Testament subject and it makes absolute sense. The descendants of the Israelite nation had trouble letting go of the kingdom. The Former Prophets spoke of the new kingdom to come. And, God desires to reign. He desires to be amongst His people. *"I will be their God; they will be My people"*. So, we keep our eyes Heavenward for the King, yet He has a Household Steward to shepherd His flock on Earth.

Christ the Prophet

"God, who at various times and in various ways spoke in time past to the fathers by the prophets, has in these last days spoken to us by His Son..." (Hebrews 1:1 &2a).

This was teaching the 'will' of God. He taught Gospel, the coming New testament. Christ came preaching and teaching the things of the Kingdom of God. He modeled it through His behavior. He spent time illuminating the Old Testament and how it would be fulfilled. He also prophesied about the things to come including how His death and resurrection figured into the salvation mystery.

"And we know that the Son of God has come and given us an understanding, that we may know Him who is true; and we are in Him who is true; in His Son Jesus Christ. This is the true God and eternal life." 1 John 5:20.

Christ Our High Priest

"Here is the main point: We have a High Priest who sat down in the place of honor beside the throne of the majestic God in heaven. There he ministers in the heavenly Tabernacle, the true place of worship that was built by the Lord and not by human hands." (Hebrews 8:1-2)

The book of Hebrews fills us with visual pictures of Christ's priesthood seemingly from beginning to end. I encourage you to read it in its entirety.

In John Chapter 2, Jesus addresses the Pharisees, and caught them off guard..." *Destroy this temple and I will rebuild it in 3 days...".* John goes on to say that He was talking about a new temple, His body.

We are also Temples of the Living God...Our bodies are members of Christ himself.

> *Shall I then take the members of Christ and unite them with a prostitute? Never! Do you not know that he who unites himself with a prostitute is one with her in body? For it is said, "The two will become one flesh." But whoever is united with the LORD is one with him in spirit. Flee from sexual immorality. All other sins a person commits are outside the body, but whoever sins sexually, sins against their own body.*

> *We abide in Him, and He abides in us (John 6)*

Christ is the sole Mediator. *(Hebrews 8 and 9).* In chapter 10, we will get into this subject more in-depth, but here it is in a nutshell. At Calvary, the blood-soaked curtain was rent. The Tabernacle isn't gone forever; it was rebuilt. We all have access as ministers of reconciliation. As priests of the Melchizedekian order, we offer bread and wine.

Christ is the same today, as yesterday. So, He ministers at the Heavenly Tabernacle on our behalf. In return, we receive the Body, Blood, Soul, and Divinity in the consummation of our sin atonement, and reconciliation once again with God and the body of Christ.

Bringing it together

Throughout the Old Testament, God never commanded a certain type of earthly government. Much of His point was to teach us how to treat each other within our social constructs. The aspect of free will seems to play a prominent role in covenanting and in structuring governance, always needing the cooperation of the people.

God's patience is repeatedly evident while He attempts to guide His people. He consents, anoints, and warns about different forms of governance, while evidently waiting for the people to reject His reign.

Unity was another important guiding principle. How would they remain pure to the "Teachings of Moses", to the covenants surrounding their national "communion" at the Tabernacle, and in their relationships? The nation went from unified under Moses to the dysfunctional anarchy of the period of Judges. Then, on to an earthly King.

They sought to regain the lost unity, both as an identity and with God. It was never regained. It was never restored. Many failed to see the restoration in Christ. They had a tendency to fail to see, not like what they heard, and mistakenly kill their prophets.

Understanding the three Ketarim helps us when we study the culture into which Christ spoke; it was also the culture that hosted His Church. The Church needs to be seen in this light. We also need to understand why and how Christ occupies the three offices of the Ketarim; the office of the king, the office of prophet, and the office of our high priest.

The books of the *Former Prophets* or the historical books of Joshua, Judges, 1&2 Samuel, 1&2 Kings, along with 1&2 Chronicles tell the story of Israel from Moses to its resurrection after the Babylonian exile. However, rabbinical schools don't see that as the main purpose.

The main purpose is to develop and teach God's covenant with the Israelite people. This covenant gave the tribes the responsibility to create a Holy Commonwealth in the land that God gave them. Just as the New Testament, these books don't attempt a full historical record. Rather, they should be viewed as an expression of central ideas of prophetic Judaism from a moralistic point of view.

> *"The New (Testament) is in the Old concealed…*
> *The Old (Testament) is in the New revealed" Augustine*

The books of Samuel have turned from the Monarchal (civil) perspective of Judges and to a prophetic point of view of the nation. The books of Kings are essentially about political aspects of the civil governance and the books of Chronicles from the point of view of the priesthood; the three Ketarim.[6]

THE CHURCH THAT EMERGED

Chapter 6: Samuel: The Prophet led Regime

"The rise of a prophet who was trained within the [priesthood] but shifts to the [office of the prophet]"-Prof. Daniel Elazar

e've gained just a little insight into how contemporary Jewish scholars see the Book of Joshua as the ideal model for the nation of Israel to live out the *Holy Commonwealth*. We've also been introduced to the ideas of the distinct domains of authority that developed. It almost seems unimaginable that the nation fell apart so quickly during the era of the Judges. But here we are.

The writer of the Book of Judges was certainly pro-monarchy. And, we'll see Samuel wasn't. We're reminded again, *"For in those days there were no king in Israel, so everyone did what was right in their own eyes"*. What a decrepit state of affairs.

The nation was obviously conscious of how poorly the loose-knit confederacy had worked politically. They were also painfully aware of how they had suffered spiritually because of how loose-knit and fragmented they had become ideologically. Socio-politically, the nation was crumbling from this anarchic approach or lack of approach.

Spiritually, we hear of repeated idolatry; we also hear of their inability to maintain and follow any central teaching, the covenant, or even the Mosaic constitution. Evidently, the time of Judges was a time of personal interpretation, or at least a local interpretation, and that led them into idolatry.

Samuel was born into the ruins of their vision for a "Holy Commonwealth". They were going to eventually deal with a fundamental regime change. Again, though puzzling, there were no provisions made for the continuance of the office of *Eved Adonai*. Apparently, there were few federal officers beyond those of the priesthood; the ministers of the national Temple.

It is a stark example, or warning, to its readers of how the Church/nation falls into anarchy when there is no central [teaching God's will] authority holding them together. Was this period God's way of showing his people that they needed more guidance than from only small independent officers (shotrim) or magistrates (*nesiim*), and elders (*zekenim*)? And later, the regional judges?

They struggled to maintain their vision in its pure form. It was a reasonably straightforward pattern of segments of the Israelites back-sliding at various times into idolatry and then repenting and returning to the "ways of the Lord". Once they were led and bound together by ideology and vision; God's vision as espoused by God's *Eved Adonai.*

The following generations became increasingly removed from this commitment to a "Holy Nation" and more concerned with their 'own' lives. Their ties as members of this nation, the society, its rituals and observances, and even the goings-on at the Tent of Meeting were by the accident of birth, and not by choice.

The Israelites primary concerns were local. They were tied to the land, their families, and neighbors. And, ideology and vision waned. In a sense, the tribal confederacy represented both the success of following God's plan and their failings because of it.

Samuel became the last of the Judges to close out the period. The Israelites were sick of their merry-go-round with God. It was devastating. As we'll see, their solution was different from God's, and Samuels as well. It was a transformational period where the entire nation dealt with a fundamental change in the way they lived and served God. It was a transformational regime change. Samuel was the last time that God directly led His people, Israel; until Jesus that is. Let that sink in:

> *I Samuel presents a picture of a prophet-led regime, or at least an attempt to restore the tribal federation by eliminating confederal anarchy through the institution of a prophet-led regime. It paints a very dynamic picture of a confederation whose principal federal office was a hereditary priesthood which is deposed in the period under discussion,* **the rise of a prophet who was trained within the Keter kehunah but shifts to the Keter torah**[the Pope begins in Keter kehunah and shifts to Keter Torah] *and his introduction of a nagid/melekh (high commissioner/king) reluctantly and out of necessity, to head the Keter Malchut, but be subordinate to the prophet.*
>
> *The discussion documents the failure of this regime to stand up to foreign military pressure, the limits of the Navi as national leader, and the error, both practical and constitutional, of trying to combine the authority and/or powers of all three domains in the hands of one person, even one chosen by*

God.[1][2]

Samuel realized that the existing regime was more than just ineffective, but it was perhaps all but dead. He sought a covenantal renewal, to strengthen civic institutions and nationalism that focused on God as it's Sovereign.

Samuel sought the old federalism under which the nation was sufficiently strong enough that it would be able to defeat the Philistines. He saw the nation under the *Eved Adonai,* God's Chief Steward as the perfect representation of God's will. Samuel sought a return to the nation, as it existed under Joshua. To Samuel, and subsequently God, the biblical presentation of the Joshua-styled regime represented the ideal leadership structure to bring about the Holy Commonwealth.

They were in charge!

Contemporary Jewish Scholars seem to have applied the importance of *Adat Bnei Yisrael* (the entire body politic) to Samuel's desire for a reconstitute regime. They weren't hearing from God…and the office of *Eved Adonai* was vacant. And, think about the domains of authority at play.

The *Keter Malkhut* was essentially local. We will see that the *Keter Torah* is described as essentially dormant. And, we assume that sacerdotal rituals were still carried on locally, as well as nationally. Let's see how this played out:

"Now the boy Samuel was ministering to the LORD before Eli. And word from the LORD was rare in those days, visions were infrequent." (1 Samuel 3:1)

This becomes a recurrent theme of the chroniclers and prophets, sages and poets, throughout the Old Testament. Let's look at a couple of Proverbs that apply to this precise time period. Notice the two different interpretations of Proverbs 29:18:

"Where there is no prophetic vision the people cast off restraint, but blessed is he who keeps the law" ESV
"When people do not accept divine guidance, they run wild. But whoever obeys the law is joyful." NLT

Do these two versions offer a distinctly different diagnosis of the recurrent theme of Judges? The answer is no. Really, it reveals that prophetic vision and divine guidance are the same things in Israel. It points to the *Eved Adonai* and his cabinet, or Magisterium. It gives light to the political battles that occurred between the *Keter Malkhut* and the *Keter Torah*; those in governance (civil rule) and those in contemplation (prophets).

Civil rule and independence of the individual held power in civil rule over the *Adat Bnei Yisrael* (the congregation of Israel). Could we also say that there is an issue with secularism? Yes, secularism reigned. Let's look at the following verses side by side:

"In those days there was no king in Israel; everyone did what was right in his own eyes." Judges17:6 & Judges 21:25 NASB

"Where there is no prophetic vision the people cast off restraint, but blessed is he who keeps the law" Proverbs 29:18 ESV

"When people do not accept divine guidance, they run wild. But whoever obeys the law is joyful." Proverbs 29:18 NLT

"Now the boy Samuel was ministering to the LORD before Eli. And word from the LORD was rare in those days, visions were infrequent." 1 Samuel 3:1 NASB

Wow, we need to read them again. Does this remind us of our landscape today? The division between God and His people; and then, Samuel and the congregation, is strikingly apparent. It finally reached a climax with the nation's (God's chosen people) demand. The demand was to amend the covenant and give them a king like everyone else.

Eli's fall, Samuel's rise

Eli was the High Priest at the Tent of Meeting in Shiloh near the close of the period of Judges. The large stone erected by Joshua in the shadow of the Tabernacle still stood as a testimony and witness to the people. He devoted himself to his ministry in the Tent of Meeting, and as one of the last Judges of Israel. In doing so, Eli spanned the domains of the national civil Judge and the Chief Priest.

Eli was a descendant of Aaron's youngest son, Ithamar. Aaron had 4 sons; however, the eldest 2 died in the Holy of Holies. They took a profane misstep by offering strange fire in the presence of the Lord, and they were killed by the fire. This led to a stern reminder from Moses, *"By those who come near Me I will be treated as holy, And before all the people I will be honored." (Leviticus 10:3)*

After the deaths of Aaron's sons, the lineage of the High Priest in Israel has descended from the families of Aaron's youngest sons, Eleazar and Ithamar. Eli, of Ithamar, had been told by God that his house would minister before God at the Tabernacle forever [10].

However, in Eli's old age, his *"eyesight had grown dim"* and he apparently could not see what was going on around him. *(1 Samuel 3:2)*. Evidently, his spiritual eyesight had gone dim as well and in his old age, he ignored the behavior of his sons.

Eli's sons were called evil and wicked. They profaned the Tabernacle of the Lord and they had little regard for the regulations of Levitical law. They used their positions for their own lusts and took pleasure taking what they wanted and when they wanted it. Usurping the law, they took their pleasure in raw meat and committed adultery with women. They did this in the sight of all of Israel, degrading the priesthood, profaning the Lord, and causing all of Israel to transgress.

This finally led Eli to confront them:

> *Why do you such things? For I hear of your evil dealings by all this people. Nay, my sons; for it is no good report that I hear: ye make the LORD's people to transgress. If one man sin against another, the judge shall judge him: but if a man sin against the LORD, who shall entreat for him? Notwithstanding they hearkened not unto the voice of their father, because the LORD would slay them.(1 Samuel 2:23-25)*

Eli's sin was not punishing his sons. His sons did not repent. Eli, in front of the entire congregation of Israel, essentially did nothing about it. The conclusion is that he honored his sons more than he honored the Lord. God laid waste to the house of Eli in response to the sins of Eli and his sons.

They would never serve as priests in the Tent of Meeting again. This led to the decimation of all the priests at Shiloh and the entire household of Eli. The Lord proclaimed, *"And I will raise me up a faithful priest." (1 Samuel 2:35)* It was in these ashes that God first raised up a new priest, Eli's foster child who was given to God by his mother, Samuel.

Samuel was given to God's plan in a similar fashion to Moses. Hannah was barren. She prayerfully begged God for a son, promised to give her son to God. He gave her a son, and she gave her son to God. He grew up learning the ways of the priesthood, like Moses, by dwelling in the house of Eli at Shiloh.

Samuel witnessed all the transgressions of the house of Eli. This led to the famous story of the first time that Samuel heard from God, but he believed that he was awakened each time by the voice of Eli. Eli realized it was God and Samuel eventually gave him the devastating news; God was going to judge the house of Eli in a grave way. He would judge *"… his house forever for the iniquity which he knew because his sons brought a curse on themselves and he did not rebuke them."*

As Samuel grew, God stayed with him. Samuel was born in an era in which a *"word from the LORD was rare in those days, visions were infrequent."* The people of God weren't accustomed to having a 'word' or 'vision' from God, but they knew God was with Samuel. He was recognized as a prophet of God. (*Keter Torah*)

> *The Lord was with Samuel as he grew up, and he let none of Samuel's words fall to the ground. And all Israel from Dan to Beersheba recognized that Samuel was attested as a prophet of the Lord. The Lord continued to appear at Shiloh, and there he revealed himself to Samuel through his word. (1 Samuel 3:19-21)*

Samuel stayed and learned in the house of Eli, but eventually, Samuel's word to Eli came upon all of Israel. The Israelites battled the Philistines without consulting the Lord. After a defeat, they decided to use the Ark of the Covenant as a good luck charm, rather than God's most Holy Place and brought it into battle. The Israelites lost 30,000 that day.

The Philistines captured the Ark of the Covenant and Eli's sons died in battle. When Eli heard this, he fell over dead. The word came to Eli's daughter in law who was about to give birth to Eli's heir. She died while giving birth to Ichabod *(no glory)* saying in her last breath, *"The glory has departed from Israel, for the ark of God has been captured."* (*1 Samuel 4*)

The Ark only remained in Philistine hands for seven months. Everywhere the Philistines placed the Ark, there was chaos. The Philistine people were afflicted with tumors wherever it was located. Each city that held the Ark, begged to get rid of it. It didn't take them long to decide to give the Ark back to Israel.

Along with the return of the Ark, the Philistines made a guilt offering of golden tumors and golden rats, hoping the God of Israel would have mercy on them, and recognized Him as superior. The Ark was discovered in the fields of

Beth Shemesh. There is, once again, a large rock that stands on the site as a memorial; a witness to the Lord.

"The large rock on which the Levites set the ark of the Lord is a witness to this day in the field of Joshua of Beth Shemesh." (1 Samuel 6:18)

Israel repented and turned back to the Lord at Mizpah in front of the Ark. Samuel acted the leader for all of Israel and said he would intercede for them before the Lord. He sacrificed a suckling lamb burnt offering to the Lord on High. In doing so, he acted as he had been taught by the priests at Shiloh. There were no other priests.

He acted in the domain of the *Keter Kehunah*. He acted as a Levite. But he had been grafted in. He was given over to God. However, while not of the family of Aaron, I Chronicles has a genealogy that lists Samuel as Kohathite Levite. Nevertheless, God accepted the offering at the hands of Samuel. *(1 Samuel 7)*

On the same day as the intercession by Samuel, the Philistines gathered to attack Israel once more. God went before the Israelites with a loud thunder that confused the Philistines, allowing the Israelites a great victory.

"Then Samuel took a stone and set it up between Mizpah and Shen. He named it Ebenezer, saying, "Thus far the Lord has helped us."(1 Samuel 7:12)

Once again, as was a tradition for Israel, Samuel took a stone [rock] to set up as a monument that would provide a permanent testimony to the congregation of Israel. As long as Samuel was alive, God protected Israel from the Philistines.

Samuel was always recognized as a prophet, as one who heard from God. In his later years, after the constitutional redesign and while still operating in the prophetic, we read of his role in the domain of the *Keter Malkhut* as a civic leader who also traveled the country each year, "judging Israel".

Samuel was a priest, a prophet, and operated in the civil domain as Judge. Think about that. I've told people I think he is the central figure in the Old Testament. It startles them. Let's see if you come to agree with me.

They demand an earthly king

Now, it came time to decide Israel's direction as a congregation and as a body politic. Samuel came to be recognized as a national leader and as one who 'heard from the Lord'. So, with this power, Samuel appoints his sons as judges over Israel. As history repeats, they soon prove themselves unworthy of the office.

There would be no more Judges. This was a crossroads. I Samuel 8 reveals the transformation:

> *Now it came to pass when Samuel was old that he made his sons judges over Israel. The name of his firstborn was Joel, and the name of his second, Abijah; they were judges in Beersheba. But his sons did not walk in his ways; they turned aside after dishonest gain, took bribes, and perverted justice. (1-3)*
> *)*

And, the *elders of Israel* (Mosaic Senate) reject Samuel's sons as leaders:

> *Then all the elders of Israel gathered and came to Samuel at Ramah, and said to him, "Look, you are old, and your sons do not walk in your ways. Now make us a king to judge us like all the nations." (4-5)*

Crossroads

Samuel desired the return to the type of regime that allowed for God to reign with God having a chief steward, or "Servant of the Lord". *[Eved Adonai]* Perhaps he saw himself as that guy. Samuel prays about their request for an earthly king, and God answers. They have ignored all that God did for them, ignored that they had served other gods, and in the end, the people rejected both God and Samuel.

> *But the thing displeased Samuel when they said, "Give us a king to judge us." So, Samuel prayed to the Lord. And the Lord said to Samuel, "Heed the voice of the people in all that they say to you; for they have not rejected you, but they have rejected Me, that I should not reign over them. According to all the works which they have done since the day that I brought them up out of Egypt, even to this day; with which they have forsaken Me and served other gods; so, they are doing to you also." (6-8)*

Monarchy movement grows

God commands Samuel to forewarn them about the king.

"Now, therefore, heed their voice. However, you shall solemnly forewarn them, and show them the behavior of the king who will reign over them." (9)

Samuel warns the nation that the king will have power over them; that the king will take what he wants from them as he reigns over them and they will be his servants.

> *So Samuel told all the words of the Lord to the people who asked him for a king. And he said, "This will be the behavior of the king who will reign over you: He will take your sons and appoint them for his own chariots and to be his horsemen, and some will run before his chariots.*
> *He will appoint captains over his thousands and captains over his fifties, will set some to plow his ground and reap his harvest, and some to make his weapons of war and equipment for his chariots. He will take your daughters to be perfumers, cooks, and bakers. And he will take the best of your fields, your vineyards, and your olive groves, and give them to his servants.*
>
> *He will take a tenth of your grain and your vintage and give it to his officers and servants. And he will take your male servants, your female servants, your finest young men, and your donkeys, and put them to his work. He will take a tenth of your sheep. And you will be his servants. And you will cry out in that day because of your king whom you have chosen for yourselves, and the Lord will not hear you in that day. (10-18)*

Israel refused to hear and obey Samuel and they demanded a king in spite of God's warning. They didn't care to heed the warning.

> *Nevertheless, the people refused to obey the voice of Samuel; and they said, "No, but we will have a king over us, that we also may be like all the nations, and that our king may judge us and go out before us and fight our battles." And Samuel heard all the words of the people, and he repeated them in the hearing of the Lord. So, the Lord said to Samuel, "Heed their voice and make them a king. [nagid]" And Samuel said to the men of Israel, "Every man go to his city. (19-22)*

The assembled tribal representatives understood Samuel heard from God and was relaying His voice, but they weren't there to reaffirm the existing covenant. They weren't there to affirm Samuel's hope for a return to a Mosaic style regime of old. They wanted constitutional reform. God reassured Samuel not to take it personally and to give them what they wanted.

During the exchange, the assembly always requested a king [melekh] and Samuel always responded back offering something different. He used the word nagid. [high commissioner] So how did it get to this? [2]

Dealing with Saul

The establishment of a royal family was repeatedly rejected as a structural component of governance in Israel prior to David. Moses' sons did not study the ways of the Lord. Aaron's eldest sons died in the Sanctuary, and Gideon's, Eli's, and Samuel's sons weren't considered fit to follow in their father's footsteps. So, Samuel had a dilemma.

His sons had *"dishonest gain and accepted bribes and perverted justice". (1 Samuel 8:3)* Samuel expressed bitter hostility to the idea of the establishment of a monarchy but reluctantly acquiesced to God's command and in quick fashion, the institution of the monarchy is dealt with systemically, and in a workmanlike manner. [1][2]

God chose Saul to become their new leader and directed Samuel to expect his arrival. Samuel proceeded to anoint Saul to a position that could be considered less than that of a king. Saul was repeatedly referred to as *"**ruler** over My people Israel" (1 Samuel 9:16)* during the introduction of their new leader. The office Samuel advocated was that of *nagid*. The *nagid [High Commissioner]* did not apparently carry the powers associated with a king, nor was it hereditary. Yet, God anointed Saul as 'ruler' and the Spirit of God fell upon him.

Following the anointing of Saul as governor *(nagid)*, Samuel summoned the *Adat Bnei Yisrael*(the congregation of Israel*)* to Mitzpah, the new shrine, for a constitutional assembly similar to that of old. The ceremony began with the reminder that they had rejected God's leadership and that He had delivered them from all their troubles.

They were also reminded that even considering all God had done; they still demanded a king to rule over them. They were presented with their governor *(nagid)*, the new constitution, and the rights and duties of their new ruler. Yet, those assembled elected a king using the term, *melekh*. *"Long live the king!" (1 Samuel 10)*

The civil constitution for the new regime needed to remain faithful to the framework of the old, and of the Torah. Samuel wrote down the new law of the kingdom *[mishpat hamelukhah]*, the political structure was redesigned, and they adjourned. Saul didn't last that long, however. [4]

The limited authority granted Saul represented a lingering desire to restore the national unity that existed during the days of Moses and Joshua. We must understand how much Samuel's power was diminished. But he humbled himself and stayed faithful to God

Samuel still saw the governor *[nagid]*, who held executive powers, as being held in check by the *[Keter Torah]* and his mediation of God's word. Remember, none of Samuel's words fell to the ground. So, while he officially stepped down, Samuel stayed in the public arena and kept close tabs on the new ruler; whose main task was to keep Saul within the limits of the covenant.

This would lead to Saul's demise; he was the transitional figure who was still really part of the older tradition. Samuel intended to keep the 'monarchy' limited in scope with more in common with a federal republican tradition where God acted as its Sovereign. The tension between the two domains was to become a trademark of the entire monarchal period.

Samuel's farewell speech was another all-out attack on the monarchy, calling the peoples demand for a king, evil. This marked the third time that Samuel addressed the entire congregation of Israel about the sin of rejecting God as their 'king'. He again chronicles all that God had done for the people of Israel and their ancestors. He reminded them of the times when the people forsook the Lord and wandered off to serve other gods only to plead again for deliverance.

Yet, they rejected God. *"No, we want a king to rule over us'—even though the Lord your God was your king. Now here is the king [Saul] you have chosen, the one you asked for; see, the Lord has set a king over you"* (1 Samuel 12:12-13) He continues, telling Israel that they need to realize the evil, *"And you will realize what an evil thing you did in the eyes of the Lord when you asked for a king."(12:17)*

Samuel concludes the speech doubling down on an important tenet of their sinful agreement. If they obey and don't rebel against both the king or God, and remain faithful in their hearts, all will go well with them. However, they are tied to their ruler. If either of them strays from God's commands, His *"hand will be against them"*. Samuel ends:…

"Yet if you persist in doing evil, both you and your king will perish." (12:25)

A couple of paragraphs later, we read that Saul ignored Samuel. He didn't wait for Samuel to arrive to sacrifice both the burnt offering and the fellowship offering before the Lord. An arrogant Saul took it upon himself to make the offering, and in doing so, he usurped the domains of the prophetic and the priesthood.

Saul took upon himself the authority granted the other domains and ignored the limits of his authority as governor. *(See the difference!)* Samuel arrived and shouted, *"What have you done?" (13:11)* He told Saul that God had been ready to establish his kingdom for all time, but now that wouldn't happen. Because Saul didn't keep the Lord's commandment, *that Samuel had given him,* Saul's kingdom would not endure. *(1 Samuel 13)*

The saga illustrates the tension between Samuel and Saul. Saul didn't hear directly from the Lord. He needed Samuel, but he apparently didn't see it that way. The office of *Eved Adonai* heard from God directly, allowing God to lead. But, now these two needed to essentially coexist and the more limited role of Saul as governor is easier to see.

Next, Saul ignores God's direct commands, albeit through Samuel. Saul is ordered to destroy everything in battle and not to take any spoils, not even the best of the animals. He didn't see the point of it, so he kept the best of the herd. Once again, Samuel shows up, this time God has spoken.

Samuel heard from the Lord, *"I regret that I have made Saul king because he has turned away from me and has not carried out my instructions."(1 Samuel 15)* Saul proclaimed that he had followed the commands of the Lord, but Samuel begged to differ. Saul did evil in the eyes of the Lord by taking plunder that God had commanded to be destroyed. *"But I did obey!"* Saul replied. To which Samuel stated:

> *Does the Lord delight in burnt offerings and sacrifices as much as in obeying the Lord? To obey is better than sacrifice, and to heed is better than the fat of rams. For rebellion is like the sin of divination, and arrogance like the evil of idolatry. Because you have rejected the word of the Lord, he has rejected you as king." (1 Samuel 15:22-23)*

Saul immediately confessed his sin and asked for forgiveness. But it was too late. He had rejected the word of the Lord, as heard through Samuel, and in the process, God had rejected him as a suitable leader for His inheritance.

Bringing it together

The three domains of the Ketarim were operating in Samuel's life: Samuel was adopted into a house that taught him the role and duties of the priesthood. He learned at the Tabernacle in Shiloh. He also learned from the chief priest; the *Kohen Gadol*. The biblical record of Samuel's life reveals that he was recognized as a priest by the nation and he offered sacrifices before them to the Lord. *(1 Samuel 7)*

Samuel was recognized as a prophet. The entire *Adat Bnei Yisrael* accepted the words that Samuel spoke on God's behalf as being, in fact, God's words. The nation hadn't regularly been hearing *"word from the Lord"*, but Samuel was different. So much so, that God didn't *"let any of his words fall to the ground"*. *(1 Samuel 3)*

Samuel was also a national civil leader. As the national leader, he spoke at national ceremonies and presided over the covenantal and constitutional assemblies that changed the regime dynamics that changed their national structure. He also spent much of his old age traveling the countryside judging Israel. *(1 Samuel 7)*

There hasn't been a more transformative figure in Israelite history. Samuel operated in all three domains of the Ketarim and in the highest office of each. He was the last to successfully straddle the domains of the Ketarim and the divisions of authority between the prophetic (constitutional interpretation) and the civil became institutionalized by the end of the Judges period. Was this a type of Christ? Christ was the next and last to operate in all three offices.

Samuel's early life was like Moses' early life, having been grafted into a leading family that would teach him the priestly functions. He also heard from the Lord and led His *inheritance* in a similar fashion to Moses. This has led the rabbinic discourse to suggest that Samuel was *above* that of Moses and Aaron because of his role as interim high priest in the post-Eli era, and the consensus is always that Samuel was *equal* to Moses and Aaron. *(Berachot 31B)* *"Moses and Aaron were among His priests, and Samuel among those who invoke His Name,"* *(Psalms 99:6)* [3]

Still, the people proclaim,… *"Long live the "melekh" [king]…"*

Samuel was the last to attempt to straddle both domains; (his two official titles normally being a judge and a prophet). This was certainly to restore the office of *Eved Adonai*. He also gained authority within the decimated priesthood. He apparently *was* the priesthood. What a time was it to be alive, or at least to witness?

Samuel attempted to restore the vision of a Holy Commonwealth as the goal for the nation of Israel; a goal viewed as mandated by God. The institution of the monarchy would abandon God's direct rule over His people and ultimately lead away from the dream of a Holy Commonwealth led by God. Ultimately, perhaps considering Samuel's hope, subsequent dynasties were judged by their faithfulness to God's will. For whatever reason, Samuel failed. [2]

And, the band played on…

Chapter 7: The Earthly Kingdom

"'No, we want a king to rule over us'—even though the Lord your God was your king."
I Samuel 12:12

As we've become painfully aware, there was a wrestling match that was enacted solely by the children of God. God's desire has been to dwell amongst His people. He would be their God. They would be His people. There has been, even to our day, a wrestling match. It is a game of musical thrones if you will. Just where is that throne? Who's in charge? And, so on.

The throne was now on earth. The earthly kingdom placed an intermediary between God and His people. The *Servant of the Lord* always conveyed God's will with God remaining Sovereign. This really changed things.

We will continue to try to highlight the aspects of the Davidic-styled kingdom that would have an impact on what the early Church may look like. The cultural elements and the relationship between the domains of authority will also impact our view of the Church that emerged. Moses, Joshua, and Samuel represented a Prophetic led regime.

David would represent a 'civil' led regime. He would have to cooperate with both the priestly and prophetic domains and not fall into the same traps that Saul did. He would also need to work to resurrect the priestly abyss left by Eli's sin.

The following illustration of the apparent eyewitness account of a ratification ceremony of a king in the land of Connacht, Ireland, was astonishingly like how I viewed an Ancient Israelite ratification ceremony may be like. It is also possibly reminiscent of an ancient ordination.

It was found while researching my ancestry and I have no idea where it came from. But I thought that it was a great resource to use to begin this chapter. The ceremony apparently had roots that may have gone back a few thousand years.

The installation of the Ardri, (High King) was held at Canrfree near Tulsk, where for ages the Connacht kings had been inaugurated.

The ceremony took place on an old cairn of stones on top of which rested the coronation stone. It was an elaborate affair and was attended by many bishops and principal chiefs or sub kings of Connacht. O'Mulconry gave the new king his wand, O'Flanagan was his High Steward, O'Flaherty and O'Malley had command of the fleet, O'Kelly was Chief Treasurer, etc. *Mageraghty was given special honour and received gifts of cattle and sheep from the new king as an indication of the special relationship between the O'Conor's and Mageraghtys. (Both shared a common ancestry).*

An eyewitness account of the inauguration of Cathal Crovedearg O'Conor (1201-1224) records that O'Conor gave Mageraghty 'twelve score milch cows, twelve score sheep and twelve score cows". At the ceremony, it was decreed that the twelve dynasts or sub-chiefs of Connacht should be present. In addition to those named above were O'Flynn, O'Hanly, O'Fallon, O'Beirne, O'Concanon, O'Heyne, O'Shaughessy and O'Teigh. The latter was the chief of the household of the King of Connacht. The record states that 'forty-eight townlands constituted the patrimony of each of his four royal chiefs'.

Preceding the inauguration, the king would march down from Rathcrogan with his retinue of abbots, bishops, chieftains, sub-chieftains, and statesmen. When they reached the top of the cairn the king placed his sword in front of the stone as a symbol that he would rule his of kingship, and a golden slipper which was placed on his right foot. He then walked around the stone three times in a clockwise direction giving him plenty of time to view his newfound lands. To take his oath of allegiance he would step on top of the stone and place his foot in the imprint of two footprints that were carved into the stone by the first king of Connacht.

The coronation stone had the same significance to the Irish that the Stone of Scone has to the Scots. Upon it, the Kings of Scotland were crowned. The Stone of Scone was a gift to the Scots by the Irish in the year 500. It is said, (though not proved)

95

that in ancient times there was a larger stone that was split in two. The Irish kept one part and the other was given by Fergus to the Scots. In the Scottish crowning ceremony, the stone was placed under the king's throne. After Cromwell subdued the Scots, the English transported the Stone of Scone to Westminster Abbey, England. There it remained for centuries until a few years ago when at the persistence of Scottish Nationals, it was returned to Scotland. And you might ask, "whatever happened to the Irish coronation stone?" Well, I'm happy to report that it still exists, though it would seem, it is not held in the same esteem as the Scots have for the Stone of Scone. It now rests at Clonalis House, the ancestral home of the O'Conor Don, on land owned by the O'Conors for 1500 years." (found in annals online)

This eight-hundred-year-old account of the coronation ceremony above suggests that it had been done that way for hundreds of years. The ceremony apparently followed a long traditional ritual for the installation of the new high king. This illustration should help us in our perception of the earthly kingdom of the Israelites; a kingdom in which God, through Samuel, warned the nation about.

The elaborate account can give us insight into the Church that Emerged. Through additional research, it seems Mulconry was probably a bishop. There was a High Steward, and many other offices of the royal court, or cabinet, are named. There is a chief of the household named O'Teigh among the many officials. There looks to have been 12 different tribes in the kingdom that were full of political figures that governed at various levels.

From a local perspective, the illustration reveals local and regional officials. Even though the names are different, we could say that they had mayors, councils, and governors. There were familial ties and local connections to clans and a specific tribe. Each of these clans apparently gave of their crops and livestock to the monarchy just as God had warned. The kingdom of the Ancient Israelites was much the same way.

Lastly, the account reveals a separation of the *Keter Torah* and the *Keter Malkhut*. The ratification ceremony has an apparent politically "representative" tone. There is also a suggested "anointing" aspect of the ceremony with the approval of the bishops, abbots and certainly priests in attendance. The *Keter*

Torah (prophets, teachers) and the *Keter Kehunah* (priests) were accessory to any apparent direct governance of the kingdom. Their attendance suggests that they had influence in the kingdom and the royal family itself.

David's Rise

Interestingly, we find that even though David had been anointed by God as King of Israel. He still had to go through trials to gain the nation's acceptance. First, God instructs Samuel to seek out David to anoint him as the king to replace Saul. This was done in secret to enable the entire nation, through their tribal leaders, to recognize David as their national leader.

It was done to maintain the framework of the covenantal agreement between God and the congregation of Israel. David, though anointed, and granted God's Charisma, would need to ascend through covenantal channels between the people and their leaders, and David himself.

Secondly, David gained access to Saul's inner circle as a musician and poet. Saul was depressed, plagued by mental and emotional issues. In noticing this, one of Saul's entourage suggests that a young musician, a harpist, could provide some relief to Saul's mood. After being invited to the court, David's music provided that, albeit temporary, relief.

And thirdly, even though David is still at home and not yet mobilized into the confrontations with the Philistines, he seizes on an opportunity for recognition by singly volunteering to fight, and then defeat, Goliath after arriving on the scene with food for his brothers. *(1 Samuel Ch.16 & 17)*

From the very beginning, David reveals many of the characteristics he will need to ascend politically, acquire power, and then to secure that power. He showed modesty while still being overtly confident in acting proactively to seize opportunities. David was said to be handsome and talented, capable of garnering the support of powerful people even in some of the higher institutions of the nation. He showed himself to be a young man with new and original ideas and had a military competence that he would need to ascend to national power.

David did not immediately ascend to the highest office and there were several milestones along the way. The path was strewn with trials and potential pitfalls. He learned to form alliances and protect himself from those who were out to get him.

He gained access to the "inner court" through his music, but he was also a popular hero. He gained experience in politics and knowledge of the court's inner workings. He formed friendships as he grew in power.

David's popularity exceeded that of Saul's and that created Saul's contempt.

David was far from innocent as he seemed to seek the public's admiration. However, David was able to sidestep the snares that Saul had set for David's harm. He entered the royal family by delivering the foreskins that Saul required for the hand of his daughter, Michal. Now, instead of just being a part of Saul's court, he was a part of the royal family.

A special relationship grows between David and Saul's oldest son Jonathan, who would be heir to the throne. The friendship eventually requires Jonathan to make the unenviable choice between his father and his friend.

David becomes a political refugee. During this time, his following continues to grow. He is increasingly adept at covenanting along the way. He garners the support of the remnants of the priesthood. This becomes the beginning of his legitimacy.

David continues to grow both militarily and politically through alliances and co-opting of various groups and institutions. Ultimately, Saul is defeated.

Through a series of Saul's missteps and David's sidesteps, Saul is killed in battle. David decides to take advantage of the vacuum that is created. After asking God, David moves to Hebron, the seat of the government for the house of Judah. It's also Judah's spiritual center.

The men of Judah covenanted with David to anoint him, king, over "the house of Judah" and David became the king of the house of Judah alone. *(II Samuel 2:1-4).* It was seven years and six months before he became the king of the entire nation through a separate covenant.

After several years of turmoil, they covenanted with David to become the King over all of Israel, both the houses of Judah and of the house of Israel. The same blueprint is continually used in Israel and it was used in the agreement. The assembly showed that they understood that God has appointed David *nagid* (high commissioner) as Saul 's successor. Still, the assembly of the people of the Israelite nation, anoint him *melekh* (king). The dual formula of the *melekh* of the people being God's *nagid* carries on in the land.

> *Then came all the tribes of Israel to David unto Hebron, and spoke, saying: "Behold, we are thy bone and thy flesh. In times past, when Saul was king over us, it was thou that didst lead out and bring in Israel; and the Lord said to thee:* **'Thou shalt feed My people Israel, and thou shalt be prince over Israel.'"** *[Jesus said this to Peter] So all the elders of Israel came to Hebron, and King David made a covenant with them in Hebron before the Lord, and they anointed David king over Israel." (II*

Samuel 5:1-3)

The mantle of kingship used the required combination of God's designation through the prophets and the popular consent of the people through separate agreements with the elders of Judah and Israel.

David's Reign

Let the politicking begin. David quickly moved to consolidate power by attacking and capturing the City of Jerusalem. He then made Jerusalem the nation's capital. The effects were twofold. First, it removed the Canaanite settlement that occupied the land between the Southern tribes and the Northern ones.

Secondly, it created a "federal district" outside of the jurisdiction of any of the existing tribal lands. The federal monarchy had created its own district, literally known as the "City of David". David moved both his family and his royal court to the city and began building a 'grand' home and a dynamic capital.

David learned from the failures of the past and built upon the base of the old tribal federation. He grafted the mantle of kingship onto the existing governing base who became increasingly subordinate to the king and his court. The *Keter Malkhut* was continually strengthened through the developing bureaucracy. The bureaucracy included the inner circle of the royal court, a cabinet, and the "sons of David" (his loyal supporters). *(II Samuel 8:15-17)*

The royal court included representatives from the domains of the priesthood and the prophets, while the cabinet seems to have represented a group from across the civil and military elite. There was also a small standing army.

This army was ultimately tied to the king first and foremost and regularly extinguished continual revolts and claims to power. This gave David the tools necessary to develop a ruling class, to increasingly legitimize the concept of a 'royal' family, and to establish most of the fundamental powers of the office of the king. David was quite successful in consolidating power, both in his office and in his royal court, by centralizing the overall power of the government.

He did not try to abolish the tripartite division of *Ketaric* authority, but only to control it. David learned from Saul. Instead of trying to eliminate traditional institutions of the Israelite polity, he resurrected their identities and co-opted them. In relatively short order, David's forces retook lands and defeated the Philistines. Ultimately, this led the Philistines to transfer the Ark of the Covenant into David's hands.

He brought the Ark to the federal district, Jerusalem. The priesthood was resurrected out of Eli's ashes and a new priestly family, the Zadokites, descendants from Aaron's last remaining son, were anointed guardians of the Ark. By doing so, David strengthened the *Keter Kehunah* who would be essentially beholden to him. Thereby, David gained some control over it.

Similarly, the wisdom that David gained through Saul's reign led him to deal with the *Keter Torah*, in much the same way. At David's encouragement, leading prophets resided in his court. Their powers were reaffirmed, and they were given 'free rein' to criticize and denounce transgressions without any fear of retaliation.

While these prophets were free to exercise this authority, they were also somewhat tied to David. So, David had remobilized the basic lines of authority and what could be considered Sovereign covenantal ties, he also realized that he could subtly manipulate the office to serve the king.

Both the eventual adoption of the dynastic principle and the building of the Temple were examples of David's interaction with the prophets, and with God through them. David brought a leading prophet, Nathan, into the royal court *(II Samuel 7)* to be a personal advisor.

Through Nathan, David requests God's permission to build a Temple for the Ark. Initially, Nathan was inclined to grant David's request. However, that night Nathan dreamt that Lord didn't need it. The word of the Lord revealed that the Temple would violate the Israelite spirit of the simplicity of the traditional Wilderness Tabernacle.

God also instructs Nathan to remind David that he is, in fact, God's *negidim* (high commissioner) as his descendants would also be *negidim*. The paradigm of a dynastic monarchy is being formed. Nathan reports that God would then assure this dynastic principle and his heir would be permitted to build God's house.

David acknowledged the constitutional credibility of the dream through the *Keter Torah*. So, he responds in a prayer of mutual agreement to consummate the covenant. The permanent dominion of the house of David has been secured.

David's Fall

The Bible portrays both David's strengths and weaknesses. His greatest transgression of the law included adultery and murder. He sent a Hittite to the battlefield knowing he would die to both keep it secret and to take the Hittites wife, Bathsheba.

The adulterous union of David and Bathsheba produced a son, Solomon, who later became heir to the throne of David, and ultimately established the dynastic principle. With David 's fall, he realizes that he is subjected to the judgment of God through the prophets. And, both would be needed to establish this dynastic structure and to once again amend the Israelite constitution. David would need forgiveness, also reparation.

David has consolidated the *Keter Torah* into his royal court. For this, David must pay a steep price. The dynastic standard had not been added to the covenant and there was no precedent for a hereditary monarchy. The quest for power and wealth, both in the Royal court and especially David's children, is well documented.

In the final battle for the throne, David was essentially forced to name Solomon, Bathsheba's son, his successor. This also made Bathsheba *Gebirah* Queen Mother during Solomon's reign. In the next chapter, we delve into the office of the *Gebirah* Queen Mother in the kingdoms of the Israelite nation.

Adonijah had attempted a coup to seize the birthright by garnering sizable support, but Solomon also had substantial support. Remember, Solomon was Bathsheba's son. Nathan, who was the lead prophet of his generation and a personal consultant to David *(II Samuel 7)*, became the swing vote.

He mobilized Bathsheba to intercede with the king and ask for David to anoint Solomon to the throne. In a clearly orchestrated volley, both Bathsheba and Nathan appear before David. They force David to see that their lives would be surrendered if Adonijah were to ascend to the office of the king. This essentially ties David's hands and Solomon is the heir.

David will need to garner the support of all three *Ketarim* in order to get the entire nation to ratify the amending of the constitution to reflect the new system to pass on the mantle of kingship. If Solomon was to rightfully ascend to the throne, David would need both the prophetic and priestly domains to publicly declare their support for a hereditary monarchy.

Chief representatives of all three *Ketaric* branches of the national government were summoned: the high priest, the prophet, and the steward of the royal court declared support for the new process at a public ceremony. The gathering of the Edah would be required to affirm and ratify this new process at the ceremony. The ceremony is similar to the one that installed the king in Connacht…

And King David said, "Call to me Zadok the priest, Nathan the prophet, and Benaiah the son of Jehoiada." So, they came before the king. The king also said to them, "Take with you the servants of your lord, and have

Solomon my son ride on my own mule and take him down to Gihon. There let Zadok the priest and Nathan the prophet anoint him king over Israel; and blow the horn, and say, 'Long live King Solomon!'

Then you shall come up after him, and he shall come and sit on my throne, and he shall be king in my place. For I have appointed him to be ruler over Israel and Judah." Benaiah the son of Jehoiada answered the king and said, "Amen! May the LORD *God of my lord the king says so too. As the* LORD *has been with my lord the king, even so, may He be with Solomon, and make his throne greater than the throne of my lord King David."*

So Zadok the priest, Nathan the prophet, Benaiah the son of Jehoiada, the Cherethites, and the Pelethites went down and had Solomon ride on King David's mule, and took him to Gihon. Then Zadok the priest took a horn of oil from the tabernacle and anointed Solomon. And they blew the horn, and all the people said, "Long live King Solomon!" And all the people went up after him, and the people played the flutes and rejoiced with great joy so that the earth seemed to split with their sound." 1Kings (1:32-40)

Solomon follows that all too familiar Path

In a strange exchange of 'matter of fact' house-keeping before David dies, he reminds Solomon not to fall into the pitfalls of Saul by recognizing the divisions of authority, to honor the traditional way of the Torah, *and…* to kill those who might try to seize the throne from him.

Solomon was extremely gifted and obviously anointed to fulfill the role to sit on the throne as successor to David with Bathsheba as Queen Mother. He was skilled at bureaucratic reform and centralizing power while under the watchful eyes of his prophetic counterparts and the *Keter Kehunah* didn't seem opposed initially. They saw it as a way to implement God's will more efficiently.[5]

As part of the transformation, Solomon would need to transform Israelite ideology to justify a fixed place of worship; the Temple. God had always objected to a fixed place of worship in the past. The Ark of the Covenant and the Wilderness Tabernacle were always completely portable, and God could move them at will. Through a series of prayers and confirmations, the constitution is amended to the centralization with one caveat. If he or his heirs would violate the constitution, both the Temple and the land would be destroyed. *(II Chronicles 7)* [5]

Well, to make a long story short, Solomon fell into the sins of so many of his ancestors. Many of his wives were pagan, of other religions, and served other gods. Solomon built chapels around the Temple that served these other gods. Solomon tolerated other religions and the *'smoke from other altars rose in the shadow of the Temple'*.

"...and his heart was not fully devoted to the LORD his God, as the heart of David his father had been." 1 Kings 11:1-4

God graciously tried, as He does each one of us, to turn Solomon back. But his apostasy was complete, and God finally appeared to Solomon on the QT. He told him that he would take the kingdom away from Solomon and his heirs. *"Since you have not kept my covenant and have disobeyed my laws, I will tear the kingdom away..."* However, God was still gracious to Solomon and evidently honored the covenant until after his death. He also did it through nature channels. The Kingdom was torn apart. There were 10 tribes that succeeded. The Israelite kingdom has not been put back together again.

"Then you will cry out in that day because of your king whom you have chosen for yourselves, but the LORD will not answer you in that day." 1 Samuel 8-18

Chief (High) Servant in the House of David

Did the Davidic Kingdom have a high steward? A chief servant, or steward? Yes! When you read the Old Testament Accounts of the Davidic Kingdom period, we realize that the system of offices, officials, courts, and authorities was quite complex. There was always someone in charge.

Sometimes we see interpretations of court administrations, or household, or royal court administrations, etc. There are a few biblical accounts in which we can see that they mirror the Chief Servant, or Steward as Eliezer did in Abraham's household. They weren't technically *"Servants of the Lord"* because of the earthly throne. But most still called God, their Master.

The prophet Isaiah, who prophesied during later kings of Judah, admonishes Chief Steward. Shebna, who at one time oversaw the royal household.

Isaiah 22:15 "Thus says the Lord GOD of hosts, "Come, go to this steward, To Shebna, who is in charge of the royal household, NASB

The lambasting goes on for a couple of verses before Shebna is replaced by Eliakim, the son of Hilkiah. This Chief Steward was entrusted with the keys to watch over the kingdom, the keys of the house of David with the delegated authority that the keys represented.

> *Isaiah 22:20-24 "And it shall come to pass in that day, that I will call my servant Eliakim, the son of Helkiam. And I will clothe him with thy robe, and will strengthen him with thy girdle, and will give thy power into his hand: and he shall be as a father* **(calling priests father)** *to the inhabitants of Jerusalem, and to the house of Judah. And I will lay the key of the house of David upon his shoulder:* **and he shall open, and none shall shut: and he shall shut, and none shall open.** *And I will fasten him as a peg in a sure place: and he shall be for a throne of glory to the house of his father. And they shall hang upon him all the glory of his father's house, diverse kinds of vessels, every little vessel: from the vessels of cups even to every instrument of music."*

Isaiah explains the power this Chief Steward will have; the steward who has the kingdoms keys. He shall be clothed with the kings (God's) robe, strengthened with the king's (God's) girdle, and [His] power shall be put into this steward's hand. We can see that pride and self-service will lead to the Chief Servant's replacement, otherwise, the Steward will be protected by God himself.

We can also see that when Shebna was to be replaced, God did it. The enormous power the steward has in the keys is explained, "...he shall open, and none shall shut; and he shall shut, and none shall open." We'll see how this passage is used by both Jesus and in the epistles for our understanding of the Church in later chapters.

The biblical narration of the office of the High (chief) Steward is even more elaborate. In II Kings 18:18-32 we see that Shebna has been reduced to that of a scribe. He became the Eliakim's new secretary.

The king sends Eliakim out to meet the field commander in his place, to speak for him in his absence. In Isaiah's biblical account, Eliakim's responsibilities, and the authority of his office are recounted several times. This was the office of the High Steward or the Chief Servant in the hose of David.

These passages reveal the importance of the office's authority in the absence of the king. It is a successive and ongoing office within the kingdom, fixed in a sure place by God. The 'peg', who possesses the keys, is a mark of glory in the house of David, the house of God, and the kingdom.

Obadiah

Long after the era of Judges, there arose a strange man named Obadiah. This was well after the split of the tribes after Solomon. The name Obadiah is a possible biblical theophoric-al name (embedded theological name because of the meaning). But his name really means…are you ready, Servant of the Lord? Was his name, Obadiah, placed there in the midst of a kingdom?

In the northern Kingdom, there was a powerful king named Ahab. He had a Chief servant named…Obadiah. You will see many translations of the bible call his office different names. Names such as the Palace Administrator, Governor, or that he was the steward of the house and had charge over the household, and so on. He was the Chief Servant or Chief Steward of the house.

He greatly feared the Lord. His faithfulness led him to hide 100 of God's prophets in caves to protect them from Jezebel. Of course, we all know Elijah also hid from Jezebel. Interestingly, the estranged Jezebel is never called a Queen Mother. We get it though.

But, because of Obadiah's faithful actions, Rabbinical tradition, and many Orthodox traditions believe that he received the prophetic gift. The Chief Servant of the Household, Obadiah, was the same prophet of the Book of Obadiah.

If this is so, there is a couple of interesting tidbits. An old Rabbinical tradition places his burial place at the same site as Elisha's and John the Baptists at Sebastia. And, there are some interesting prophetic teaching:

Adherence to the golden rule. As one has done, it shall be done to him (Obadiah 1:15).

Humility is better than arrogance, for arrogance is self-deceptive. It deceives the heart (Obadiah 1: 2-4)

Whether or not these are the same Obadiah(s), doesn't really matter, but it makes perfect sense. As we will see in the next chapter, operating in the domain of the prophetic, or teaching domain, would be expected. But what does matter, we see this same office operating under an earthly king when the throne was here on earth.

Chief Servant Verses

Here is a sampling of verses that point us at the Chief Servant,…

"And he that was over the house, and he that was over the city, the elders…"2Kings10:5

"And Ahishar was over the household" 1Kings4:6

"and over the storehouses in the fields, in the cities, and in the villages, and in the castles, was Jehonathan the son of Uzziah:"1Chronicles27:25

Bringing it together

The kingdom of the Israelites lasted less than a thousand years, most those years in turmoil and disarray. We need to face the fact that it was as God said,

"And you will cry out in that day because of your king whom you have chosen for yourselves, and the Lord will not hear you in that day." 1 Samuel 8:18 NKJV

As my mother would have put it, "they've got "kingdoms" on the brain", like I had pawsickos (popsicles) on the brain. God had a kingdom issue with his chosen people. They decided they wanted to be like other nations with a king, but was the appointment of a king mandatory?

God long sought to reign over his people, however, He never mandated a specific form of government in the Old Testament. It is quite indecisive about the entire idea of the monarchy, choosing to rather explore issues of governance from many different angles.

Until Jesus speaks repeatedly of the kingdom, we are unsure as to whether the entire idea of a monarchal regime was "consistent with a covenantal system".[9] It most definitely wasn't God's idea. We've seen that. Jesus spoke to them on their terms. They still had *"kingdoms on the brain"*. So, Jesus expressed the new relationship with God in a way they could understand. It became a kingdom.

Even though God authorized the kingship, we are left wondering whether He had truly blessed it, or merely acquiesced. This question seems to "haunt" the Israelite people from the book of Judges with Gideon and Samuel to the disappearance of the monarchy and beyond.

Three things are made clear about the role of the king: he is bound by covenant (brit) with God, he is bound by covenants among the assembly of Israelites, and he is bound by the constitution (Torah). Kings are repeatedly reminded that, in God's view, they are *negidim, (negid)* or only high commissioners. This tradition worked to limit the propensity for monarchic self-aggrandizement.

The tripartite system is now known as the three Ketarim (crowns) fully blossomed with the onset of the monarchal period. Earth-bound humans were given primary importance in civil governance of the Israelite nation. This threw the importance of God out the window. The time God directly reigned was over. The *Eved Adonai* was gone. And, the *Keter Torah* was extensively diminished. They heard less from God.

Prophets were relegated to an ancillary role in the kingdom, but they still acted as kingmakers and at times king-breakers, and as critics of both the king and of the condition of the heart of the nation as well. Yet, the *Keter Malkhut* had ascended to the "top of the heap" in the struggle for power and governance in the life of 'people of God".

The role of the *Keter Kehunah* was resurrected and again tethered the people to God through ritual and sacerdotal proceedings. So, the groundwork for the tripartite divisions of authority between civil (essentially secular), prophetic (or constitutional interpretation), and priestly became entrenched in the framework of the monarchal era. But there was a collateral effect, it lowered God's status as Sovereign.

Solomon's sins and idolatry, along with the growing arrogance of the ruling class, led to Solomon's son Rehoboam, being denied throne by the ten northern tribes. They failed to ratify his coronation. *(I Kings 12; II Chronicles 10).*

In the aftermath, the two kingdoms operated differently. The South lost most of its federal identities with the dominance of Judah, however, in the North, the tribal federation remained strong until its fall. The fall of the northern kingdom marked the end of the first monarchal epoch and the end of the tribal federation as an entity in the history of the Israelites.

In the post-tribal federation period, there was a brief period of reform. King Josiah's reform restored the Book of Deuteronomy as the basis for the constitution of his regime. He returned to the idea that the polity should be based on tripartite covenant; a covenant between, God and Israel, God and the king, the king and Israel, all of which needed to be in acknowledgment of God as Sovereign who was represented by his prophets in the day to day matters of relevance within the kingdom. *(II Chronicles 23:1-2,21; and 34:29-32).* This could be considered a necessity for their identity to survive the destruction of the First Temple, ending the era. (586 BCE)

So, why is all this important to us? We're of a new covenant, aren't we? It's the only way we will see the authentic first Church, The Church that Emerged.

We'll use this as we move toward that Church and illuminate the various aspects and characteristics of Church that grew out of a gang of 12 on the hills of Judea.

It will help us understand what Jesus talked about, who He talked to, and why He talked to them. It will show us how we came the Old Testament concealed the New, and the New reveals the Old. Christ spoke to these people and this nation. It is out of there His Church emerged. We'll see the Church, highly modeled on the past societies, and one that is most definitely visible.

Chapter 8: Gebirah: Queen Mother of the Kingdom

"Then said he to the disciple, Behold your mother! And from that hour that disciple took her to his own home." John 19:27

J ezebel is one of the most prominent figures of the Old Testament. For good reason, and not good ones. The evils of Jezebel are well known. What isn't known is that she wasn't a queen. Nope. Nada. I looked again doing a bible word search for her name. She is never called a queen. Yes, she's married to King Ahab.

But Israelites didn't have queens that way. Kings normally had many wives, but they only had one mother. They didn't have many queens. They had one Queen Mother. *(Gebirah) Strong's #1377*

"Nebuchadnezzar led King Jehoiachin away as a captive to Babylon, along with the **queen-mother***, his wives and officials, and all Jerusalem's elite" (2Kings 24:15NLT)*

We only see biblical *Gebirahs* in the unified and the southern kingdom and not in the north. The Queen Mother *Gebirah,* in the Kingdom of Judah, was the King's chief Counselor, and the most vital and influential member of his royal court. You'll be surprised to find out that she had a throne and a crown. She was also held responsible before God. What? You say. Follow along. Here Jeremiah is referring to the same incident as in 2Kings above:

"Say to the king and the queen mother (Gebirah), "Come down from your thrones and sit in the dust, for your glorious crowns will soon be snatched from your heads."(Jeremiah 13:18)NLT

The Beginning: The New Eve
I'm going to start in Genesis as I did with the *Eved Adonai;* however, we're

going to begin to extend into the Gospel period out of necessity. I'm going to start with the protoevangelium—the first gospel…Mankind's fall from grace in the garden and God's plan for redemption. St. Irenaeus explained it this way:

> *Just as the former-that is, Eve-was seduced by the words of an angel so that she turned away from God by disobeying his word, so the latter-Mary-received the good news from an angel's announcement in such a way as to give birth to God by obeying his word; and as the former was seduced so that she disobeyed God, the latter let herself be convinced to obey God, and so the Virgin Mary became the advocate of the virgin Eve. And as the human race was subjected to death by a virgin, it was liberated by a Virgin; a virgin's disobedience was thus counterbalanced by a Virgin's obedience..." (Adv. Haer., V, 19, 1). (cir.200)*

Now, of course, this blows some people's minds; NOT **Mary**! they freak out. Well, we just introduced the *Gebirah* of the Davidic Kingdom, who we'll expand on soon, and we are going to explore some of the Matriarchs of the Old Testament. T*oxic* feminism has gripped our culture in a way that refuses to even look and celebrate the wonders of the *better* gender. The gender that sheds blood in cooperation with the creator. So, let's celebrate and put some verses together.

"And I will put enmity Between you and the woman, and between your seed and her Seed; He shall bruise your head, And you shall bruise His heel. (Gen.3:15)

"It was added because of transgressions, till the Seed should come to whom the promise was made; (Gal. 3:19)… But when the fulness of the time was come, God sent forth his Son, made of a woman, made under the law…. to redeem those under the Law, that we might receive our adoption as sons. [and daughters]" (Gal 4:4-5)

It is Mary that bridged the Old Testament and the New Testament. Christ triumphed over Adam's disobedience, sin and death through His sacrificial death and glorious resurrection as a new Adam.[1] We became *"new creatures in Christ"*.

Mary became a new Eve when she was obedient to God. From the angel Gabriel's announcement that she was the woman that was chosen to receive the "promised Seed" to her witnessing Christ's Passion on Calvary, she cooperated with God's salvation plan.

Eve was born out of the side of Adam. At Calvary, in a glorious mystery,

Christ, bears the Church, His bride, from His side, as His Mother is given as the *Gebirah* to the Church. Don't worry it will all become clear later.

Eve was stamped with the seal of perfection, with complete wisdom and beauty; covered with precious stones and gold *[Ezekiel 28:12-13]* She was adorned with twenty-four decorations that depict the women of Israel. *[Isaiah 3:18-24]* Eve's name meant "mother of the living" and when Christ gave His mother to the Church at the cross, she became the "mother of those who truly live." The Eve anew.

Israel's Matriarch's

In Chapter 2, we uncovered God's Plan of Redemption. Here we will recount God's Plan of Salvation. It's time to move on to the Old Testament Matriarchs. Salvation was protected through Israel's Matriarchs who protected the lineage of the Christ.

They also all provide a link between Eve and the Kingdoms Queen Mothers. In a profound way, they all are devoted to a prophetic vision that leads to the announcement of the Messiah and the Virgin Mary. So, it's difficult to develop this chapter into a distinctly political 'Early Church development' point of view.

Here is a short description of some of the Matriarchs of the Old Testament and how this insight helps us with the big picture. It also helps us see how important they are.

Sarah

Sarah was the great matriarch who protected the authentic lineage that would become the nation of Israel. She was the only woman to be called *Gebirah* outside of the Davidic Kingdom. This was before the kingdom. This was in the Household of God. Hence, she wasn't a Queen Mother. She would become the *Great Lady,* mother of a great nation through faith. Abraham and Sarah freely responded to this Divine invitation by faith…to salvation and onward to a nation of a great people.

Sarah was old and barren, chosen to give this miraculous birth to the nation. Mary was young and a Virgin, the "Chosen Daughter of Israel", to give a miraculous birth to the Messiah. Both were conceived by faith. Sarah's barrenness ended when the *Lord* proclaimed it to Abraham by saying,

"Is anything too marvelous for the Lord to do? At the appointed time, about this next

year, I will return to you, and Sarah will have a son" (Gen 18:14)

And the angel Gabriel announced Christ's birth to Mary,
"The Holy Spirit will come upon you, and the power of the Most High will overshadow you. Therefore, the child to be born will be called holy, the Son of God ... for nothing will be impossible for God" (Lk 1:35, 37).

Rebekah
"The girl was very beautiful, a virgin, untouched by man."[Gen 24:16]

"She is the most clever and authoritative of the matriarchs, and yet she epitomizes womanly beauty and virtue, in her conduct (her virginity, her actions at the well), in her energetic speech, in her thoughtful courtesy, and in her self-assurance. " [3]

Rebekah is the second matriarch of Israel. She is sterile until she prays to God for deliverance from her barren womb. She gives birth to Esau and Jacob, but she seems to prefer Jacob. She, like Sarah, protects the lineage of the Messiah through cleverness and mediation yet we also find that it was through the grace of God. Like Mary, evidently, God made it known to Rebekah ahead of time so that His elective plan would continue.

Paul tells us it was God's plan of Salvation… and He told Rebekah:

"…but by Him who calls-she was told, "The older shall serve the younger" (Rm 9:10-12).

Rebekah cooperated and was obedient to God's plan of Salvation. Rebekah was a virgin with single-minded fidelity, love of predilection and faithful virtue is extolled upon the matriarchs and the accounts of the Blessed Virgin in the New Testament.[4]

Rachel
Once again, as is the pattern, Rachel was sterile and with great sorrow reached out to God. She finally gave birth to Joseph and to Benjamin. Joseph was sold into slavery by her brothers to be used to fulfill God's purpose. Rachel is a story

of unparalleled love and unparalleled sorrow.

She gained God's ear by speaking of love and family relationships, but also how they are lived out and experienced in life. She knew too well the suffering this brought her, but through her sacrifice, Israel was eventually rescued and saved. Mary endures the Cross at Calvary as a Sorrowful Mother at the death and resurrection of the Messiah.[4]

Leah

Leah is recognized, one way or another, as the mother of 10 of the tribes of Israel, recognized as the 'Leah tribes. She is known to have given birth to six sons and the sons of one of her slaves are reckoned as hers as well. Like Rachel, she was no stranger to self-sacrifice, devotion to family life, and the virtues of parenting.

Through God's Divine Providence, Leah is the matriarch of both Moses and of David. This puts Leah in the lineage of Jesus. Later, Mary gives birth to the Messiah who is the descendant of Judah (son of Leah).[4]

Deborah

Deborah, as Judge *(Keter Torah) prophetically* calls on the people of Israel to *"walk in the way of the Torah"*. Deborah is recognized as a Mother of Israel in the Tradition of Israel. [Pseudo-Philo] Mary also, exhorts the servants at the wedding at Cana to *"Do as Jesus tells them"*.

Deborah's song, in Judges chapter 5, is a reflection about water and glory. She exhorts Israel to *"glory in the Lord"*. At Cana, Christ changes water into wine manifesting His glory prompting belief to those in attendance.

The victorious woman in the song is considered *"Blessed amongst women" [Judges 5:24]* provides similarities between Deborah, Jael (poem subject), and the Virgin Mary. When Mary visits Elizabeth, she is greeted…*" Mother of my Lord…Blessed amongst women…all nations will call you blessed." [4]*

Jochebed

As the mother of Moses, Miriam, and Aaron, Jochebed is considered in Jewish tradition as a "Mother of Israel". We learn that she is a Levite, *"born of the tribe of Levi, born to the tribe in Egypt."* Israel has ceased having children due to the persecution by the Pharaoh. However, Miriam convinces her parents to secretly stay together and shortly after, true to her prophetic calling, she foresees the birth and calling of her brother Moses.

"My mother will give birth to a son who will be the savior of Israel" (Sothah 12b-13a).

Moses is then 'rescued' from the waters of the Nile, and unknowingly the Pharaoh allows Moses' own mother to raise him for the daughter of the Pharaoh.[4]

Ruth

Ruth was also placed among the "Mothers of Israel". The Targum states:

> *… you are the one that arrived…protected under the shadow of the Majesty of God….you will be liberated from judgement of Gehenna because you have a place among Sarah, Rebekah, Rachel, and Leah…the Mothers of Israel [7]*

Ruth, on many levels, represents a *"shadow of things to come"*. The story of Ruth personifies Israel's relationship with God apart which there can be no other God. Ruth seems to represent Israel while her husband symbolizes God. Or, we can see Boaz as a figure Christ and Ruth symbolizing the Church.

Ruth illuminates the *hesed* (lovingkindness) of God, and the *hesed* in the heart of a woman. She mirrors the blessed Virgin Mary's heart as an active respondent to God…

"All the Lord has said, we will heed and do" [Ex24:7] "I am Ruth, your handmaid."

Mary matched this obedience and humility before the Lord.

"Behold the handmaid of the Lord, be it done to me according to your word" [Luke 1:38]

The great Matriarchs and those known as the 'Mothers of Israel' exhibit profound qualities rooted in undying faith and devotion. They are women of grace and loyalty who, when committed to obedience show profound insight into God's plan of Salvation.

Mothers, who give themselves fully to it; will many times sacrifice and suffer for it. Their commitment is to family and children with purity is an untold virtue that is pleasing and wonderful in the eyes of God. To the list of the "Mothers of

Israel", like adding to Mount Rushmore, I would like to nominate Hannah.

As was the norm, she also could not give birth. She prayed for a child and God provided. She gave her son to God as she promised. Her son, Samuel, was a pre-figured image of Christ. The last before Christ to hold all three offices in Israel.

We're starting to get a better picture now. God's Plan of Redemption, and now His Plan of Salvation is amazing. And, we didn't know. Psst...we're just getting started. Let's move on to expand our understanding of the office of the Queen Mother in the book of Esther.

Esther: A Jewish Queen Mother among the pagans?

The book of Esther presents perhaps the best picture of the Old Testament office of the *Gebirah*. It gives us the best insight into the dignity; the power and authority; and the privileges of the Old Testament Queen Mother. Strangely, it is the extraordinary story of a pagan king and his Jewish wife, Esther. And even more remarkable, it was when Israel was in exile in Babylon. So, while the king wasn't a Davidic king, this will give us insight as we navigate through the Davidic Queen Mothers.

During Israel's Babylonian exile, the Persian kings tolerated the Jews, and many enjoyed great favor and advancement in this atmosphere. Esther is the perfect example of someone who prospered in a favorable climate.

King Ahasuerus grew attracted to her... *"loved Esther more than all the women, and she found grace and favor in his sight more than all the virgins, so that he set the royal crown on her head" (Esther 2:17)* Esther's beauty, faithfulness, and virtue made this Jewish maiden stand out among the kings wives. She became exalted above the rest as his most cherished queen.

Esther became entangled in a dispute with a newly appointed Grand Vizier, Haman, who had an intense dislike for the Jews. The atmosphere toward the Jews in the kingdom completely changed and persecution increased as Haman sought to eliminate them in the kingdom. Haman lied to the king, telling him that the Jews planned to rebel and plotted an uprising. He convinced the king to issue a proclamation to put every Jew in the kingdom to death. Esther was faced with a dilemma.

Once the Edict became known to Esther's relatives, they came to her begging for intercession before the king. However, she was also a Jew, and she was not called by the king.

All the king's servants and the people of the king's provinces know that for any man or woman who comes to the king to the inner court who is not summoned, he has but one law, that he be put to death unless the king holds out to him the golden scepter so that he may live. And I have not been summoned to come to the king for these thirty days." (Esther 4:11)

What happened? Esther interceded for the people before the king, but it was with much anxiety. She prepared by gathering the local Jews around her to come alongside her for prayer and fasting. She clothed herself with the robes of the Queen Mother and with fear and trembling she went to see the king. Upon entering the throne room, the king greeted her with loving-kindness, He *"comforted her with soothing words, and said to her, 'What is it, Esther? I am your brother. Take courage; you shall not die, for our law applies only to the people. Come near'"* (15:8-10). [5]

Esther courageously explained the plot to her king interceding for her people. The king removed the Edict to put the Jews to death and executed the Grand Vizier for his treachery in their place. Esther alone was exempted from the severity of the king's law. Let's reflect on that.

Queen Esther was spared from the curse of death from the law. Her people, Israel, came to experience freedom through her intercession with the king, adorned in the robes in her royal dignity before the king.

We now see that the Queen Mother was a faithful and highly regarded counselor to her son, the King. The people repeatedly came to the Queen Mother for help, and she interceded for them, going to her son on their behalf

.

Gebirah: Queen mother

Ok, your right. The favorite wife of a pagan king who happened to be Jewish did not become a Queen Mother. I know, Queen Mothers only existed in the Davidic line. They did not appear in the Northern Kingdom, and Esther was the esteemed wife of a pagan king while the Israelites were in exile. We'll see that Esther's story radiates some of the virtuous merits that are common in the Judah's Queen Mothers and as a type of the Blessed Virgin Mary.

In the book of 1Kings, we learn that David had 700 wives and 300 concubines. Yet, most think the Queen was his wife. As we've already learned, instead of choosing amongst his wives, the role of *Gebirah* went to his one and only mother. There were also times that the Queen Mother remained as her grandson took the throne. Here, King Solomon receives his mother as she comes to intercede for Adonijah.

"When Bathsheba went to King Solomon to speak to him for Adonijah, the king stood up to meet her, bowed down to her and sat down on his throne. He had a throne brought for the king's mother, and she sat down at his right hand." [2 Kings 2:19]

Are we surprised? The king bowed before his mother and the king had a throne placed at his right hand for her! It was the highest position of honor; to occupy the seat at the right hand of the king. She was the chief confidant and chief councilor who had more influence than anyone else in the kingdom. What happens next? *"...Ask it, my mother, for I will not refuse you."*

When we see the whole interaction, we see the same principle of influence.

> *Now Adonijah, the son of Haggith, went to Bathsheba, Solomon's mother. Bathsheba asked him, "Do you come peacefully?" He answered, "Yes, peacefully." Then he added, "I have something to say to you." "You may say it," she replied. "As you know," he said, "the kingdom was mine. All Israel looked to me as their king. But things changed, and the kingdom has gone to my brother; for it has come to him from the Lord.*
>
> *Now I have one request to make of you. Do not refuse me." "You may make it," she said. So, he continued, "Please ask King Solomon—he will not refuse you—to give me Abishag the Shunammite as my wife." "Very well," Bathsheba replied, "I will speak to the king for you."*
>
> *When Bathsheba went to King Solomon to speak to him for Adonijah, the king stood up to meet her, bowed down to her and sat down on his throne. He had a throne brought for the king's mother, and she sat down at his right hand. "I have one small request to make of you," she said. "Do not refuse me." The king replied, "Make it, my mother; I will not refuse you." (1 Kings 2:13-20)*

We can see that scripture gives us ample evidence of the office of the Queen Mother in the House of David. We see that this royal office has transcended its early roots in the Abrahamic Covenant's Household of God and navigated all the way to the Monarchy under Mosaic Law.

This position of authority was afforded the mothers of the kings in the House of David, within Judah. They were apparently required at both state and religious functions, within the royal courts and cabinets, and had responsibilities

117

representative of their crown, and high seat of influence within the kingdom.

There is overwhelming evidence that this royal title continued in Judah as long as the House of David reigned. It is also hard to argue that this office was crowned, adorned with a robe, and was seated on a throne next to the king. We know from Scripture that the Queen Mother regularly exercised this influence with their son, as counselor *[2Chronicles 22:3]* and as intercessor *[1Kings 2:13-20]*. This extended to their grandsons (*I.e. Maacah: 1 Kings 15 with her grandson Asa*)

> ***Note:*** Catholics call the King of kings (in the line of David) mother, who has also ascended into Heaven and is seated at His right hand... The Queen of Heaven. This is where it comes from and technically, it should be the Queen Mother of Heaven. It has been popular to try to tie Mary to a pagan Egyptian queen. But this isn't so.

Jeremiah makes the distinction clearly. Whenever he is describing the Egyptian goddess, he uses the word *Meleketh (queen)*. Jeremiah uses the word *Gebirah* for the Queen Mother of the Judahite king in the Davidic House. He clearly makes the distinction.

> *"You are the glory of Jerusalem, the surpassing joy of Israel; you are the splendid boast of our people" [Judith 15:9]*

Here are just a few passages which refer to the office of the *Gebirah [NJB translation]*

- *Kings 15:13: He even deprived his grandmother Maacah of the dignity of Great Lady [Gebirah] for having made an obscenity for Asherah...*
- *Kings 10:13: he met the brothers of Ahaziah king of Judah. 'Who are you?' he asked. 'We are Ahaziah's brothers,' they replied, 'and we are on our way to pay our respects to the king's sons and the queen mother's (Gebirah) sons.'*
- *Chronicles 15:16: King Asa even deprived his (grand) mother Maacah of the dignity of Great Lady (Gebirah) for having made an obscenity for Asherah.*
- *Jeremiah 13:18: Tell the king and the Queen mother (Gebirah), 'Sit in a lower place, since your glorious crown has fallen from your head.*

- *Jeremiah 29:2: This was after King Jechoniah had left Jerusalem with the Queen mother (Gebirah), the eunuchs, the chief men of Judah and Jerusalem, and the blacksmiths and metalworkers.*

All the king's Mothers

It is little recognized and highly significant that every Davidic king has the Queen Mother listed along with her son in Sacred Scripture. The name of each Queen Mother of the House of David is introduced in each reign of the Davidic Kings. *[i.e. 1 Kings 14:21; 15:9-10; 22:42; 2 Kings 12:2; 14:2; 15:2; 15:33; 18:2; 21:2; 21:19; 22:1; 23:31; 23:36; 24:8; 24:18].*

Throughout 1&2 Kings and 1&2 Chronicles, the Queen Mother is named when her son assumes the Davidic throne and there are very few exceptions. [2 Kings 8:17-18], King Ahaz [2 Kings 16:2-3], and King Asa [1 Kings 15:10]. However, there seems to have been extenuating circumstances in each case.

The Queen Mothers of Israel (table)

1. *Jeremiah 29:2: This was after King Jechoniah had left Jerusalem with the Queen mother (Gebirah), the eunuchs, the chief men of Judah and Jerusalem, and the blacksmiths and metalworkers.* 1. Rehoboam 930-913	Son of Solomon Mother: Naamah the Ammonite	*1Kings 11:42-14:31 2 Chronicles 9:31-12:16*
2. Abijam (Abijah) 913-911	Son of Rehoboam Mother: Maacah descendantof David's son Absalom	*1Kings 14:31-15:8 2 Chronicles 13:1-23*

3. Asa 911-870	Son of Abijam Gebirah = grandmother Maacah	*1 Kings 15:8-24* *2 Chronicles 13:23-* *16:14*
4. Jehoshaphat 870-848	Son of Asa Mother: Azubah	*1 Kings 15:24-22;* *41-51* *2 Chronicles 17:1-* *21:1*
5. Jehoram 848-841	Son of Jehoshaphat Mother:?	*2 Kings 8:16-24* *2 Chronicles 21:1-* *20*
6. Ahaziah 841	Son of Jehoram Mother: Athaliah	*2 Kings 8:24-29;* *9:14-26* *2 Chronicles 22:1-12*
7. Athaliah (Queen Mother) 841-835	Daughter of Ahab and Jezebel of Israel	*2 Kings 11:1-20* *2 Chronicles 22:1-15*
8. Jehoash (Joash) 835-796	Grandson of Athaliah and son of Ahaziah; Mother: Zibiah (Beersheba)	*1 Kings 11:1-12:21* *2 Chronicles 22:10-* *23; 24:27*
9. Amaziah 796-781	Son of Jehoash Mother: Jehoaddan	*2 Kings 14:1-22* *2 Chronicles 26:1-23*
10. Uzziah 781-740	Son of Amaziah Mother: Jecoliah	*2 Kings 15:1-7* *2 Chronicles 26:23-* *27:9*
11. Jotham	Son of Uzziah	*2 Kings 15:32-38*

740-736	Mother: Jerushah	*2 Chronicles 26:9-27:9*
12. Ahaz 736-716	Son of Jotham Mother: ?	*2 Kings 15:38-16:20 2 Chronicles 27:9-28:27*
13. Hezekiah 716-687	Son of Ahaz Mother: Abijah	*2 Kings 16:20; 18:1-20:21 2 Chronicles 28:27-32:33*
14. Manasseh 697-642	Son of Hezekiah Mother: Hephzibah	*2 Kings 21:1-18 2 Chronicles 32:33-33:20*
15. Amon 642-640	Son of Manasseh Mother: Meshullemeth	*2 Kings 21:18-26 2 Chronicles 33:20-25*
16. Josiah 640-609	Son of Amon Mother: Jedidiah	*2 Kings 21:26-23:30 2 Chronicles 33:25-35:27*
17. Jehoahaz 609	Son of Josiah Mother: Hamutal	*2 Kings 23:30-34 2 Chronicles 36:5-8*
18. Jehoiakim	Son of Josiah Brother of Jehoahaz Mother: Zebidah	*2 Kings 23:34-24:6 2 Chronicles 36:5-8*
19. Jehoiachin 598-597	Son of Jehoiakim Mother: Nehusta	*2 Kings 24:6-17 2 Chronicles 36:8-10*

20. Zedekiah 597-587/6	Son of Josiah Parental uncle of Jehoiachin Mother: Hamital	*2 Kings 24:17-25:30* *2 Chronicles 36:10-13;* *Ezekiel 17:13-16*

Wedding at Cana

The wedding of Cana has a great deal packed in this event early in Christ's life. For now, let's just jump into one of the happenings at the wedding. In a later chapter, we'll revisit this jamb packed event. It must have been a marriage feast of a relative and in Judah, that would mean it went on for seven days. So, they ran out of wine.

Mary intercedes for the people; friends, family, and locals who had gathered. She went to Jesus. *"They have no wine!"* Jesus responded back to his mother, *"Woman, what is that to me, my time has not come!"* Now, I always thought that Jesus was being rude…at least it concerned me. But what was happening? There are two simple things that we can immediately see without much thought.

First, "Woman" (capital W) would be relating to the Genesis verse and her role as the new Eve. The second half of His response confirms this. (Think Gen 3:15) Was she expecting Him to reveal His Divinity? His time had not come to step into His role as the New Adam. He was still years from the Garden; the Garden of Gethsemane. Still, in obedience to His mother, He begins His journey.

Second, He does not call her mother. She is not yet the *Gebirah*. She is not yet the Queen Mother. It would have been significant if He would have. Still, Christ does as His Mother asks…

"of course, [mother]"…Ask it, my mother, for I will not refuse you." Mary turns to them and says…*"do everything the [Lord] the [King of kings] tells you to do."*

The Ark of the New Covenant

"In the beginning was the Word, and the Word was with God, and the Word was God." [John1:1]

God's desire was always to dwell among His people, and He would be their God. *Our God reigns.* So, He gave instructions to build a Tent of Meeting, and an Ark of the Covenant that would be behind the veil in the Holy of Holies.

This Ark, deep inside the Tabernacle needed to be perfect, made of Acacia wood and it would be adorned with gold. The Ark was filled with the stone tablets of the Covenant, the rod of Aaron that budded, and a golden jar of manna. Note: The Law was outside the Ark!

The Shekinah of God, like a cloud, would descend on the Ark, and would "overshadow "it. The glory of the Lord would fill the Tabernacle. All of God's people were required to make pilgrimage three times a year to give thanksgiving with Festivals before the Lord. The Tabernacle altar was a "Ministry of Reconciliation" that kept the people reconciled to their God.

The dwelling place of the Ark, inside the Holy of Holies, was so Holy that people died in the innermost parts of the Tabernacle when they treated it with disregard and irreverently. Even two of Aaron's own sons were overcome and died.

During a special transport returning the Ark to Israel after David rescued it from the Philistines, a soldier died just touching it in an attempt to save it from falling. This led David to leave it in the hill country of Judah for three months, where it was and to cry out, *"How can the ark of the Lord come to me?"* [1 Sam 6:1-2]

The Virgin Mary bridged the Old Covenant and the New Covenant. We are reminded, Eve was *"stamped with the seal of perfection"*. The sages and rabbis saw with prophetic insight, the "Mothers of Israel" as being protected in the *shadow* of the Majesty of God and saved from Gehenna. Mary, in obedience to God, received His word gladly and the Shekinah of God fell upon the Blessed Virgin Mary. *"All things would be made new"*.

> *"The angel answered and said to her, "The Holy Spirit will come upon you, and the power of the Most High will overshadow you; and for that reason, the holy Child shall be called the Son of God." [Luke 1:35]*

Mary would bear a son, The Son of God. And the Son of Man. *"...The Word was with God...The Word was God"* The stone Word of the Old Covenant would pass away. It was being replaced by the Living Word. Her womb carried the Word of God made flesh, the true Bread that comes down from Heaven and brings eternal life.

St. Gregory, a third-century Church father, proclaimed Mary... who is truly an ark—*"gold within and gold without, and she has received in her womb all the treasures of the sanctuary."* Mary was the Ark of the New Covenant.

"Hail, full of grace, the Lord is with you!" [Luke 1:28]

Luke's account of the visitation used the typology of the Ark of the Old Covenant to reveal the Blessed Virgin Mary's role in God's Plan of Salvation in a clear and precise way as the Ark of the New Covenant. Mary, the Ark of the New Covenant as pure as the Ark of Old. Let's look at the direct Scripture comparisons. I never saw it before!

Ark Comparison (table)

Old Ark of the Covenant	Virgin Mary, The New Ark
God the Holy Spirit overshadowed and then indwelled the Ark. The Ark became the dwelling place of the presence of God [Exodus 40:34-35]	God the Holy Spirit overshadowed and then indwelled Mary. At that time Mary's womb became the dwelling place of the presence of God [Luke 1:35].
The Ark contained the Ten Commandments [the words of God in stone], a pot of manna, and Aaron's rod that came back to life [Deuteronomy 10:3-5; Hebrews 9:4].	The womb of the Virgin contained Jesus: the living Word of God enfleshed, the living bread from heaven, "the Branch" (Messianic title) who would die but come back to life [Luke 1:35].
The Ark traveled to the hill country of Judah to rest in the house of Obed-edom [2 Samuel 6:1-11]	Mary traveled to the hill country of Judah (Judea) to the home of Elizabeth [Luke 1:39]
Dressed in a priestly	John the Baptist, son of a

ephod, King David approached the Ark and danced and leaped for joy [2 Samuel 6:14]	priest who would himself becomes a priest, leaped for joy in Elizabeth's womb at the approach of Mary [Luke 1:43]
David shouted for joy in the presence of God and the holy Ark [2 Samuel 6:15]	Elizabeth exclaimed with a loud cry of joy in the presence of God within Mary [Luke 1:42]
David asked, "How is it that the Ark of the Lord comes to me?" [2 Samuel 6:9]	Elizabeth asks, "Why is this granted unto me, that the mother of my Lord should come to me?" [Luke 1:43]
The Ark remained in the house of Obed-edom for 3 months [2 Samuel 6:11]	Mary remained in the house of her cousin Elizabeth for 3 months [Luke 1:56].
The house of Obed-edom was blessed by the presence of the Ark [2 Samuel 6:11]	The word "blessed" is used 3 times concerning Mary at Elizabeth's house. [Luke 1:39-45]
The Ark returned to its sanctuary and eventually ends up in Jerusalem where the presence and glory of God is revealed in the newly built Temple [2 Samuel 6:12; 1 Kings 8:9-11]	Mary returned home from visiting Elizabeth and eventually comes to Jerusalem, where she presents God the Son in the Temple [Luke 1:56; 2:21-22]

God made Aaron's rod (which would be kept in the Ark) return to life and budded to prove he was the legitimate High Priest [*Numbers 17:8*].	God would resurrect His Son, who had become enfleshed in Mary's womb and born to bring salvation to all mankind, to prove He is the eternal High Priest [*Hebrews 4:14*].
When the Ark was outside the Holy of Holies [when it was being transported] it was to be covered with a blue veil [*Numbers 4:4-6*]	In Mary's appearances outside of heaven, visionaries testify that she wears a blue veil.
In *Revelation 11:19* John sees the Ark of the Covenant in heaven [this is the last verse of chapter 11]	In *Revelation 12:1* John sees Mary in heaven. It is the same vision Juan Diego saw of Mary in 1531 — the Woman clothed with the sun and standing on the moon.

Bringing it together

This is the first chapter that we traversed from Genesis and into the Gospels. The role of *"Mother of our Lord"* transcends the Old and the New as the Virgin Mary's obedience bridges to two Covenants. So, why the confusion about the Mother of God?

Many hate that title, but it points to the Divinity of Christ carried in her womb. It does not speak to any divinity of Mary who was completely submitted and sheltered in the *shadow* of God. No one believes her to be the mother of the Triune Godhead. Let's take look.

When Mary arose and she went to the hill country of Judea to visit Elizabeth near *Ein Kerem*. The Ark had once resided a stone throw away at Abu Ghosh. So, both made the same journey to the same hill country of Judea. When Mary arrived and Elizabeth heard her greeting, the baby, John the Baptist, leaped in her womb. She was filled with the Holy Spirit and asks,

> *Blessed are you among women and blessed is the fruit of your womb! And why is this granted me, that the* **mother of my Lord** *should come to me? For behold, when the voice of your greeting came to my ears, the babe in my womb leaped for joy. And blessed is she who believed that there would be a fulfillment of what was spoken to her from the Lord" [Luke 1:39-45]*

Finally, what must have shocked first century Jews was John's discovery of the Ark. Jeremiah hid the Ark prior to Babylonian exile and the Ark had never adorned the second Temple, now John found it. In the last verse of Revelation chapter 11, John sees the Ark in Heaven. *"Then God's temple in heaven was opened, and the ark of his covenant was seen within his temple."*

But, wait, was this the same ark? His very next sentence, his next verse, was even more shocking, we're about to see the Ark…

> *And a great portent appeared in heaven, a woman clothed with the sun, with the moon under her feet, and on her head a crown of twelve stars; she was with child" [Rev 12:1-2] ….. she brought forth a male child, one who is to rule all the nations with a rod of iron, but her child was caught up to God and to his throne, [Rev 12:5]*

> *"Hail, full of grace, the Lord is with you!" [Luke 1:28]*

Chapter 9: Passover: The Beginning of Life

"Recognize in this bread, what hung on the cross and in this Chalice what flowed from His Side…"
St. Augustine

C hrist held up the Chalice…It was Thursday. It was the Passover Seder; the first night of Unleavened Bread. It was the night He was betrayed. He held up the third cup. The. Third. Cup. He was Christ, Our Passover. Let's contrast the Old some. Jewish Rabbis credit the daily morning and evening sacrifice of a lamb to Abraham's first sacrifice of a lamb in place of Isaac. Humankind has always seemed determined that someone, or something, has to pay for their transgressions. There must be the shedding of blood for our sins.

Through the gate at the Temple, Israelites strained to see past the guards just to get a glimpse at the taking of a life. It was a surrogate life; a life that should have been their own. Or, they watched for the red ribbon to become white as the scapegoat wandered into the wilderness apparently never to be seen again. Jesus came to say…no, no more, I'll take your place.

This was not that. Yes, Christ mediated the altar at that Tabernacle. This was not that. Christ, Our Passover, is not that. The Israelites sacrificed the Passover lambs. That would also be a prefigurement of Christ. *(John 1:29)*. We know that this is the first of the many and varied ways Christ fulfilled the "Old" sacrifices. It's important to ponder this difference in our relationship with God.

Christ was participating in the Passover vigil. The meal was the Passover Seder commemorating the first Passover. We know that the Passover freed them from Egypt. They were called out, set apart, sanctified and baptized in the waters of the Red Sea. This delivered them from their past. That began the "Counting of Omer" as they grew in knowledge of God.

Christ, our Passover is not the old Passover. How does that work? Let's begin by exploring the ritual of the Passover Seder and the four cups of the meal. It reveals itself as a *"shadow of things to come"* for us today.

> On the night that Christ was betrayed, He
> held up a cup. It was the third cup.
> He said, "Do this." Do the third cup.
> Do you 'do' the third cup? Many do!

The Passover Seder

A theme that was reinforced throughout the Old Testament is one of a 'set order' of things. At times, we see that God's instructions need to be carried out to a tee, (David placing the Ark of the Covenant in a cart and a Levite died) or when God allows for some leeway, permitting his people to set up the process and procedures for (civil governance). Either way, instructions, and procedures were important to the Israelites, especially pertaining to the absolutes of the tabernacle and the sacrifices to God.

The Passover Seder (set order) is a highly liturgical ritual on the vigil of the Passover. Every participant of the Passover Seder sees themselves as having joined the Exodus out of Bondage. They come alongside their ancestors as the journey is made present during the Seder. All partakers have been personally been called out of Egypt, sanctified, and cleansed.

This liturgical service brings forward the past enabling the Jewish people to bond and remember, from where they came. Jewish tradition explains this:

> *From generation to generation everyone must consider himself as having personally gone out of Egypt. Therefore, we must thank Him [God] and praise Him who led our fathers and us through these wonderful things out of slavery to freedom"* (Mishna Pes. 10, 5).

Only those obligated, or chosen, could partake of the unblemished Pascal lamb that fateful night in Egypt. Apostates could not partake of the lamb. Neither could someone steeped in sin or outsiders (non-Jews) who were not in "communion" with the body. They would need to 'remove' the leaven from their midst. The blood was painted on the doorframes… and the rest is history.

Haggadah

The Haggadah (the story of the Passover) is central to the vigil meal of Passover. The little book of the Passover is also known as the Haggadah. Family members gathered with wives and children at the same table. This enabled everyone's participation in the give and take Litany that fulfills the Scriptural command: *"Thou shalt tell thy son on that day."*

There were "set orders" for each day, and each sacrifice at the altar in the Tabernacle, and all things pertaining to the service of God. The Passover Seder (set order) is also one of the times that order is mandatory. So, the Passover liturgy is embedded in the meal as 15 'stations', or steps, of the Passover Seder.

Just like the four steps in God's Plan of Redemption, there are four cups of the Passover. And, just like the Redemptive Plan, life is lived in the middle of the four cups. The four cups are milestones along the way. But there are 15 stations of significance that are stopping points as the meal progresses.

It is a liturgical journey with ritual prayer. There are well-defined parts of the meal that symbolically point to and remind them of both the bitterness and also the joys of their cumulative past. During the Maggid portion, there is a Litany of four questions asked and answered that bring the participants to the night of the first Passover.

As the Seder service moves along and each step is unveiled and made present, Psalms 113 through 118 and finally 136, are incorporated into the Haggadah story. They are either prayed, chanted, or sang at various points during the evening.

The Psalms confirm the story and affirm their experience. They mirror the Israelite journey out of bondage in Egypt and onto nationhood, set apart to God, in their new land. Psalms 113-118 are known as the Hallel.

Portions of the Hallel are recited at different times during the service. Psalms 113 and 114 are recited at the beginning. And the entire Hallel is recited between the third and fourth cup as an act of praise and thanksgiving for what God has done.

As the Psalms follow the Exodus story, we see it begin with the sanctification out of Egypt and onto Mount Sinai. They grow in their relationship with God during Psalms 113 and 114. The Psalms soon brings us to Aaron's priestly ministry and the judgment of God amongst His people with the giving of the Torah. By Psalm 116 they are giving thanks for the Law and confirm it as their guiding covenant with God.

Finally, the Hallel moves to the time where God dwells amongst His people, apparently in the Promised Land. When you read through these Psalms, one can readily see how they dovetail with both the Passover Seder and the Exodus itself, expressed through poetic prose.

This is just another way they live the Exodus. It's always about the Exodus. The Seder overlays and restates the four steps of the Redemptive Plan of God as well as the Pilgrimage Festivals. We will see that the four cups not only enjoin but will again cover the same Journey.

Christ, Our Passover, piques my interest and I'm sure it does yours as well. He held up the third cup.

The Four Cups

> *Therefore, say to the Israelites: 'I am the LORD, and I will bring you out from under the yoke of the Egyptians. I will free you from being slaves to them, and I will redeem you with an outstretched arm and with mighty acts of judgment. I will take you as my own people, and I will be your God. Then you will know that I am the LORD your God, who brought you out from under the yoke of the Egyptians." (Exodus 6:6-7)*

One…two…three…four…First-cup second-cup…third cup…fourth-cup.
Passover…   Pentecost…   Tabernacles… And, it is finished.

One…two…three…four.

I will bring you out…I will deliver you…I will redeem you…I will take you as My people.

It was Thursday. The vigil of the Passover. The evening that Christ was betrayed. He held up the cup…the third cup. He said, "Do THIS in memory of Me". Ahh…do what? Well, do the third cup… WHAT?!?! What's up with that?

Paul called this cup "The cup of blessing that we bless." That's the third cup. It's the cup of blessing. "The cup of blessing which we bless, is it not the communion of the blood of Christ? The bread which we break, is it not the communion of the body of Christ?" 1Cor 10:16 NKJV

There is overwhelming agreement that Christ held up the third cup amongst scholars. The biblical narrative distinctly lists two cups during the Supper service. We also know of the fourth cup on the cross; the climactic finale when the soldier lifted the wine to Christ's lips…It. Is. Finished! Bingo! Finito! But, what's that?

Wait for it...Passover, Pentecost, Tabernacles... Finito!

We know of at least three cups at the Last Supper. Most look at the Last Supper account in the book of Luke and find the four cups. Popular Commentaries seem to agree that the Passover/ Last Supper account must have included the four cups.

Through Old Testament verses and the different Gospel accounts, they arrive at consensus...the four Cups. For instance, Luke 22:17, Luke 22:18, Luke 22:20, and Luke 22:42. In verse 42, Christ prays about the fourth cup at Gethsemane...the fourth cup on the cross.

The Rabbinical schools that grew in the Post Temple era attempted to record their customs for fear of losing the culture forever. This was called the Oral Torah, or (how they did 'church' as we would say). One of these books is the Mishnah.

> *The Mishnah says (Pes. x. 1) that even the poorest man in Israel should not drink less than four cups of wine on this occasion, this number being justified by the four words employed in Ex. vi. 6-7 for the delivery of Israel from Egypt."* (Jewish Encyclopedia)

The four cups from the perspective of Exodus chapter 6 are...

- The Cup of Sanctification   "I will bring you out" Called out and sanctified
- The Cup of Deliverance/Judgment   "I will deliver you" Confirmed in the Covenant
- The Cup of Redemption/Blessing   "I will redeem you" Blessing and Thanksgiving
- The Cup of Praise/Hope/Kingdom/Salvation/Restoration   "I will take you for My people"

The 4 cups are drunk in the following order throughout the Seder:

- Drink the 1st Cup with Kiddush (at the start of the Seder).
- Drink the 2nd Cup after the Maggid (telling of Passover story).

- Drink the 3rd Cup after Birkat Hamazon (Also, pour Elijah's cup in anticipation for final redemption and coming Messiah.)
- Drink the 4th Cup after Hallel (Psalms of praise).

One...Two...Three...Four.

The four cups represent the four steps of deliverance from Egypt and on to their relationship with God...God's Redemptive Plan. You will find different words for the various cups and sometimes slightly different stages. Some look at the first stage being Passover and the last cup being the marriage of the nation through the Covenant at Sinai. Most, however, look at the climax (fourth cup) as our eternal and final destination.

Both can really be acceptable views, and both be accurate. So, as a *shadow of things to come*, the Israelites Journey that ends in the Promised Land, can be also seen as our eternal destination, our resting place in Heaven.

Both are equally worthy of reflection; this completely dovetails their journey and ours. So, let's summarize the four cups of the Passover Seder meal in light of the unmistakable correlation.

The First Cup: (Kiddush) The Kiddush Cup basically means "to make holy" (Kiddush). To begin the Seder service, the participants partake of the First cup over which a prayer of blessing has taken place.

This is also known as the Cup of Sanctification. They were called out. They were gathered and banded together. They were cleansed in the Red Sea. And, so the Seder begins. This Kiddush cup also opens each of the other three Pilgrimage Festivals. The prayer is to bless and 'make holy' the events of the festival.

The Second Cup: (Maggid) The Maggid Cup is "the telling of the story of the Exodus". After the first cup and before the second cup, the story of the Exodus journey is told through the Haggadah. A young child begins the Litany of the four questions. The questions are then answered back by the (*Maggid*) preacher or teacher.

The Cup of Deliverance (Maggid): addresses their journey to Sinai. They grew in their understanding and reliance upon God. They hoped to escape the judgment or wrath of God. They Confirmed this relationship. And, they confirmed their freedom. Along with this freedom came responsibility. Along with this freedom came the Law. They confirmed their freedom and they confirmed the Law. With this, they drink the second cup.

B'Chol dor vador: If this seems to be getting repetitive, it's because it is. **Everything** is about this. It must be important. Each individual and generation should look at themselves as having personally been brought out of bondage in Egypt. It transcends time and is made present for them. It is not enough to recall in a symbolic sense, but each participant is responsible to commemorate their personal deliverance from Egypt.

The Third Cup: (Barech) *"The Cup of Blessing that we bless"* Passover participants eat the main Seder meal prior to the third cup. There are seven symbolic courses in the meal that contains the well-known unblemished Pascal lamb and the unleavened bread. From the bitterness of slavery to the saltiness of the Sea, each brings to memory of parts of the Exodus. It's always about their plight. Their relationship.

This is also the Cup of Redemption… The Cup of Thanksgiving. God revealed Himself as the same promise-keeping and covenant-making God of Abraham. The one who was fulfilling His promise to Abraham through them. God revealed Himself in a more personal way than with Abraham, Isaac, and Jacob with the giving of the Mosaic Law.

With that, there was more responsibility. Now He seeks a relationship through the ratified covenant. Many see this as a Betrothal Cup. I agree. This is exactly what it is! And, only the bride and groom could drink of the cup. Wine is always a symbol in the Old Testament of blood. A sign of things to come.

Then he took the Book of the Covenant and read it to the people, who replied, *"All that the LORD has spoken we will do, and we will be obedient. So, Moses took the blood, sprinkled it on the people, and said, "This is the blood of the covenant that the Lord has made with you according to these words"*

This verse is mindful of a piece of the Betrothal/marriage contract of Jewish Tradition. After time to grow spiritually, the couple gathers under a four-poster canvas *Chuppah*, a symbol of the home they make together, and they take their vows. It reminds us of our own four-poster beds, perhaps.

This is the cup that Jesus rose, this blood, is the cup of the Last Supper. The third cup. "The cup of blessing that we bless". I know you are getting it. I know you see it. Just wait, it gets better. Remember, you won't be able to un-see it again. It will soon demand action…as God always does.

"From everyone who has been given much, much will be demanded; and from the one who has been entrusted with much, much more will be asked" Luke 12:48

> ***Point of Reflection:*** Tradition claims in the Midrash that only 1/5, or 20%, a mere remnant, were saved. The remaining died in the (plague) darkness. Many of the remaining remnants may not have even looked for redemption or even wanted it. With this, they drink the fourth cup.

The Fourth Cup: (Hallel) The fourth cup has many names. The Cup of Praise, or of Future Hope. It is the idea of the kingdom and of restoration. It is the climax of the evening and it points to a final destination. …"I will take you for my people."

Most Christian Commentaries point to this as our eternal destiny. In terms of the Israelites, they were gathered to become a nation. They landed as was promised by God. The promise being "I will be their God, and they will be my people" in a new land as a 'nation among the nations' that is set apart onto God. After the third cup, it is about praise and trust, and of dependence, provision, and thanksgiving.

They finish the final four Psalms of the Hallel. These Psalms move us from Sinai and across the Jordan. Psalm 136 was added later in the Great Hallel. This Psalm summarizes the entire Journey and their relationship with God. And, with that, the Passover Seder comes to its climactic end. Let's look at it from a slightly different angle.

The Three Pilgrimages

One…two…three…and four.   Passover…Pentecost…Tabernacles…
It is Finished.

Let's look at the 3 pilgrimages. Life is lived between the four cups. The festivals celebrate those times for the nation of Israel, but also for us in the post-Calvary era in the New Covenant.

God commanded the people of Israel to come to see Him. Whether they were on the move, at Shiloh, or eventually in Jerusalem, the Israelites made pilgrimage 3 times a year to the Temple or the Tabernacle. They appeared before the Lord.

The festivals have both agricultural and spiritual significance. They were the major spring, summer, and fall festivals, but they are also associated with the Exodus journey. They have been irrevocably linked to the central narrative of God's deliverance from bondage.

Passover. The Passover is the first of the seven-day feasts as commanded by God. It was a spring feast that is viewed as a beginning to the crop season and eventual harvest. Interestingly, it is also associated with the offering of first fruits.

It remembers the calling out of the nation from Israel…the first fruits of barley. We've discussed the Passover earlier, so we won't discuss it here. Firstfruits connect us to the Passover event; the first fruits of God's Chosen People.

The Passover Seder reenacts the events of that night. It also makes it alive again. It is fitting that this is the meal that Christ and His disciples partook of on the night He was betrayed. It restates their lives and shows us ours.

The Counting of Omer: The Counting of Omer was the evening counting of the days between Passover and Shavuot. It was a time of preparation for the Mount Sinai experience. They prepared to receive the Torah at Sinai as Moses would soon reveal. It was a time of sacrifice and a time of growth. The Israelites were forbidden certain life practices to grow in spiritual preparation and anticipation for the giving of the Torah at Sinai.

This may remind many of the Church's preparation during both Lent and Advent. I recently received a quote about a Rabbi's pondering this time. It was:…

"The Israelites were only freed from Egypt at Passover in order to receive the Torah at Sinai".

So, the Counting of the Omer illustrates the Israelite nation's deep conviction to receive the Torah and practice it in their own life. The grew in knowledge of God in this preparation. Once again, this points us to their ratification and confirmation of the Law as their marriage covenant.

Pentecost: The *Shavuot* festival begins after the counting of the weeks. It is on the 50th day. Hence, Pentecost. It commemorates the giving of the Law at Mount Sinai. As an agricultural festival, it would be considered a mid-season feast.

The Exodus is considered God's unmerited gift. Now, instead of simple gifts, the game has been elevated with the reception of the Mosaic Law. The relationship becomes more complex and the potential for judgment is introduced. The people are deemed to have grown spiritually and more is required through both individual and corporate participation and cooperation.

Many Jewish families decorate their homes with flowers and greenery on the fiftieth day (Shavuot) to resemble a Chuppah. A Chuppah is a cloth canopy decorated with flowers and greenery that hang from four posts. The Israelite or Jewish couple would stand under in a marriage ceremony. This symbolizes the home the couple will make together. The day of Pentecost (Shavuot) is the mystical day...a day...

> ...*in which Moses the matchmaker brought the bride (the nation of Israel) to Mount Sinai. The bride entered the Chuppah (Mount Sinai) for the marriage ceremony with God. The (ketubah) marital contract was the Mosaic Law...the marital covenant." (quote from unknown Rabbi)*

Traditionally, participants stay up all night before the day of Pentecost studying the Torah growing in knowledge. This keeps them vigilant as opposed to when the Law was given, the nation fell asleep that night and were unprepared... Moses needed to wake them for the event. They would enter the spiritual *'Chuppah'*, the nation confirmed, and Moses ratified the commitment with the sprinkling of the blood.

Feast of Tabernacles: This festival commemorates the time period between the marital ceremony at Sinai and the entrance into the promised land. They celebrate God's loving-kindness *(hesed),* His trustworthiness, and His Provision in the wilderness.

It is a festival of Thanksgiving. The last agricultural festival of the planting season. It is a time of harvesting. But the festival's religious significance commemorates the nation's total reliance on God's will during their time in the desert.

We are reminded of the Hymn, *"Bringing in the Sheaves"*. Christ spoke of this time.

Then he said to his disciples, "The harvest is plentiful, but the laborers are few; therefore, ask the Lord of the harvest to send out laborers into his harvest." (Matthew 9:38-39)

Even today, people live in *Sukkahs*, temporary tents or booths, for the duration of the festival. They 'remember' the time in the wilderness when they lived in these temporary structures for 40 years as God led them to the Promised Land.

God provided them with daily bread, their daily Manna, each morning the entire time in the wilderness up until the day that they crossed the Jordan into the Promised Land.

"You shall live in booths seven days; all citizens in Israel shall live in booths, in order that future generations may know that I made the Israelite people live in booths when I brought them out of the land of Egypt" Lev. 23: 42-43

Interestingly, the 7-day feast became an 8-day feast along the way. On the first and eighth day, they were to do no work. The eighth day was the most special. It could be construed that the Sabbath became a workday, and Sunday (the first and eighth day) became a day of rest. The eighth day became the best. Does this foreshadow the Risen Lord on Sunday morning? I don't know. I haven't really studied it, but it's something to ponder.

So, once again it's 1, 2, 3, and 4. Passover, Pentecost, Tabernacles, and it is finished. Their journey was finished the day they entered the Promised Land. God made these festivals mandatory with a pilgrimage to first the Wilderness Tabernacle, and later the Temple.

Both the story of the Exodus from Egypt and the three pilgrimages dovetail together for a unifying and synergistic tale of God's relationship with His chosen people. It became astounding simple for me to see, as I'm sure it is for you. It becomes easy to see why Christ and His disciples gained so much notoriety and how easily the Hebrews became believers. But, let's finally begin to tie these things together.

Our Journey Revealed
The New (Testament) is in the Old (Testament) Concealed
The Old (Testament) is in the New (Testament) Revealed
Saint Augustine

We've arrived at the place where we can see our basic journey…our Salvation. The trials and tribulations of the plight of the Israelite nation reveal ours. As Augustine explained, we wouldn't see it if we never looked. It would remain concealed. Let's begin this process of revealing that Church. The Church once delivered.

The Last Supper

Let's see Christ as our Passover. We are at the Last Supper. Peter and John found the furnished upper room that Jesus told them to expect to find. They prepared for the Passover. The hour came, they reclined and…Here's the gist of it.

"I have eagerly desired to eat this Passover with you before I suffer. For I tell you, I will not eat it again until it finds fulfillment in the kingdom of God."(Luke 22:15)

After taking the cup, he gave thanks and said,

> *Take this and divide it among you. For I tell you I will not drink again from the fruit of the vine until the kingdom of God comes."(Luke 22:16)*
> *And he took bread, gave thanks and broke it, and gave it to them, saying, "This is my body given for you; do this in remembrance of me."*
> *In the same way, after the supper he took the cup, saying, "This cup is the new covenant in my blood, which is poured out for you.(Luke 22:16-18)*

This is the third cup.

Our Redemption Plan

Let's expand on Christ as our Passover. Paul develops it here:…

> *Get rid of the old yeast, so that you may be a new unleavened batch—as you really are. For Christ, our Passover lamb has been sacrificed. Therefore, let us keep the Festival **[Tabernacles],** not with the old bread leavened with malice and wickedness, but with the unleavened bread of sincerity and truth **[Eucharist].** (1 Corinthians 5: 7-8)*

> *For when **we were** in the flesh, the motions of sins, which **were** by the **law,** did work in our members to bring forth fruit unto death. But now **we** are **delivered** from the **law,** that being dead wherein **we were** held; that **we** should serve in newness of spirit, and not in the oldness of the letter. What shall **we** say then? Is the **law** sin? God forbid. (Romans 7:6)*

We were delivered from our sins. We were delivered from the Law. We rid ourselves of the "Old" and grab hold of the "New". Through Christ, we transcend the Old Law, and that we should serve the truth with the newness o spirit. Christ is our Passover.

Israel was delivered from the bondage of Egypt. The Church was delivered from the bondage of the Law. Israel was called out of Egypt to create their own nation. The Church was called out of Judea to make disciples of all peoples. They were called out and landed in the center of the known world, Rome. We Passed Over…already. There is a great Feast in remembrance of the event. We keep the Festival. It is the Easter Tridium.

- **Holy Thursday.** This was the Passover vigil with the Seder meal. It was the night He was betrayed. He was turned over for 3 nights of darkness
- **Good Friday.** It was the Day of His Passion. It was the day He drank the fourth cup. He pronounced His mother as Gebirah. And, in that, He said, *"It is Finished"*.
- **Holy Saturday.** It was the great Sabbath. There were 40 hours o darkness from Friday evening to the Empty Tomb on Sunday morning
- **Resurrection Sunday.** Light has come into the World. It is a new day The Lord's day. We rest in Christ.

Salvation History Repeats

Salvation history tends to repeat itself. The past reveals itself to be a shadow of things to come. God's Plan of Salvation remains the same. And, God's Plan of Redemption plays out identically in the New Testament.

Passover: So, with Christ, we have Passed Over. We have been delivered and called out. The Church has been gathered. We are Sanctified.

Baptism: The Israelites were baptized in the Red Sea, cleansed of their past…every man, woman, and child. The disciple's baptized entire families because of its importance. Today we baptize children as soon as we can. They are gathered into the Church and protected from the sins of old.

Counting of Omer: The Church spent 50 days beyond the empty tomb growing in the knowledge of the kingdom. Christ appeared. He spent this time with them showing them the fulfillment. He was the same Promise-keeping Covenant-making Son of God, that died for them. Today, every man, woman and child spend time after their baptism learning and growing in the knowledge of Christ.

Pentecost: 50 days from the empty tomb came Pentecost. Moses came down from the Mountain and proclaimed the Old. The people confirmed the agreement and a nation is formed. Peter came down from the Upper Room and proclaimed the New. The people confirmed the New agreement and a Church is formed.

Tabernacles: Christ combined all the sacrifices and the Manna that came down from Heaven into one sacrifice. Just as with Israel, Christ provides the true Manna until the day we are confronted with our personal Jordan.

Jordan: Israel crossed the Jordan into the Promised Land. We cross our personal Jordan as we enter our Promise.

Purgatory: The washing of the Jordan may symbolize our final cleansing in Purgatory. Just a suggestion. If so, the Old Ark was held up in the middle of the Jordan as they crossed. Is the Ark of the New Covenant in the midst of our crossing? Of, our Purgatory to aid our crossing? Asking for a friend.

Tabernacles

Recognize in this bread what hung on the cross and in this chalice, what flowed from His side...whatever was in many and varied ways announced beforehand in the sacrifices of the Old Testament pertains to this one sacrifice which is revealed in the New Testament. Saint Augustine Sermon 3.2 circa 410AD

So, here we are. The sacrifice of the cross combines all the sacrifices of the Old Testament. Every one of them. The sacrifice of the cross was not just the unblemished Lamb of the Passover. It. Was. ALL...of the many and varied sacrifices. The Council of Trent affirmed this more than a millennium later.

It is, finally, that sacrifice that was prefigured by various types of sacrifices during the period of nature and of the law, which, namely, comprises all the good things signified by them, as being the consummation and perfection of them all."(The Canons and Decrees of the Council of Trent) [4]

Old Tabernacle Sacrifices

The machinations at the Tabernacle was Israel's *Ministry of Reconciliation.* The Tabernacle restored their relationship with God. It also maintained it. The Israelites brought their offerings to the gate and the outer court. They peered at the goings-on, but they couldn't partake. The priests made the offering for them. As part of the sacrifice, the priests ate the offering. For most offerings, it was required. They ate the Lamb. They ate the sacrifice.

Here's a list of the five main "many and varied" sacrifices, or Korbanot. They are the Burnt Offering, Grain Offering, Fellowship Offering, Sin Offering, and the Guilt Offering.

Burnt Offering: This offering was the oldest and most common in Israel. The burnt offering meant *ascension* in Hebrew. It represented total submission to God's will. As the name suggests, it was to be completely burnt up. The priests could not eat it.

Sin Offering: The sin offering was offered to atone and purge sin. It can be for the individual or the community. It was an expression of sorrow and the desire to be reconciled to God. For the average person's sin, only the priests eat the sacrifice.

Guilt Offering: This offering is atoning for the "sin of stealing from the altar". This means for a sin that a person is unsure it was a sin. They were encouraged to make this sacrifice if they were concerned about it, to be reconciled. It was only eaten by the priests.

Peace Offering: This offering expresses thankfulness and gratefulness to God. This sacrifice doesn't have anything to do with sin. A portion is completely burnt as offering to God. The remainder is eaten by the one making the offering and their family.

Food and Drink Offering: This offering is for the devotion to the fruits of our labor to God. A portion is completely burned as an offering to God, and the remainder was only eaten by priests.

There were also morning and evening sacrifices of first-year lambs. They were to be a continual burnt sacrifice that never ended. *(Numbers 28:6)* The evening lamb was to slowly burn all night and until the next morning's sacrifice. This was to be done day after day.

> *Now this is that which thou shalt offer upon the altar; two lambs of the first-year day by day continually. The one lamb thou shalt offer in the morning; and the other lamb thou shalt offer at evening"* (Exodus 29:38-39)
> This is what *"Works of the Law"* meant. Christ ended it all.

Our Tabernacle

The veil of the Temple was torn from top to bottom. Christ did it. He unceasingly ministers at the true sanctuary in Heaven on our behalf. He combined all the sacrifices into His one sacrifice when He offered Himself for us. He is the same yesterday, today, and forever. He reaches through the veil to touch…you. For your sins. For relationship.

Where 2 or more are gathered, He offers Himself, on the Tabernacles on earth. We do this as He told us, this is His body, and this is His blood, it was shed for you. The same yesterday, today and tomorrow He explodes by the barriers of time and becomes present in the atonement for your sins.

And, we, the Kohanim (priest) partake of the Lamb. The sacrificial offering for your sin isn't complete, until…You. Eat. The. Lamb.

Let's dig into the Mass, the source and the summit of the faith. We enter into His rest. Many, though unbelief, never enter the Sanctuary of His rest'

Chapter 10: The Mass: Enter into the Holy of Holies

"Eternal Father, I offer you the Body and Blood, Soul and Divinity, of Your dearly beloved Son, our Lord Jesus Christ, in atonement for our sins..."
Chaplet of Divine Mercy prayer

So, what is the Mass? What is happening? The short answer is this...it's the only way you can worship God. It's the only way you will be in relationship and reconciled to Him. It is the source and summit of your faith. Do you believe in Christ? Well, this is where the rubber meets the road. As Jesus said, this is the "works" that you need to do, to believe in Christ in the Mass. *(John 6)*

Let's see how this works. At the Passover vigil...

> *The Lord Jesus, on the night he was betrayed, took bread, and when he had given thanks, he broke it and said, "This is my body, which is for you; do this in remembrance of me." In the same way, after **supper** he took the **[third]** cup, saying, "This cup is the new covenant in my blood; do this, whenever you drink it, in remembrance of me". (1 Corinthians 11: 23-25)*

This is the epicenter of the Mass. It was Christ's command during the Passover Seder. The problem is, the Church has Passed over...from Old to New, delivered from the bondage of the Law. Each of us, with the aid of the Church's sacerdotal duties, participate in our own coming of age as we join the body of Christ.

While the festival of our Passover through Christ is celebrated through the Sacred Tridium, we also remember it at every Mass. He was the Passover Lamb, but we've also witnessed that it is much more. He took upon himself all aspects of the many and varied sacrifices of the Old Testament.

The Passover was a sort of 'first fruits' in what became an elaborate system of pilgrimages and sacrificial offerings that the Israelites made in relationship with their God. He turned them all into one sacrifice. He became the perpetual morning and evening sacrifice. He became the burnt offering and the sin offering. He became them all, in this one sacrifice.

Yes, it's a mystery...a mystery to all of us... The *many and varied* aspects of the mystery of the Eucharist needs to be understood. Let's wander through Hebrews to gain more insight.

> *It is important that the mystery of the Eucharist should shine out before the eyes of the faithful in its true light. It should be considered in all its different aspects, and the real relationships which, as the Church teaches, are known to exist between these various aspects of the mystery should be so understood by the faithful as to be reflected in their lives Eucharisticum Mysterium (1967)*

Hebrews: Do We Neglect So Great A Salvation?

Step by step, the book of Hebrews illustrates the Mystery of the Mass more than any other. It contrasts the Old way of the Tabernacle with the New Way of the Tabernacle. Hebrews articulately define the priesthood of Christ, the fulfillment of the Law and the Prophets, and paints Christ as the author and perfecter of the faith.

> *"All things Old have passed away, all things have become New"*

Paul warns that people are falling away because they don't even try to understand the Gospel. They are still spiritual infants that should have grown to maturity to discern between good and evil. He pushes past the elementary teaching not wanting to lay again the foundation. He then addresses the repercussions of those who knew Christ and fall away. They couldn't be brought back to repentance. This. Is. Not. Once. Saved.

It is impossible for those:

> *who have once been enlightened, who have **tasted the heavenly gift**, who have shared in the Holy Spirit, who have tasted the goodness of the word of God and the powers of the coming age and who have fallen away, to be brought back to repentance."(Hebrews 6:4)*

The heavenly gift. ...tasted the heavenly gift. There are people who have been enlightened. There were people who knew sacred scripture. There are people who have shared in the Holy Spirit. There are people who understood the power of the coming age. Obviously, once- saved, always saved, is certainly not true.

The heavenly gift is not scripture. And, they didn't even have the New Testament. It isn't the Holy Spirit. It is the Eucharist. Paul talked about it all the time. Christ also revealed it to us. It's what we need to believe. Christ told us that this is the 'work' of believing. Maybe, it was missed by your pastor. Let's first lay the foundation. Paul does this throughout Hebrews.

Paul began to once again lay it out....

Christ is a priest forever. He is a priest in the order of Melchizedek and not Levite. He is our High (Chief) Priest. This gives us the understanding that this priesthood would have something to do with bread and wine.

Our hope in God's unchanging oath. "The Lord has sworn and will not change His mind". The purple curtain was torn from top to bottom. We enter the inner place led by Jesus, who entered on our behalf.

Melchizedek was without mother and father. Without the beginning of days or ending of life...much like the Son of God, he remains a priest forever. Christ has a permanent and perfect priesthood, not needing to make offerings for Himself

This is the main point, as Paul says, we have a High Priest who perpetually ministers in the true Sanctuary, and the true Tabernacle, on our behalf. The earthly tabernacle was a shadow of the one in Heaven. He offers His body and His blood for you. The (New) Covenant, or Tabernacle, made the (Old) Tabernacle obsolete.

The Old Tabernacle did not clear the consciences of those who worshipped there. They approached God through that Old altar, the nation's mechanism of repentance. *"Except ye repent ye shall all likewise perish" (Luke 13:3)*. The new altar was outside of the Wilderness Tabernacle. Paul confirmed:

> *Do not be carried away by all kinds of strange teachings. It is good for our hearts to be strengthened by grace, not by eating ceremonial foods, which is of no benefit to those who do so. We have an altar from which those who minister at the tabernacle have no right to eat." (Hebrews13: 9-10)*

In this same breath, Paul tells us that this one sacrifice is available to you today. It is the same sacrifice. *"Jesus Christ is the same yesterday and today and forever"*.

So, we have an altar. We are priests. And priests, are required to eat the sin offering. This is the same today, as it has always been.

The Sole Mediator

The book of Hebrews describes Christ as the Sole Mediator. This is one place where all of Evangelicalism and Protestantism misrepresents a verse as an excuse for a multitude of ill-conceived reasons. I used to do it myself. You can't do it. Don't do it.

The verses are used to justify the "Jesus and me" mentality, the 'bible alone' crowd, the 'we don't need a church' crowd, the 'we only confess or sins to Jesus' group, and so on, and so on. The trouble is that's not the truth. In fact, there is a multitude of verses that completely contradict Protestant oral traditions.

But, that's for another time. What does Paul actually say it is? He proclaims that we need to seek the truth; to be lovers of the truth. Let's seek the truth in the two verses, in context.

In *1 Timothy chapter 2*, Paul explains that he is ordained as an Apostle and teacher. It is God's desire that all be saved. But that they would need to come to the knowledge of the truth. That knowledge is that Christ alone, the Sole Mediator, was the one mediator between God and man. It is because He gave Himself as a ransom for all people, whether Jew or Gentile. For. The Whole. World.

At this juncture, Paul was pointing directly to the cross. He is contrasting the New again, with the Old Testament Tabernacle, and the Law itself. It is not any of the aforementioned appropriated traditions that co-opt this verse. But, let's see if we're right, let check out Hebrews.

In *Hebrews chapter 9*, Paul gives us a long essay on the design and operation of the Old Testament Tabernacle. He then contrasts it with the New Covenant Tabernacle, the true Tabernacle. Christ ministers unceasingly at the true Heavenly tabernacle. There is no need for the continual and repetitive bloody sacrifices required by the Law.

Christ accomplished it all. The continual and perpetual offerings are no longer necessary. Christ fulfilled them all. He transformed them into His one sacrifice, to be continual and perpetual across all ages and for all who come to Him.

Paul explains the blood of the old altar was of no avail. Christ shattered the abyss of this altar. If the old altar was enough, there would be no need for the New. **It is for the is reason, Christ is the Sole Mediator**. No one else could repair that breach.

> *For this reason, He is the mediator of a new covenant, so that, since a death has taken place for the redemption of the transgressions that were committed under the first covenant, those who have been called may receive the promise of the eternal inheritance."(Hebrews 9:15)*

So, we have confirmation. It wasn't about any of the bogus aforementioned claims. It was about The Old Testament altar.... Not confessing sins...Not Jesus alone.

A Nation or Church of Priests:

"Lord, we pray you to take away our wickedness from us, so that we may worthily enter into the Holy of Holies with pure minds, through Christ our Lord. Amen."
Irish Aufer a Nobis [7]

Originally, the *Adat B'nai Yisrael* [entire body] would have all been part of the priesthood; they would have access to the innermost places where God dwelt. He would be their God and they would be His people.

This would depart from the hereditary Priesthood of the Egyptians and everyone would have a role. However, the golden calf incident derailed that prospect. So, access to the tabernacle was limited to a family of trained priests who served in the tabernacle and in the sacrifices at the Brazen Altar.

Leviticus, the biblical manual for the priesthood in the Old Testament, did a couple of things. First, it spelled out the necessary steps to maintain integrity in God's house. And second, the reader of Leviticus realized that they weren't trained in matters of the ministerial priesthood.

In Israel, there were High Priests, like Eli and Samuel who, along with the ministerial priesthood who worked at the Tabernacle in service of the Lord. There were also Levite priests served sacerdotally across the nation aiding in the spiritual life of the Israelites. However, it was only the ministerial priesthood could 'enter in' past the gate and into the inner courts of the Old tabernacle.

As New Covenant priests, we are welcome to 'enter in' to the sanctuary. We enter where the lay Israelites were prohibited from entering. However, we too, have trained and ordained priests to maintain this liturgical integrity. "God will not be mocked".

The veil was rent, torn from top to bottom. The Temple was destroyed.

Christ built His Temple in the three days following His crucifixion. There was a new Altar. This was the Altar at which all believers could eat; the royal priesthood.

The body of Christ is now called a royal priesthood, and a nation of priests. The Church also recognizes these three categories: Christ as High Priest, the ordained ministerial priesthood, and the common priesthood of believers.

The entire laity, (the *Edah*) the whole Church (nation or kingdom of God) has access to the new Tabernacle. All those who were baptized in the Father, Son and Holy Ghost "enter in" through the gate, into the sanctuary, and partake of the sacrifice. We are priests of the "Melchizedekian Rite" who, under our High Priest, bring the transformational offering of unleavened bread and wine to the New altar.

All believers are called to be *"Ambassadors for Christ"* and ambassadors for the *"Ministry of Reconciliation".* The good news is the proclamation of the need to return to a "state of grace" with our "Lord". We confess our egregious sins, receive absolution, and are once again received by the bridegroom at Mass in this new and intimate way.

The Ordained (ministerial) Priesthood

(Deacons, Presbytery, and the Episcopate):

The Pauline letters to Titus and Timothy clearly define the qualifications necessary for Deacons, Elder/Priests, and Bishops. They took these offices very seriously. As we've seen, the Israelites ordained people to take an office. Paul also addresses the ordination into these offices. Part of this process included the laying on of hands.

The new "Ministry of Reconciliation" was available *"wherever 2 or more are gathered".* This ministry was led by a priest (presbyter) who was trained in the ministry. The Levitical rites and rituals fulfilled, there was now new Melchizedekian liturgical form in local churches across cities and nations.

The liturgy would not be ransacked with a willy nilly organization. There was a "set order". There was a necessity to maintain order; to follow the teachings of the Apostles. *"God be not mocked",* so it would be necessary to maintain order and solemnity. The purity of the reconciling ministry was a difficult task in the ever-expanding reach of Christianity.

The early presbytery was the parish priest. (new *Keter Kehunah*) The local priest was the local facilitator of the "Ministry of Reconciliation". The presbyters were constantly beseeched by the Apostles, and later the Bishops, to keep to that which they were taught.

From the beginning, these men devoted themselves to training and prayer to keep the sacrifice (breaking of bread) pure. The common use of the term 'Elders' may well have been an appropriate term for these first ministers. They were chosen from amongst the Congregation being recognized as mature and faithful.

However, this office is more accurately recognized in the priestly domain. The local priest(s), who kept to the teachings of the Apostles, administered it in strikingly similar fashion today.

The Bishop:

The office of Bishop also hasn't changed that much since the earliest times. The Bishop provides oversight on a regional scale. Today, this authority or diocese is within delineated by established boundaries surrounding a city. In the early church, we see this also emanated from a central hub, usually, a City, although with more blurred extended boundaries. (The Church at Corinth, the Church at Ephesus).

The Bishop was generally first a local presbyter who grew in reliability and trust; to shepherd the flock. Along with their priestly responsibilities, they took on a teaching *(Keter Torah)* role that remained submitted to the *Teachings of the Apostles* and brought the 'will' of God to their geographic area.

Christ, Our High Priest:

This can't be stated enough. Christ has entered the true and innermost sanctuary. He continues to minister on our behalf. He multiplies His Body and Blood just as He did the wine and bread during His earthly ministry. No one will go hungry. We enter through the rent curtain.

The ministerial priest *consecrates* the Melchizedekian bread and wine in cooperation with Christ. It is Christ who accomplishes the "Transubstantiation" through His perpetual priesthood by ministering at the Heavenly tabernacle. The local ordained priest, *In Persona Christi,* is the active and necessary earthly participant in the paschal mystery and ministry of reconciliation. Christ reaches from the Heavenly Tabernacle to the Tabernacle at Mass as the priest stands in as Christ's earthly representative.

The Bread of Life

Let's recall that the nation of Israel "remembers" and celebrates their trust in God's provision during Tabernacles. They "remember" their reliance on God's provision in the wilderness. God supplied the manna, daily.... their daily bread. Every morning the nation gathered this bread [manna]. (except the Sabbath).

It didn't matter how much a person gathered, it was still only enough for one 'omer', or one day. So, they relied on God for their daily provision. In 1 Corinthians 10, the Apostle Paul referred to this time, "and they all ate the same spiritual food." Christ, as our High Priest and our "sacrificial Lamb", brought all our needs onto himself. All the varied sacrifices and God's provisions were combined to one source.

That source was Christ Himself. Christ provided the miraculous provision of wine at the wedding of Cana. He multiplied the bread for all to eat. These spiritual provisions were a shadow of the True Provision that was to come. He explains the culmination of all of this was in His body and His blood in John chapter 6.

We used to remind each other that Christ's words are in red...So, pay attention. There's a lot of red words in John chapter 6. So, yep, pay attention. And, when Jesus says, "Verily, verily" or "Very truly, I tell you", well this is SERIOUS! We need to pay double...quadruple attention.

John chapter 6 is one of those times. It begins with a multiplication of the bread just to remind us. But, the gist of the entire discourse was the Manna. It is the true Manna. As Paul put it, "our spiritual food" has come down from Heaven...our daily bread.

> **Side Note:** We pray, "... *Give us this day, Our Daily Bread*". *Our Daily Bread* is **NOT** a publication of scripture verses, daily devotions, and inspirational stories. Though this may all well be good, Or Daily Bread is not bible verses at all. It is Christ's body, and Christ told you so. The mere belief that it is what the *Our Daily Bread* publication says it is, leads you away from the truth, and away from God.

Christ tells the Pharisees and scribes,

> *...you do not believe the one he sent. You study the Scriptures diligently because you think that in them you have eternal life. These are the very Scriptures that testify about me, yet you refuse to come to me to have life. (John 5:38-40)*

Wow, scripture doesn't give me eternal life!... Christ does! How? Well, Christ was just about to tell us what to believe. Immediately after telling them that scripture does not give them eternal life, He went on to give the *Bread of Life* discourse.

We all recognize the importance of John 3. Christ tells Nicodemus that he needs to believe in Him to have eternal life. He tells him that both baptism and "believing in Christ" is necessary for eternal life. Nicodemus was confused. Today we think we believe. But, do we? Here Christ tells us what He meant by "believe in Him".

Note to self: Believing in Scripture is **not** believing in Christ!

Very Truly #1) The apostles are looking for Jesus. When they find Him Christ tells them not to work for food that spoils. (Works???) But, to work for food that has eternal life.

I didn't see it at first, but Christ **JUST** contrasted the Manna of Old to the coming New provision. The disciples apparently saw the relationship immediately. It led them to ask... *"What must we do to do the works God requires?"* To which Jesus responded, The **work** of God is this: *"to **believe in the one he has sent.**"*

The disciples understood Christ's reference to the Old manna in the wilderness, so they asked this question,

*"What sign then will you give that we may see it and **believe you**? What will you do? Our ancestors ate the manna in the wilderness; as it is written: '**He gave them bread from heaven to eat.**'"*

Very Truly #2) Jesus tells them that it wouldn't be Moses who gave them bread from Heaven, but God the Father has given them the **true bread**... *"For the bread of God is the bread that comes down from heaven and gives life to the world."* We can see why the disciples would always want this bread to eat.

Jesus continues, *"I am the **bread of life.** [not scripture] Whoever comes to me will never go hungry, and whoever believes in me will never be thirsty. But as I told you, you have seen me and **still, you do not believe.**"* ...There is growing unrest.

Jesus addresses the issue of the will of the Father, *"For my Father's will is that everyone who looks to the Son **and believes in him shall have eternal life**, and I will raise them up at the last day."* The grumbling and growing unbelief grew, especially amongst the Jews.

Very Truly #3) Jesus doubles down. No other words are necessary.

*"the one who believes has eternal life. ...I am the bread of life. Your ancestors ate the manna in the wilderness, yet they died. But here is the bread that comes down from heaven, which anyone may eat and not die. I am the living bread that came down from heaven. Whoever eats this bread will live forever. **This bread is my flesh**, which I will give for the life of the world."*

Wow! The Jews were freaked out now!

Very Truly #4) Rut Roh, we get a triple-down. The discourse intensifies as Christ continues:

> **unless you eat the flesh of the Son of Man and drink his blood, you have no life in you. Whoever eats my flesh and drinks my blood has eternal life,** *and I will raise them up at the last day. For my flesh is real food and my blood is real drink.* **Whoever eats my flesh and drinks my blood remains in me, and I in them.** *Just as the living Father sent me and I live because of the Father, so the one who feeds on me will live because of me. This is* **the bread that came down from heaven**. *Your ancestors ate manna and died, but whoever feeds on this bread will live forever.*

At this point, minds must have been exploding and blood must have been shooting out of their eyeballs. This...This was this some sort of cannibalism?? The Law wouldn't allow for that! Many of the disciples and Jews left. They couldn't handle it and proclaimed that the teaching was too hard. It was unbelievable.

Apparently, Jesus watched them as they walked away. He didn't run after them and say, "Wait, wait! I didn't mean it! It was just symbolic. Not real, just a symbol. I meant the Old Manna was more real...and true." No, Christ said..." *Does this offend you...It is the Spirit who gives life...[My Words] are full of Spirit and life....yet,...some of you still do not believe."*

Jesus turned to the disciples and asked them if they were leaving too. Peter responded, *"Lord, where shall we go? You have the words [full of spirit and life] of eternal life. We have come to believe and know that you are the Holy One of God".* It is through grace, and through the works of our faith in the Pascal mystery on the Altar; His Body and his Blood, that we believe.

John 6 6 6 *"As a result of this many of His disciples withdrew and were not walking* *with Him anymore." (John 6:66)* Blood was forbidden in the Old Testament. So was cannibalism. Difficult teaching indeed. Those who didn't believe in the body and blood of Christ walked away...John 6 6 6.

While teaching about the Lords Supper, Paul stated, *"they eat from the same spiritual food, and they drink from the same spiritual cup. (the third cup)"* ...and later..." *They have tasted the Heavenly Gift".* Have you? Does He 'know' you? Does He abide in you, and you in Him? We are to be ambassadors of this Ministry of Reconciliation...the True Manna...from the confession and absolution of our sins...to the ongoing reunion with Christ on the marital bed of the altar. "Be ye reconciled".

Peter summed it up this way:

> *Repent (by way of the New altar, the Ministry of Reconciliation) and be baptized every one of you, (by way of the laver) in the name of Jesus Christ for the remission of sins, and ye shall receive the gift of the Holy Ghost, (enter into the kingdom, or heavenly tabernacle)" (Acts 2:38).*

Side note: I attended a service with a family member at their church. Of course, it was their monthly communion service, and I couldn't partake. The pastor repeated several times, that it was just a symbol. He was right. They don't approach the altar. Afterward, we discussed Communion with Christ as His Real flesh and His real blood.

My relatives saw it the same as the Pharisees did. They saw it the same as John 6 6 6. My jaw dropped. I looked at my wife. She was surprised too. They didn't believe. One of my relatives replied, "I don't want to think that I eat Jesus." I suggested some bible study. But that was that.

Sacramentarian-ism

A Sacramentarian is a person, a church, or a denomination that believes that the elements of the Eucharist are purely symbolic in nature and that there is no real presence of Christ. They believe that the consecrated bread and wine of the Eucharist are only metaphorical and that there is no physical presence of the body and blood of Christ.

Hence, the sacrament of the Eucharist is relegated to just a symbolic memory that is offered on occasion [or less], and not the center of Christian life or the center of weekly worship. Worship is then merely a concert-like atmosphere

THE CHURCH THAT EMERGED

followed by holding your bible high… "This my bible!" *(yet, the Ark of the Covenant in the Holy of Holies remained ever-present to the Israelites)*

Sacramentarian-ism in the post-Reformation world makes perfect sense. Everything was, and is, up for debate. All things can be deconstructed until the debater(s) or the de-constructor(s) are satisfied. The repeated disagreements and schisms led to churches to be once, twice, and thrice removed from the new altar; the of the New Covenant.

> *"We have an [new] altar from which those who serve the [old altar] tabernacle have no right to eat." (Hebrews 13:10)*

They are also first, second, and third removed, have split from the Church, and from unity with the body, the *"one, Holy, Catholic, and Apostolic* Church. The truth of what "belief in Christ" is, has been completely removed. Paul sternly reminded the Corinthians of the reality,

> *Therefore, whosoever shall eat this bread, and drink this cup of the Lord, unworthily, shall be guilty of the body and blood of the Lord. But let a man examine himself, and so let him eat of that bread, and drink of that cup. For he that eats and drinks unworthily, eats and drinks judgment to himself,* **not discerning the Lord's body**. *For this cause, many are weak and sickly among you, and many sleep" (1 Corinthians 11:30)*

The symbolic offering of communion, away from the new altar, naturally becomes less important. Protestant Theologians would be correct. In that case, as was the case of my relative's church, communion is symbolic, and not genuine relationship.

This doesn't change the reality at the New Altar and the New Tabernacle. It doesn't change the truth of the real presence in the Eucharist that comes down from the Heavenly Tabernacle. Christ told us so.

To the Sacramentarian: Your senses would be real. You would have removed yourself from the Body. You have separated yourself from the Heavenly Tabernacle. You don't believe. So, you sing and worship the bible. You may even have copies of *Our Daily Bread* on your coffee table. Inspirational indeed, but not belief in your true "daily bread". It recalls the familiar question, "When you don't feel close to God, guess who moved?"

The reformers sought a unifying doctrine on the Eucharist but failed. Early Calvinists, Lutherans, and Anglicans would certainly be surprised at the views of their spiritual descendants.

Martin Luther fought Sacramentarian-ism until his death. He once wrote, *"I*

would rather drink blood with the Papists than mere wine with the Zwinglians [enthusiasts]!"
[6] Today, all but a couple of Protestant and/or Evangelical denominations are Sacramentarians with their Wonder bread and Welch's grape juice. Some ignore any symbolic communion altogether. They unknowingly ignore the center of a Christian's life with their God.

The Mass

The Mass today is a highly structured liturgy reminiscent of the Levitical rituals at the Old tabernacle and the Passover Seder. Likewise, the Jerusalem council is the first of the Church councils that have convened several times over the centuries to protect and delineate the deposit of faith. They are cairn guideposts that mark the historical road.

While the Church councils addressed doctrinal issues, the Mysteries of both the Eucharist and the liturgy of the Mass are also regularly laid out systematically. The call for renewal and re-education of the laity to bring a new zeal and devotion to the Mass is continually seen as essential. Councils continually refocus us back to a renewed understanding of the Mass. It is the center of Church life. [1][2]

The councils explained that the Mass, the Lord's Supper, *"is at the same time and inseparably"*: connected to the many and varied sacrifices of Old...as the *"consummation and perfection of them all".[3]* The conclusion is made that the Mass is, therefore, *"the sacrifice and sacred meal belong to the same mystery-so much so that they are linked by the closest bond". [1]*

- *A sacrifice in which the Sacrifice of the Cross is perpetuated;*
- *A memorial of the death and resurrection of the Lord, who said "do this in memory of me" (Luke 22:19);*
- *A sacred banquet in which, through the communion of the Body and Blood of the Lord, the People of God share the benefits of the Paschal Sacrifice, renew the New Covenant which God has made with man once for all through the Blood of Christ, and in faith and hope foreshadow and anticipate the eschatological banquet in the kingdom of the Father, proclaiming the Lord's death "till His coming"]*

What's Happening during Mass
We have entered the sanctuary. It is a place the common Israelite could never

go. There is a procession as the ministerial priest enters the Tabernacle.

- There is an ever-lit red light that is like the old Tabernacle light. The Son of God is present in the Tabernacle.
- Just like the Pentecost at Sinai and the Pentecost at the base of the Upper Room, the Covenant is reaffirmed. It is confirmed through the New Covenant Creed.
- The local body spiritually unifies with the "universal" Church. It connects to the unending hymns of praise through unending prayer and supplication.
- Just like the varied offerings at the old Tabernacle, this offering is petitioned for distinctly personal, and corporate reasons. There are both silent, and corporate petitions. And, the laity spiritually unites to confirm the prayers of the many.
- We pray as Christ taught…" *Our Father…give us this day, Our Daily Bread".*
- The common priesthood in the Melchizedekian rite, approach the altar with an offering of bread and wine.
- Through the words of Christ and the liturgical ritual, the laity through the priest mysteriously make supplication toward the Heavenly Tabernacle. The curtain is torn, and the priest stands at the local altar "in the person of Christ" on earth.
- Once the unleavened bread and the cup of wine are lifted and the Eucharistic Prayer is offered, it mysteriously transformed into the Body, Blood, Soul, and Divinity of Christ.
- This fulfills all the sacrifices of the old Tabernacle, it reminds us of our deliverance from the Law and provides us with our Daily Bread, the Manna (John 6)
- The bridegroom and the bride unite. They are once again reconciled. He abides in us, and we in Him. *(does He know you, or will He say, "Depart…I never knew you")*
- The Tabernacle and God's presence is once again secured. And, the perpetual Light remains.
- There are a final blessing and supplication. The priest(s) leave the sanctuary and the laity files out after.

This is a bullet-point summary of the primary "stations" of the Mass. It is similar to the 'set order' of the rituals and ceremonies that comprised the life of the nation of Israel in their relationship with God. Today, people don't make any of those connections. The comparisons with the Old Testament are few.

The relationships between the Old and the New Covenant Gospel are just not made. Israel attempted intimacy between God and His people, through the gate, past the altar drenched in blood, past the Brazen Laver, and then on to the blood-soaked veil that undoubtedly strained at containing the Shekinah of God's brilliance that bore witness in Israel.

Today, the gate, the veil and the doors of the sanctuary were thrown open and we are invited to 'enter in'…

> *The Church constantly draws her life from the redeeming sacrifice; she approaches it not only through faith-filled remembrance but also through a real contact since this sacrifice is made present ever anew, sacramentally perpetuated, in every community which offers it at the hands of the consecrated minister.*
>
> *The Eucharist thus applies to men and women today the* **reconciliation** *won once for all by Christ for mankind in every age. "The sacrifice of Christ [on the cross] and the sacrifice of the Eucharist are one single sacrifice". Saint John Chrysostom put it well: "We always offer the same Lamb, not one today and another tomorrow, but always the same one. For this reason, the sacrifice is always only one… Even now we offer that victim who was once offered and who will never be consumed". Ecclessia De Eucharista [2]*

It is necessary for the Eucharist to *"shine out before the eyes of the faithful in its true light,…all its different aspects, and the real relationships…,[It] should be so understood by the faithful as to be reflected in their lives". [1]*

The Council of Trent defined the relationship between Christ and the fulfillment of the Old Testament sacrifices. The Sacrifice of the Mass:

> *It is, finally, that sacrifice that was prefigured by various types of sacrifices during the period of nature and of the law, which, namely, comprises all the good things signified by them, as being the consummation and perfection of them all."* It also reaffirms, *"It is one and the same victim here offering himself by the ministry of his priests, who then offered Himself on the cross;*

it is only the manner of offering that is different". [3]

The Church always conjoins the Passover, the Last Supper, and the Old Testament sacrifices,

> *Our Savior at the Last Supper on the night when He was betrayed instituted the Eucharistic Sacrifice of His Body and Blood so that He might perpetuate the Sacrifice of the Cross throughout the centuries till His coming. He thus entrusted to the Church, His beloved Spouse, a memorial of His death and resurrection: a sacrament of love, a sign of unity, a bond of charity, a paschal meal in which Christ is eaten, the mind filled with grace, and a pledge of future glory given to us."[1][5]*

The Mass is a celebration, but it is also a [perpetual] sacrifice, and the Mass along with the Church is a hospital. It is where frail and wounded people come looking for healing and a reunion with their Father in Heaven.

The sacrifice of the Mass and the whole Ministry of Reconciliation is for healing the wounded. The two work in tandem to heal the hurts and wounds of the body. Through the grace of God, it brings back unity and communion of the entire body of Christ. That's what makes the perpetual nature of Christ's sacrifice understandable. We couldn't make it through this life without Him.

It is a view from the pew. It is a view with nose pressed against the glass, from outside the gate. The gate where our predecessors brought their offerings; offerings for healing, offerings for thanksgiving, offerings for peace, for relationship, and even with confusion; they offered, we still offer. Christ still ministers to this day. We partake.

Where two or more are gathered, He has made himself present. We partake of the Heavenly Gift; we partake of the body and blood, Soul and Divinity, of Christ. He is made present for us; for our sins; for our intentions; for our prayers. We are reunited with Christ. We are once again made clean through the ministry of reconciliation that began with our confession and culminated with the consummation of our relationship.

Chapter 11: In Christ: Our God reigns...again

"The law and the prophets were until John; [call no man father or teacher] since then the good news of the Kingdom of God is preached, and everyone enters it violently." (Luke 16:16)

The Holiest place in the Temple has been empty for about 600 years. There was no Ark. They went through the motions of the Altar and the sacrifices, but God never dwelt there. It was just a ghost of its past glory. The throne has been empty for almost as long. There was no king in Israel. Their land was occupied and then occupied again. When would God answer? When would they have a king once again? When would the Kingdom of Judah be restored in the land of His Promise? Or, specifically Judea.

Christ entered through the Golden Gate. They would have their earthly king. He triumphantly rode in on a white stallion to take his place on the throne. They would be freed. The half-Jew puppet king Herod would be king no more. Jesus would fulfill the prophecies in the way they determined. He would fulfill their dreams. WAIT... Full. Stop.

That's not what happened.

There was a triumphant entry in the Jew's recent past. Simon, the Maccabee, won their freedom and entered Jerusalem as High Priest, and was a great leader. The event was recorded...

"And entered into it ... with thanksgiving, and branches of palm trees, and with harps, and cymbals, and with viols, and hymns, and songs."(1 Maccabees 13:51)

After this triumphant entry, the Romans flipped this victory upside down. Eventually, they appointed a half-Jew, Herod, as a puppet king who they called *"King of the Jews" (sound familiar?)*. With rumors mounting, he became concerned that his power was challenged. The Messiah was rumored to be born in Bethlehem. He set about killing all the firstborns to protect this power.

The Sanhedrin were against Herod's rule. His tax policies supported his lavish lifestyle. Herod ignored many of the demands the Pharisees made regarding the Temple's construction. And, he replaced many Temple priests with more Hellenistic priests to garner support within their ranks, thus alienating the Sadducees.

Then came Christ. He approached for His Triumphal Entry into the city through the Golden Gate (Gate of Mercy) He stopped. He looked on the city from afar and wept over it. A donkey and a colt were summoned. The donkey represented the Jews encumbered by the Law and the colt represented the wildness of the Gentiles.

Several hundred thousand people had descended on Jerusalem in advance of Passover. And, they knew of Jesus. When Christ rode into Jerusalem, people on the route laid down their clothes and waved palm branches before Him. They sang Psalm 118. (the same psalm is recited or sang near the end of the Passover Seder.)

"Blessed is He who comes in the name of the Lord. We bless you from the house of the Lord ...." (Psalm 118:25-26)

The very next day, Christ entered the Temple Court. It was bustling with activity because of the influx of Jewish Pilgrims. The House of the Lord was being mocked and had become profane. Christ threw people out, chastised them, and turned over tables while running the money changers off.

The courtyard became chaotic, but Christ still drew people to Him. The children, the blind and the lame arrived when they heard Jesus was teaching there, *"Hosanna, Hosanna, to the Son of David."*. But His fate was sealed. Whether the Pharisees were protecting themselves from Herod or protecting their own power. They had enough.

The Pharisees were also too late, however. They could not stop Jesus as Messiah. Three days later, Christ assembled with His closest for the Passover Seder. He was soon to hold up the third cup.

Musical Thrones

Once again, they had "kingdoms on the brain". When was God going to reestablish the earthly kingdom again? When is He going to rebuild the Temple? Well, He did, in a new way. Jews and Gentiles have become one. The Kingdom of Heaven has been established. The true Tabernacle is in operation.

God's not going backward. He is not going to restore the Old Temple sacrifices. We've been told that if that was enough, there would have been no need for a change. And, remember Samuel, God was never for an earthly king. In fact, He said that when they screwed it up, He wouldn't be there to rescue them.

They wail at the wall. Most Orthodox Jews believe they need to wait upon God to restore these things and see contemporary Israel as man's attempt at restoration. It's strange to see an amalgamation that is both a worldly and secular democracy as the essence of this restoration. It is not a Theocracy. This is quite the distinction.

What happened. The Apostle Matthew repeatedly points to a "Kingdom of God" or "Kingdom of Heaven". This has to do with the throne of God. Man, in his thinking, has created a game of musical thrones. Where's the throne? And, who sits on it. We need to remember Samuel. God is Sovereign. The monarchy is in Heaven. Our. God. Reigns. Period.

"Our God Reigns" is the key. God has always described it this way… *"I will be their God, and they will be my people".* Israel adopted the idea that there must be a king. Israel became stuck on it. Therefore, God told Samuel that Israel had not rejected Samuel personally, but had rejected God. Since that time, God has not directly led "His people".

The monarchal perspective in the Gospel of Matthew always directs the reader to the fact that the throne, or Sovereignty, is in Heaven. He wrote in terms the Jews could relate to. So did Christ. We now have a kingdom. It's defined for man's comprehension. Christ the King. It's truly about this… *" I will be their God; they will be My people."* His Sovereignty restored.

Kingship of God

"He went through every city and village, preaching and bringing the glad tidings (good news) of the kingdom of God." (Luke 8:1)

Instead of the Israelite nation witnessing as the Holy nation of the one true God to the kingdoms and nation-states around them, the Church became that holy body, the Holy Commonwealth, and ultimately the Kingdom of God. The Old covenant was fulfilled. The *"time" [Kairos] is [also] "fulfilled".* It was the appointed time.

Upon Christ's death and resurrection, the fullness of both the Old Covenant and the appointed time arrived. The New Covenant ushered in a time where God's reign was renewed through His Son. The 'kingdom' terminology of the

New Covenant had arrived.

"The law and the prophets were until John; [call no man father or teacher] since then the good news of the Kingdom of God is preached, and everyone enters it violently." (Luke 16:16)

The time between John the Baptist and Christ's Passion was a transitional time. During this time, the Kingdom of God and of Heaven are *"forcefully advanced"*. And, we know this Kingdom is still violently thrust forward. *(Matthew 11:12)*

The Church Militant are those on earth who still war against the things of this world; against *"the rulers of the darkness of this world, against spiritual wickedness in high places" (Ephesians 6:12)*. And, the Church Triumphant is the communion of saints, who root on the Church Militant, are the members of the body of the bride of Christ who are in Heaven.

The New Covenant re-established the reign of God. It re-established His Sovereignty over those who choose to serve Him. The ideology of 'kingdom' terminology had been on the collective brain of the *Adat B'nai Yisrael* for as much as a thousand years.

So, for the first time since Samuel attempted to strengthen God's Sovereignty through renewed nationalism and the *Eved Adonai* as God's Chief Servant, God's direct reign over His people was being restored. That's what the "kingdom" of God...is.

The theological jostling of the relationship between God and mankind has inevitably revolved around the kingship of God. The term "Kingdom of God" does not appear in the Hebrew Bible, but the concepts of a monarchy certainly do. The monarchy wasn't instigated by God, it was promoted by the people.

God desired a relationship in which He would dwell and rule His people. The relationship led to a 'musical chairs' over the seat of authority. Would the people look to Him as a divine ruler, or reject Him? The 'musical chairs or thrones' of kings, and of God, took twists and turns.

The description of God's relationship with people of the New Covenant settled on that of a monarchy in the good news brought by Christ. The New covenant returned God as Sovereign Lord and King, with His seat in Heaven; as the true king.

When Christ spoke, He spoke into this history and this culture. The people of the province of Judah understood quite well. The throne would be in Heaven and there was an earthly council, a royal court. They also understood that on earth there would be a Chief Servant appointed by the king and patriarch of the New Covenant. It had *always* been so...

Christ and His disciples came preaching the glad tidings of God. They came preaching the glad tidings of the Household of... and the Kingdom of God.

"Now after John was arrested, Jesus came into Galilee, preaching the good news of God, and saying, "The time is fulfilled, and the Kingdom of God has drawn near; repent, and believe the good news[of the kingdom of God]" (Mark 1:14-15)

He would need a Chief Servant. He would be a "Servant of the Lord". Let's see how Christ did this.

Christ's office of Chief Servant

And I say also to you, that you are Peter (Petros), and on this rock (Petras) I will build my church; and the gates of hell shall not prevail against it. And I will give to you the keys of the kingdom of heaven: and whatever you shall bind on earth shall be bound in heaven: and whatever you shall loose on earth shall be loosed in heaven." Matthew 16:17-18 AKJV

This verse has long been ground zero in the debate over the office of the Chief Servant in the Kingdom of the New Covenant. Boisterous volleys of verse and note; the dueling of banjos and the clanging of cymbals lead to the rampant deconstruction of the biblical verses that support a reader's predetermined outcome.

However, as was foretold in Ezekiel, God will...

*Just as I pleaded with your fathers in the wilderness of the land of Egypt, so will I plead with you, saith the Lord God I will cause you to pass under the rod and will bring you **into the tradition** [bond; constructs] of the covenant. (Ezekiel 20: 36-37) [2]*

God will bring us to what has already been constructed. The structure and tradition of the Church are already there. I don't need to build it or deconstruct it. I need to be trained in the tradition of the covenant and not reinvent it.

Implications in the interpretation of Matthew 16:17-18 are profound... Is Peter the Chief Servant, or was it upon Peter's faith that the Church was built?

Was this a perpetual office, or Peter's faith. Here's the deal. Peter's faith caused him to ascend to the permanent office of *Eved Adonai*. Get it?

One side says Matthew didn't get it. God's Providence failed, and we are confused. Why...because Jesus said "Cephas" and not "Petros". The other denies the possibility of the chair of Peter all together...it was Peter's faith. FULL...STAHP! Well-meaning, but predisposed, interpreters argue on.

Here's the deal...Jesus appointed Peter as *Eved Adonai*; in the tradition of a Chief Servant. It was a well-established Salvation history. God would once again be Sovereign Lord and would entrust a "Servant of the Lord". The restoration of His reign, the Kingdom of God, would follow the *constructs [tradition] of the covenant* and restore the office.

When we believe in God's Providence and that Matthew understood, we end up with this verse to deal with. Peter, you are *Petros* (small rock), and on the *Petras* (large immovable rock) I will build my Church... Different Right? Well, yes and no, mostly no.

The English language renders us illiterate to grammatical gender. Greek, Hebrew, and many of the European languages commonly use both grammatical genders of nouns depending on its usage. Matthew used both *Petros* and then *Petras*, both of which would be grammatically correct. Petros is grammatically masculine and *Petras* is grammatically feminine.

The verse could be written this way in many languages including Hebrew and Greek(modern Spanish, Italian, and French, etc): *"Simon, I also say to you, that you are the President(masculine), and on the Presidency(feminine) I will build my Church."* The President is the replaceable *peg* and the Presidency is not.

Upon exploring the Greek Lexicon and Concordance, the same phrase could be written in several ways:

- Simon, you are the *Leitourgos (masculine),* and on the *Leitourgia (feminine)* I will build my Church. *Leitourgos* is a public servant (*peg*), a public minister [administrator]. *Leitourgia* is the office of the public servant. The *Leitourgos* is a replaceable peg and the *Leitourgia* is not.

- Simon, you are the *Hiereus (masculine)* and on the *Hierateia (feminine)* I will build my Church. *Hiereus* is a priest and *Hierateia* is the office of the priesthood. The priest is a peg that can be moved and changed, but the office of the priesthood cannot.

- The office of the deacon is *(Diakonia)* is feminine, as is the office of the overseer or bishop *(Episcope)*. The offices are immovable.

> **Side Note:** *Hierateia,* the priesthood…" *archy*" means "rule". Hierarchy is the priestly rule. *"Render onto Ceasar"* addresses the fact that there will be a competing secular civil rule…there will be Hierarchal, and legal precepts, from within the Church. Out of the priesthood, Bishops get elected…They receive teaching authority in the Prophetic domain of the *Keter Torah.* It all blends together into a unified whole… *"for the edification of the entire body".*

French, Italian, and Spanish dictionaries reveal a consistent pattern of grammatical gender for nouns. Offices and Titles are almost always feminine. Matthew's gender-*izing* of the term in the verse makes sense. He had to. Linguistically the small stone(masculine) and large stone(feminine) imagery are grammatically correct. This effectively creates the perpetual office of Chief Servant.

Matthew didn't believe that the office was going anywhere. The office would be a receiver or receivership, and Peter would be inserted into the chair, or into the office. Isaiah, in chapter 22, uses the same basic imagery when describing the office of the Chief Servant in the House of David. The officeholder was described as a peg.

*"I will drive him like a peg into a firm place; he will be **a seat** of honor for the house of his father."* (Isaiah 22;23)

One could argue that the office is less in stature to the *Eved Adonai.* That could be, but it points to Christ's Lordship. This Servant is Chief Servant of the Lord. Whether *Eved Elohim* or the *Nagid* from the days of an earthly kingdom, it remains the same. Let's look at two parallel verses you might not know to exist.

The Lord said to David, **'Thou shalt feed (shepherd) My people Israel, and thou shalt be a prince (captain or rule) over Israel.'** *(2 Samuel 5:2).*

Our Lord Jesus challenges Peter in the same way… **"…Feed (shepherd) My sheep…Peter…Tend (watch over, take care of, rule) My sheep, Peter,…Feed My sheep."**

So, while challenging Peter, He was also anointing Peter for his ministry as the Chief Servant of the Church. This was an ordination. Peter was to lead, shepherd, feed, and take care of those that Jesus entrusted to him. The office takes its rightful place in the King's court, and *"...the gates of hell shall not prevail against it."*

Peter wasn't ascending to the role of the King, Peter would oversee all that Christ, our King had, the household of God. He took on the role that existed since the first covenant between God and Abraham. As a matter of biblical history, there is an astonishingly clear picture of what had just happened.

The use of the term "rock" in Matthew chapter 16 also has some significance in the historical *"tradition of the covenant"* of the people of God. There were cairn markers that acted as guideposts along their journey. Rock and stone monuments were erected at many points in the history of Israel that bear witness and testify as reminders to Israel...

"...and they are there unto this day" (Josh. 4:9).

Absalom's Monument helps us see this office, a new "seat[chair] of Moses", from a different perspective. Christ had no children. Neither did Absalom. Absalom named a stone pillar after himself so it would perpetually stand.

> *"During his lifetime Absalom had taken a pillar and erected it in the King's Valley as a monument to himself, for he thought, "I have no son to carry on the memory of my name." He named the pillar after himself, and it is called Absalom's Monument to this day." (2 Samuel 18:18)*

Gone is the hereditary earthly monarchy. Christ perpetually reigns, seated at the right hand of the Father. The stone pillar remains. His Chief Servant is responsible for carrying on the memory of His name; to carry on His legacy, and to preserve the once delivered Gospel of the Kingdom.

While Jesus was appointing Peter to the position of Chief Servant, he gave him the keys to the kingdom. With those keys, Peter would be able to bind and loose.

"...and whatever you shall bind on earth shall be bound in heaven: and whatever you shall loose on earth shall be loosed in heaven.".

In an almost identical dialogue in Isaiah 22, Eliakim is appointed the Chief Servant, replacing Shebna in the House of David. The keys were given to Eliakim...

"...And I will lay the key of the house of David upon his shoulder: and he shall open, and none shall shut, and he shall shut, and none shall open. (Isaiah 22)

The Seventy

One of Moses' first acts was to ordain a Council of 70 to teach and Judge Israel. We see that they operated in both civil and teaching (prophetic) domains of authority. The "Judgement" was in accordance with the Law. So, teaching and Judging amounted to much the same. Eventually, the Sanhedrin carried on the [constructs] of tradition during Christ's ministry.

Jesus made a distinct differentiation between the Old and New. There was a new sheriff in town. He challenged the status quo, by sending out His own Council of Seventy. They went to cities and towns ahead of Christ's arrival. There would be a new authority. There would be a New Covenant.

(I call it a Council of Seventy to keep it consistent. From Moses' first Council to Jesus, we read of fluctuations between 70 to 72. Perhaps including a *Nasi* or president.)

Christ's Seventy was always there in the background. They served as needed. They were in Jerusalem for His Passion, they were there during the 40 days after His Resurrection, and they were in prayer in the Upper Room as they awaited the Holy Ghost on the 50th day.

In contrast, the Pharisees, Sadducees, and scribes that chased Jesus around were normally of the Sanhedrin. They continually pelted Him with questions attempting to trip Him up. *"Abraham is OUR father"* is one of those times.

Call no man Father

What a can of worms this has become. Jesus did not make a commandment to abstain from calling anyone father. We are to honor our father and our mother. So, what was he saying? When we read the text, we immediately see that Christ was differentiating between the Old Covenant and the New Covenant.

The Pharisees represented the Old, and Christ represented the New. So, essentially the Pharisees were defending their faith and their ancestry. "Abraham is our Father", or Moses is our Teacher" was their defense. Jesus said..." *Umm, no...Just no!"* (*my paraphrase*)

Father Abraham was the "father of many nations". He was the father of

Isaac and the grandfather of Jacob, the forefathers of the Hebraic and Jewish religion. He was the great-grandfather of the patriarchs of the twelve tribes of Israel.

There is a Jewish Passover song that is like our 12 days of Christmas. *"Echad Mi Yodea"* is a litany-styled song used for memorization of the oral tradition. The song calls these three men, *The Three Fathers*. (The Patriarchs)

In Jewish tradition, Abraham is called, *Avraham Avinu, "Our father Abraham".* He is there biological Patriarch, but he is also considered the father of Judaism. Moses is called *Moshe Rabbenu- "Moses our Teacher".* He authored the Torah and is considered the greatest prophet in Judea. So, they defended their culture, and they clung to the Old.

There were several confrontations between the Sanhedrin elite and Jesus about Abraham. John chapter 8 is an example of one of these long altercations. Jesus repeatedly made the distinction between God the Father and "Their Father Abraham". He did the same with "Moses their Teacher". He turned it upside-down. The Pharisees ignored Christ..." Abraham is our Father!"

Finally, Jesus apparently tired of the repeated clashes about the Old and the New. It was about faith. It was about the Covenant. He ended the debate...He told them not to call these men *fathers*. And, don't call any of these men *Rabbis*. Period. They were to look to heaven, that's where their Father was. *(Matthew 23:9)* Everyone's Patriarch is God.

The New Testament has many of these identifiers. We are the children of God, anew, with our mother Church and our Father God. We are also, cumulatively, the bride of Christ. The Son of God and the *Prince of peace* is the groom. The Virgin Mary is our mother-in-law who intercedes for us with both our Father and our husband-her Son, so to speak.

"What therefore God has joined together (united), let no man put asunder (separate or divide)" (Mark 10:9) Don't separate yourselves, with your free will, from the other members. Don't divorce yourself from the Church, the one holy Catholic, and Apostolic Church. Adulterers beware. Settle your offenses. Pray for those in authority.

And, Father's Day is A-OK.

House of Israel

*When I will effect a new covenant with the **house of Israel** and with the **house of Judah**; Not like the covenant which I made with their fathers*

On the day when I took them by the hand to lead them out of the land of Egypt; For they did not continue in My covenant, And I did not care for them, says the Lord. "For this is the covenant that I will make with the **house of Israel** *after those days, says the Lord: I will put My laws into their minds, And I will write them on their hearts. And I will be their God, and they shall be My people. (Hebrews 8:8-10) (Jeremiah 31: 31-34)*

From the casting out of Joseph to the final division of the tribes, there was always friction and jealousy. The Northern Kingdom became known as the house of Israel, and the Southern Kingdom became known as the house of Judah. Here the prophet Jeremiah made the claim that this new covenant would be made with the house of Israel.

It must be noted that the house of Israel is not Jewish. It is not Judea. The remnants of Israel were dispersed among the nations and never returned to form an identifiable kingdom. The Northern Kingdom was lost as an independent state never to return. *"the king of Assyria captured Samaria and carried [house of] Israel away into exile to Assyria. (2 Kings 17:6).*

There is a great deal of debate and lore about just what happened to the people from both Kingdoms but especially the North. Sidestepping the multiple theories, we know that many were dispersed, exiled and deported. Some fled to other countries, and some remained as refuges in what used to be their homeland, but the kingdoms were decimated.

Christ came to *"seek and save that which is lost".* The underlying theme seems to have been, "Where is everybody?" Christ has an ongoing search of the lost people of Israel. He was going after the lost sheep. He told His disciples while amid the province of Judah,

"I was sent only to the lost sheep of the house of Israel" (Matthew 15:24)

This has always seemed odd to me. But, when we recognize that Jesus is the "Good Shepherd", it makes sense. He wasn't setting up a Jewish kingdom and the Holy Commonwealth of the 12 tribes was no more. The tribe of Judah had "kingdoms on the brain" and they wanted the Temple restored. Christ explained it further, He told the parable of the lost sheep,

Suppose one of you has a hundred sheep and loses one of them. Doesn't he leave the ninety-nine in the open country and go after the lost sheep until he finds it? And when he

finds it, he joyfully puts it on his shoulders…" (Luke 15:4-5)

The challenge that confronted Christ was Judah's demand at restoration. We want our Kingdom. Aren't you the Messiah? This is the same demand made today. They wait for the same thing they have since the time of Christ. Let's have us an earthly kingdom and let's restore the Temple. They ended up crucifying Him over it.

Jesus revealed the coming changes, but they refused to see it, and they didn't hear it. They continued to seek seats in high places within the existing structure. The *Law* was sovereign, and the lawmakers ran the place. The quest for power was more important than the search for God's will. Judah just didn't get it.

Christ came at it from a different perspective. Immediately after the lost sheep parable, He tells the prodigal son story. Christ to Judah… Hello…Connected? They still didn't get it.

The missing son came back to his father having deserted the family. He spent his inheritance. There was a large celebration. What was once "lost and now was found". The son who had stayed with the father became jealous, angry, and lamented…" Where was my party?" …the house of Israel…and the house of Judah.

Professor Daniel Elazar put it this way:

> *At the same time, politics was important because the establishment of the Holy Commonwealth, later to be called God's Kingdom of Earth in some quarters, was a primary goal of the Israelite nation, a goal mandated by God. Thus, the character of Israelite political institutions was constantly judged in the Bible in terms of their success in fostering the development of the Holy Commonwealth.*
>
> *The very institution of the kingship became an issue because it involved the abandonment of God's direct rule over the people and thus was viewed by many as a departure from the path leading toward the Holy Commonwealth. Subsequent to the introduction of kingly rule, particular dynasties were judged in terms of their faithfulness to God's will in this connection. Thus, the disappearance of the ten tribes as political entities is lamented as a break in the right order of things that must be mended if the Holy Commonwealth is to be achieved." [5]*

*** I will bring you from the nations and gather you from the countries where

you have been scattered…as I pleaded with your fathers in the wilderness of the land of Egypt, so will I plead with you, saith the Lord God I will cause you to pass under the rod and will bring you into the tradition [bond; constructs] of the covenant. (Ezekiel 20: 34-37) [2]

The Transfiguration

During the verbal wars between the Old and the New, we find ourselves at the Festival of Tabernacles. The Transfiguration is one of the greatest miracles witnessed by humankind. It is considered one of the five milestones in the life of Jesus…Baptism, Transfiguration, Crucifixion, Resurrection, and Ascension.

There is much packed in the few "Transfiguration" verses. Theologians have uncovered a wealth of insight into the day Christ brought Peter, John, and James to the mountaintop. I fear that I can't do them justice. But here, I want to show the Transfiguration from a Kingdom and Church perspective. Mostly, from our Journey's perspective. Basically, how do we apply it? Then, the rest can then follow.

Chronologically, we know that the Church has entered the time of Tabernacles as it left the Upper Room on Pentecost. And, there is an overwhelming consensus that the Transfiguration occurred during, or just after, the Feast of Tabernacles. The Feast that commemorates the 40-year sojourn in the desert while living in tents which included a temporary Tabernacle for God to dwell.

Just before leaving to pray on the mountain, Jesus predicts that He would suffer greatly and die at the behest of the Chief Priests and teachers of the Law. That frightened Peter, and Christ rebuked him. He explained the "Way of the Cross" as followers having to deny themselves and take up their own cross…gloomy picture.

But, out of the blue, Christ said, *"Truly I tell you, some who are standing here will not taste death before they see that the kingdom of God has come with power." (Mark 9:1)*

It is interesting then, that they immediately left for the mountain to see the power. The Transfiguration was about to occur. First at His baptism, and then on the mountain, God says, "This is My Son…". The Apostles on the mountain would be the first to actually hear from the cloud, "This is My Son".

Moses and Elijah appeared as representatives of the Law and the Prophets. Christ transfigured surrounded by a brilliant white light. Again, Peter as "on cue" makes a connection. He wanted to make tents on the mountain. A cloud appeared from above...

"This is my Son, whom I love. Listen to him!"

God differentiated between the Old and the New. The Law and the Prophets were fulfilled. He pointed at His Son... *"Listen to Him!"* The New established.

Christ told the three that He would be crucified, Before the mountain, He told them of the power on high, now He showed them the power. And, He explained that He would rise from the dead... They pondered this power amongst themselves...What does *"rising from the dead"* mean? They would soon see.

The Ascension

On Resurrection Sunday, the tomb was empty. We were delivered from the 'works of the Law and into the grace that is Christ. Thus, the "Counting of Omer" [days] began as they Journeyed from the empty tomb to the Upper Room and Pentecost.

Just like the first "Counting of the Omer", the disciples grew in the knowledge of the Lord. They grew in knowledge of the Gospel. He proved Himself to be the same, Jesus. He was the same promise-keeping, covenant-making Lord. Thomas doubted until he poked his finger in His wounds. He was the Christ.

"By calling this covenant "new," he has made the first one obsolete; and what is obsolete and outdated will soon disappear." (Hebrews 8:13)

He showed Himself first to Mary Magdalene, then to a couple of disciples on the road to Emmaus and the Apostles. During this time, He was slowly opening the scriptures to them. He explained how all was necessary to come to pass.

"O how can you be so slow in heart to believe in all the things the prophets spoke! Was it not necessary for the Christ to suffer these things and to enter into His glory?"
(Luke 24:25)

They continued to gain insight... *"These are my words which I spoke to you while I was yet with you, that all the things written in the law of Moses and in the Prophets and Psalms about me must be fulfilled."* Their minds grew to fully grasp the meaning of the Gospel and of the Scriptures. He said to the Apostles… *"you are to be witnesses of these things."*

Christ spent 40 days with them teaching them what it all meant:…

> *he interpreted to them things pertaining to Himself in all the Scriptures.*

> *In this way, it is written that the Christ would suffer and rise from among the dead on the third day, and on the basis of His name repentance for the forgiveness of sins would be preached in all the nations -- starting out from Jerusalem,"*

> *And behold," I am sending forth upon you that which is promised by my Father. Wait here until you receive power from on high. You will be guided by the Holy Spirit, make sure you listen and receive it." (Luke 24:46-49)*

Just before His Ascension, He challenged them and gave them the Great Commission…

"Go therefore and make disciples of all the nations, baptizing them in the name of the Father and the Son and the Holy Spirit…teaching them to observe all that I commanded you; and lo, I am with you always, even to the end of the age."(Matthew 28:19-20)

He walked with them out to Bethany, the site where Christ wept over Jerusalem. He blessed them and ascended into Heaven. The disciples would gather in the Upper Room as they were told. They awaited the Promise from above. The "Counting of Omer" would soon end. They awaited the New Pentecost. The New Church would be born.

Paul

Christ their King, and their Prophet had ascended into Heaven. They awaited the promised Holy Ghost, so they decided to throw dice to replace Judas. Matthias was added to the eleven. In the meantime, Christ appeared to Paul in a unique way.

Sometime after His resurrection, Christ appeared to Paul on the road to Damascus. Paul was a Pharisee, a strong advocate for the Law, and approved of the killing of Stephen. His conversion took some persuasion And, his conversion was profound.

Paul was convinced that what happened on the road to Damascus, was indeed an encounter with the Messiah. Through this encounter, Christ gave him a unique commission. *"Go to the Gentiles and the lost sheep of the [house] of Israel."*

Later, the 12 Apostles were satisfied that Paul's "road to Damascus" story was true. They received him as commissioned to spread the Gospel to the Gentiles. Yet, Paul never saw himself as one of the 12. He was the Lesser, or Least, of the Apostles.

Bringing it Together

"Go and make disciples of all nations". The sheep where scattered. The apostle James, the first bishop of Jerusalem, was well respected for his knowledge as an orthodox Jew. He addressed his Epistle this way, *"James, a servant of God and of the Lord Jesus Christ, To the twelve tribes scattered among the nations: Greetings." (James 1:1)*

Paul was anointed to pursue the Gentiles. James was an Old Testament scholar. And, Peter was Chief Servant. There was no power grab. There was neither Jew nor Gentile, but all were in Christ. And, Christ led His Church.

Those who believed in Christ's work on the "New" altar became members of a new body politic, a new *Adat B'nai Yisrael.* That body was now transnational. It became one, holy, Catholic, and Apostolic Church. They are the Bride of Christ. They are the new Holy Commonwealth; the proverbial, "city on a hill", and the visible Church.

> *I will set up your seed after you, who will come from your body, and I will establish his kingdom. He shall build a house for My name, and I will establish* **the throne of his kingdom forever."** *(2Samuel 7:12-14)*
>
> *"For unto us a Child is born, unto us a Son is given, And the government will be upon His shoulder. And His name will be called Wonderful, Counselor, Mighty God, Everlasting Father, Prince of Peace.* **Of the increase of His government** *and peace there will be no end, upon the throne of David and over His kingdom, to* **order it and establish it with judgment and justice from that time forward, even forever.** *The zeal of the Lord of hosts will perform this."* (Isaiah 9:6-7)

Early Christian disciples understood their past. They understood the Law and the Prophets. And, they understood the Kingdom of God. They also understood *"He will never leave it or forsake it."* H. William J. Everett wrote, *"Christians seized on the Davidic covenant, therefore, to understand Jesus as God's promise to us for all the ages".*

[7]

The Old Covenant is fulfilled. The Prince of Peace sits at the right hand of the *"throne of the Majesty in the heavens"*. Christ established the government of the Church, in the *"constructs[bonds] of tradition"*. He has a Chief Servant who oversees all He owns.

He mediated the old altar of the blood of goats and oxen. Now, He offers Himself through the sacraments and the Mass in the Ministry of Reconciliation. Our mother, now the Queen Mother of Heaven, intercedes for us with the Father and Son.

We partake of the Lamb of God. It is an intimate exchange that identifies us as part of the body. We are the body of Christ, and we are His bride. In this mystical exchange in the Eucharist, we know Him, and He knows us. He abides in us, and we abide in Him.

He dwells in each member, exactly as He said; with carnal knowledge of the bride of Christ. [1] We partake of the Heavenly Gift, reconciled with the body and the Holy Trinity…. the *good news* of the Kingdom of God. Does He know you in this way? Have you amputated yourself from the bride? The union is in the bread…The Eucharist.

Filled with the Spirit, they left Pentecost having confirmed the New Covenant in Acts chapter 2. They set about making disciples.

Chapter 12: The Church that Emerged

"What therefore God has joined together (united), let no man put asunder (separate or divide)" (Mark 10:9)

It was a long journey for me, and I wasn't prepared for what I would find. But I was seeking the authentic First Church. The Acts chapter 2 Church as they left Peter's speech on Pentecost. I confess, I pictured it as a bunch of sheepherders who wandered the desert in flip-flops all day. I stereotyped. Maybe that's just me.

The culture was anything but that. It was complex. They had advanced societal structures in Rome and Greek occupations. There was also the Egyptian Hellenists creating fear that the entire culture would be Hellenization. They were redeemed out the bondage of a complex and structured society in Egypt. They created complex Davidic Kingdoms, and I thought it was all Kumbaya and sand between the toes. My bad.

Jesus faced complex pressures of Jewish entitlement. They wanted their King back, the earthly king. They ignored their transgressions to the Covenant. They had "kingdoms on the brain" just as I had popsicles on the brain when I was young. So, Jesus faced it head-on...They didn't hear Him.

The Sanhedrin Pharisees and Scribes continually confront Jesus. Jesus countered with His own seventy to directly counteract the Sanhedrin Council. There was a matrix of rituals and ceremonies that revolved around their Ministry to Reconcile both themselves and the people to God. It unceasingly emanated from the Temple at a time that it was also unsympathetically disrespected.

This *IS* the climate into which God sent His Son, and it *IS* the climate into which Christ spoke. Out of this, a New Covenant emerged. And, out of this, a Church emerged. We now can see what that Church would have looked like, how the Church Fathers would have implemented it, and what it would have looked like today.

It has been a long road. Let's look at the characteristics of the first Church. We would see the Church. This is the Church of the Apostles. They were Jews. They knew their history. They knew their culture and politics. So did Peter, and Paul, …and James. The New Testament speaks to their nation and their culture. When we see it from their perspective, we will see the Church.

Here's a quick rundown of key criteria you need to see the Church that emerged.

#1) This is Tabernacles' Time!

Moses, Aaron, and the Council of seventy descended Mt. Sinai with the Covenant. It was confirmed by the people. In the same way, Peter, the Queen Mother, and the Council of Seventy descended the Upper Room with the [New] Testament. It was confirmed by the people.

The Church was born, and the Covenant was confirmed. We know that as the Israelites left Sinai, they entered their wilderness experience. This was the time of Tabernacles. The festival commemorates the faithfulness of God's Provision in the wilderness His daily provision was the Manna.

The Church left the Upper Room and entered their Wilderness experience. Paul said, *"to keep the feast", the one sacrifice."* It is the Feast of Tabernacles. It is a celebration of God's faithfulness. Just as the first Feast, it is a feast of Thanksgiving. The faithful daily Provision is the true Manna that comes down from Heaven. It is the Eucharist.

The Church, as *"the Bride"* entered the time of Tabernacles at Pentecost and will cross the "Jordan" in the fullness of time. They will cross at the appointed time. And, they will cross into the fullness of the Kingdom. It will be the last day of God's Provision, the Manna of the Eucharist.

We enter the Church at our Baptism protected from our past. We grow in the knowledge of Christ as we approach our personal Pentecost. We confirm the Covenant and venture out on our personal wilderness trek thankful for God's daily Provision in the Eucharist.

The Church fulfills its mission as it comes alongside to help us along the way. From cradle to grave, the Church provides the Sacraments we need as we walk. The altar is the interface for our continuing relationship and our continual reconciliation with the Bridegroom.

#2) This is God's Time

Many say, "Oh, He died a long time ago, you can't sacrifice Christ again". The Church agrees He died once for all. It is one perpetual sacrifice. God's time is not our time. He sees the beginning and the end. He transcends time in a way that is a mystery to humanity's linear mindset. It all happened at once.

There are efforts to explain God's time. Philosophically, it is called *Kairotic [Kairos]* time; a passing instant. There is Chronos, our linear time, and Kairos, a passing instant that is so violently forceful…it is as an opening that appears which needs to be forcibly pushed through to achieve success.

Biblically, Kairos, God's time, is also "the appointed time in the purpose of God", a time when God's purpose is fulfilled. It is fulfilled for everyone at once. The brilliance, the Shekinah, the light transcends time. It is forcibly, in a passing instant, made present for you here and now.

This Mystery is beyond us. Minute by minute, we are linear people. Our world is linear. The true Tabernacle in Heaven is made present for you today. We need to eat His flesh and drink His blood to have eternal life. It's above my pay grade. Are we transported back to Calvary? Don't know. Is it re-presented? No. One thing is certain. It is the one sacrifice that has been made available for you. And, it was made available in an instant. That sacrifice is made present on the New altar.

#3) The Throne is in Heaven

God expressed His desire to lead His people. *"I will be their God; they will be my people"*. He was Sovereign. There was a division of authority amongst the people. They were led by the *Eved Adonai* who was accountable to God. God directly led His people.

The throne was in Heaven. The "Throne" is man's concept. It's how we explain His Sovereignty. In our wrestling with our God, there was a sort of musical chairs. They wanted the throne on earthlike other people. The earthly king would rule over them.

Matthews's Gospel focuses on our relationship from the Kingdom perspective. Christ confirmed it. Israel had *"kingdoms on the brain"*. They wanted an earthly king to ride into Jerusalem on a white stallion who would re-establish the throne on Earth.

They would serve that earthly king and God would remain.in the shadows. After several centuries, they would once again rule themselves on earth. Their power, the status quo would otherwise remain.

Christ came to re-establish the true throne. The throne would once again be in Heaven restoring the Sovereignty of God. Christ the King, we say. *'He was now their God, and they were their people'* Samuel tried to restore this type of relationship. But it is finally so. The office of *Eved Adonai* or *Servant of the Lord* has been once again instituted.

#4) The Church would be One

The Church, *Ekklesia* in Greek, means those called out as a congregation or assembly... One. Congregation. Israel was banded together by the Paschal Lamb. They were bound together, baptized, and confirmed their Covenant with God. But, also with each other. They were one nation. The wedding covenant was ratified.

They were bound together in unity by the wilderness Tabernacle. They were one people. They settled as a nation…a One. Visible. Nation. A nation settled in the Promised Land set-apart to God. Their center was always the Holiest Place. God dwelled there. And, the people communed with Him through the Old Testament tabernacle.

They lost their unity in the Land during the time of Judges. Leaders were raised up to restore that visible unity and repent from idolatry.

The Church, *Ekklesia, was* called out as congregation or assembly. They are set-apart and bound together on their own unique and parallel journey. They settled in Judea. The Church settled in the center of the Known World in obedience to Christ. It was one visible Church.

God dwells amongst them in a new way. They commune with God on the multitude of Tabernacles with the multiplication Mystery of the Eucharist. It is the Bridegroom and the bride.

Christ prayed for the unity of the body. The Apostles labored feverishly to root out strife, pride, and division. They labored preserve unity. That unity was through the Body, Blood, Soul, and Divinity on the wedding bed of the Altar.

Just like the time of Judges, this strife, pride, idolatry people wander off amputating themselves from the body. They tell themselves they are still somehow connected. But they do not commune in His one Body, the Eucharist.

#5) There is a Chief Servant

From the very beginning, there was always a Chief Servant. Abraham had a

Chief Servant in the Abrahamic Covenant. His commission was to take a lot of servants with him and seek the Bride. For. His. Son. He was the Servant of his Master.

We found that Moses and Joshua held the title of *Eved Adonai*, Servant of the Lord. Jewish scholars see the *Eved Adonai* as the highest office of the land. The humble leader submitted to God's Sovereignty while teaching the will of God. It was lost in the abundance in the age of Judges. Samuel tried to right the ship. He argued for the restoration of the office of *Servant of the Lord*.

We discovered that the complex hierarchy of the Davidic kingdom had... Chief Servants, or Prime Ministers, or Chamberlains, etc. This office oversaw all the king had. They were the keeper of the keys.

In the last chapter, we saw how Christ, the King, implemented the office. We saw the ordination, and we saw the perpetual office would continue. The first occupant was Peter. We have a 2000-year historical list of the holders of that office. Some have been Pious, and some have been Saul.

The Church has a Chief Servant. He is not a monarch. That is a Heresy. The throne is where it rightly belongs.

#6) There is a Council of Seventy

Almost immediately, Moses appointed a Council of seventy elders to judge the people. He also appointed lesser courts in tribes and cities. Both the Council of seventy and the lesser courts had full authority to judge the people. The ancient Judges were religious leaders and teachers. They would teach and judge the people's disputes and transgressions according to the Law.

Fast forward to the time of Jesus, the Sanhedrin was filled with elders from all three domains of authority. The Great Sanhedrin was the Council of seventy, plus a Nasi (president). They met at the Temple in Jerusalem and there were Lesser Sanhedrin councils that met in various locations throughout Judea.

Various political bodies such as the Pharisees and the Sadducees jockeyed for positions on the Great Council. It was this group that repeatedly confronted and challenged Jesus. It was also this group that attempted to maintain culture and traditional customs.

Christ obviously challenged the status quo. He appointed His own Council of seventy elders and sent them out amongst the people. They walked with Christ, and the Church all the way to the Upper Room on Pentecost.

The Church has maintained this Council of "Seventy". It maintains the complex administrative body reminiscent of the Davidic kingdoms of yore. The

Curia is this administrative body in the current Church. The Sacred College of the Cardinals work within this body and also act as a Cabinet. They assist and advise the office of the *Eved Adonai*.

So, the Church has this same council of "elders" filled with sages, priests, and teachers who work to maintain the tradition of the Church. They serve Christ as His ambassadors to protect and maintain the faith.

> **Side Note:** Today, many of these leaders have seemed to forget who is boss. They have forgotten where the throne is. Some treat it like their own little playground. They believe they can transform, and reform, the Church to their own desires. That desire is clouded by sin. They play…in the fields of the Lord.

#7) There is a Queen Mother

From the first Covenant with Abraham, through the Old Covenant and on to the New Covenant, there was ALWAYS a *Gebirah*. Sarah is *Gebirah* even before there was a kingdom. She became the miraculous Matriarch of a great nation. Here the word *Gebirah* was translated "Great Lady".

Sarah, the Great Lady, can also be translated as Queen, and we can see why. She was the mother and then grandmother of Israel. She would have been their confidant and counselor. She would have been their "Queen Mother". The queen was not the king's wife.

Throughout the Israelite kingdoms, there was always a Queen Mother. She was the mother of the King. She was a trusted confidant and counselor. And, she interceded for the people. We have seen that she also had a throne and a crown.

"Behold your Mother". Mary became Queen Mother at the foot of the cross. She was no longer "Woman". As with Sarah, she became a miraculous Matriarch of a great nation, the Church.

Christ gave the Church their Mother, our Mother. She cares about her children and will intercede for us. Her prayers, *"availeth much"*. If you believe in Christ, then Mary is the *"Queen of Heaven"*.

#7) There is an Altar

We also know there is an altar. The old Tabernacle was the point of reconciliation. The ministry was carried on continuously throughout the history of Israel. It was a perpetual sacrifice that bridged the abyss that manifested between themselves and their God.

Israel labored feverously in these machinations to remain in relationship with God. They took Saturdays off. They needed rest from the works of the Law at the Temple. It was a mandated rest from their transgressions.

Christ is our Rest. He was the sole Mediator of the old Tabernacles. Not Ox. Not Sheep. We have a New tabernacle. Do you believe? We have the true Tabernacles and Christ ministers unceasingly on our behalf. This is where we are. It is the season of Tabernacles.

#8) There are Bishops and Priests

The Apostles ordained priests to become Bishops in geographical areas where they evangelized. Through the laying on of hands, Apostolic succession signified the handing down of the tradition. The handed down Apostolic authority guaranteed the authenticity of the tradition. This was the faith. There was no bible.

When we think of the three *Ketarim*, Bishops were chosen from among the priestly domain. They are ordained with the teaching authority of the prophetic domain. Bishops were still priests but now had to 'keep the tradition'.

There were times when Apostles remained relatively settled in their city. James comes to mind He was an Apostle who remained in Jerusalem as Bishop. Through Apostolic succession, however, Bishops would eventually take their place.

It is odd that many scholars call this an evolution. They were Jews. They understood authority. They had more than a millennium of complex administration. They weren't stumbling around in the dark. Please.

As needs grew, they added the necessary leadership. We see that Paul gave instructions on the requirements for the selection and ordination of bishops, priests(presbyters), and deacons. They could add them as needed. These offices still exist in the Church today.

Priests operated in the domain of the priesthood just like their predecessors. Their forerunners, who labored at the Temple, were chosen and ordained from among the Levites.

The priest is called from the laity, the church of priests, to minister at the tabernacle as a wise elder, this presbyter acts as the arbiter of the body blood soul and divinity, our daily bread. We have also confirmed that there would be priests. The entire nation of Israel was supposed to partake in the priesthood.

#9) Priests need something to Sacrifice

Christ told us. It was and is unequivocal. If we believe in Christ, the work of God is to receive the true Manna, the Body and Blood, Soul and Divinity, of His sacrifice. The one true sacrifice made present for you straight from Heaven. *"What works are we to do?"*

We Are to Eat His Flesh and Drink His Blood to Have Eternal Life. This is the *work* commanded by God, to do the will of the Father. *(John 6).* This was hard teaching. He offers His Body and His Blood through the Rite of Melchizedek. It is a mystical Transubstantiation of the bread and wine of through the Melchizedekian Rite.

> *Every high priest is appointed to offer both gifts and sacrifices, and so it was necessary for this one also to have something to offer. If he were on earth, he would not be a priest, for there are already priests who offer the gifts prescribed by the law. They serve at a sanctuary that is a copy and shadow of what is in heaven... "See to it that you make everything according to the pattern shown you on the mountain." ... But in fact, the ministry Jesus has received is as superior to theirs as the covenant of which he is mediator is superior to the old one since the new covenant is established on better promises."*

Christ had (has) something to offer. He had (has) something to sacrifice. It was (is) His Flesh. It was His Blood. It was His Body. Through the new priestly rite, we receive the Eucharistic mystery that is made present for you. Christ told you. Just like the priests of the Old, you are required to partake of that one sacrifice. Through the miracle of God's time, it is made present. Otherwise, Christ would not have told you, you must eat.

We eat from the New Altar...New Covenant Melchizedekian priests need something to offer at the New Altar. If the Old altar was superior, there would be no need for a new one. The New Altar *IS* established on Christ's one sacrifice. On the New Altar, we receive the Body and Blood, Soul and Divinity, of the promised Manna from the True Tabernacle to the New Altar...the many and varied sacrifices of Old.

He held up the third cup...do this...it became all in one...in His Flesh and Blood.

#10) Unified and unceasing Hymns of praise and supplication.
The Church will always be as Malachi prophesied more than 400 years before the time of our Lord.

> *For from the rising of the sun even to the going down, my name is great among the Gentiles, and in every place, there is sacrifice [burnt offering], and there is offered to my name a clean oblation [sacrifice]: for my name is great among the Gentiles, saith the Lord of hosts." (Malachi 1:11)*

Visualize the earth's turn, as dawn continually marches forward. There is a new day. Every morning New Masses begin, unceasingly, all around the world. The Psalms are continually offered Heavenward. There are unending Hymns of praise and supplication.

Malachi prophesied of this time. There would be no end. Every place there is a clean sacrifice. And, it is continuously offered, and the True Tabernacle perpetually responds on our behalf.

I have seen estimates of between 4000 and 12,000 Masses on-going at any minute. According to Fr. George W. Kosicki, CSB, there are about "four-to-five Masses begin each second and there are approximately 8-to-9,000 Masses going on at any moment." [1]

> *"It is truly inspiring and breathtaking to consider that at any given moment thousands of Masses are being said throughout the world and the infinitely perfect sacrifice of Jesus' Body, Blood, Soul, and Divinity is being lovingly offered to the Eternal Father."[1]*

Malachi's prophesy has been fulfilled. Where 2 or more are gathered…in wilderness or jungle huts, in inner-city storefronts and charities, in parish Churches or Diocesan Cathedrals, and Abbeys and Monasteries, there are unending hymns of prayer and supplication; and Masses are being offered continually.

Whereby one priest, or groups of priests, whether the Bishop or the Pope, it remains the same…the same unending sacrifice in the Eucharistic Mass that was instituted by Christ at the Last Supper. This is the highest form of worship. We seek an intimate encounter only available through His Real Presence in the Eucharist. We are bound to Christ, the Bridegroom through this *"source and summit of faith"*.

The cup is raised…the Eucharistic Prayer echoes Malachi:

You are indeed Holy, O Lord, and all You have created rightly gives You praise… You give life to all things and make them holy, and You never cease to gather a people to yourself, so that from the rising of the sun to its setting a pure sacrifice may be offered to Your name."

The Church Emerged

*For unto us a Child is born, unto us, a Son is given, And the government will be upon His shoulder. And His name will be called Wonderful, Counselor, Mighty God, Everlasting Father, Prince of Peace. Of **the increase of His government and peace there will be no end**, upon the throne of David and over His kingdom, to order it and establish it with judgment and justice from that time forward, even forever. The zeal of the Lord of hosts will perform this." (Isaiah 9:6-7)*

The Church emerged. Time moved on. The Apostolic age ended with the death of the last Apostle John died around 100-110AD. Church Fathers of this period wrote while Apostles still lived… They became Bishops in their stead.

The Sub Apostolic age was the age of disciples who were "direct descendants" with the Apostles. The Church Fathers of this period walked with and were disciples under the Apostles. They would become Bishops in succession. Through the *"laying on of hands"*, Apostolic Succession was assured. The tradition of the Apostles would prevail.

Some of the main works of the Apostolic period are Barnabas, the disciple who accompanied Paul, Ignatius, a student of Peter, was Bishop of Antioch, Polycarp, a student of John, and Clement, who was third in the Chair of Peter.

Next, we have Church Fathers like Irenaeus, who was a student of Polycarp, and so on. Authors like the Shepherd of Hermas, Justin Martyr, Irenaeus, and Tertullian all carried on the Apostolic Tradition. They defended against erring and heretical turns.

These writers have always been esteemed by the Church. The writers were well circulated and read. At times, many of these documents were considered in the canon of the New Testament. Apostolic authorship became the defining characteristic of the Canon. This did not mean that these letters, and treatise were not valuable for teaching. They were still very close to the source.

They had the tradition. In the course of their lives, things cropped up. They addressed them. They defended the faith. Through the authors, we can grow in understanding of the Church. The more they wrote, the more we understand. We fill in the blanks. They clarified issues as they came up.

The Tradition wasn't evolving, our insight was growing. Let's look at some of the early Church Fathers. The *Didache*, or *"Teachings of the Twelve Apostles"* (c. 50-70 AD): It was one of the earliest catechisms and may well have been written while both Peter and Paul were alive.

Didache on the Bread of Life

Let no one eat and drink of your Eucharist but those **baptized** *in the name of the Lord; to this, too the saying of the Lord is applicable: 'Do not give to dogs what is sacred'". -Ch. 9:5*

"On the Lord's own day **[Sunday]***, assemble in common to break bread* **[Eucharist]** *and offer thanks;* **but first confess your sins,** *so that your sacrifice may be pure. However,* **no one quarreling with his brother may join** *your meeting until they are reconciled; your sacrifice must not be defiled. For here we have the saying of the Lord:* **'In every place and time offer me a pure sacrifice; for I am a mighty King,** *says the Lord; and my name spreads terror among the nations.'-Ch 14 (The Teaching of the Twelve Apostles) c. 50-70 CE [2]*

The Early Church Fathers

These Fathers knew more about the first Church than we do, or your pastor does. They walked with the Source. They walked with the Tradition. Their writings were held in esteem. I encourage you to study them in light of this book. Study them to find the authentic Church that emerged; the Church revealed in the New.

Here are a just few quotes that reveal the wealth of insight we find in early Church Fathers. Discover the Church that grew out of a Judean band of twelve.

On the Real Presence

Bishop Ignatius was in his 30's when Peter and Paul were martyred
"Take note of those who hold heterodox opinions on the grace of Jesus Christ which has come to us and see how contrary their opinions are to the mind of God. . .. They abstain

187

from the Eucharist and from prayer because they do not confess that the Eucharist is the flesh of our Savior Jesus Christ, flesh which suffered for our sins and which that Father, in His goodness, raised up again. They who deny the gift of God are perishing in their disputes" (Letter to the Smyrnaeans *6:2–7:1* [A.D. 110]).[3]

"Make certain, therefore, that you all observe one common Eucharist; for there is but one Body of our Lord Jesus Christ, and but one cup of union with his Blood, and one single altar of sacrifice—even as there is also but one bishop, with his clergy and my own fellow servitors, the deacons. This will ensure that all your doings are in full accord with the will of God" (Letter to the Philadelphians *4* [A.D. 110]).[4]

Justin Martyr: *"We call this food Eucharist, and no one else is permitted to partake of it, except one who believes our teaching to be true and who has been washed in the washing which is for the remission of sins and for regeneration [i.e., has received baptism] and is thereby living as Christ enjoined. For not as common bread nor common drink, do we receive these; but since Jesus Christ our Savior was made incarnate by the word of God and had both flesh and blood for our salvation, so too, as we have been taught, the food which has been made into the Eucharist by the Eucharistic prayer set down by him, and by the change of which our blood and flesh is nurtured, is both the flesh and the blood of that incarnated Jesus"* (First Apology *66* [A.D. 151]).[5]

On Baptism

Hippolytus: *"Baptize first the children, and if they can speak for themselves let them do so. Otherwise, let their parents or other relatives speak for them"* (The Apostolic Tradition *21:16* [A.D. 215]).[6]

On the Chair of Peter

Pope Clement, third in the Chair (24 years after Peter's death, Apostles still walked the earth)." ... *Accept our counsel and you will have nothing to regret. ... If anyone disobey the things which have been said by him [God] through us [i.e., that you must reinstate your leaders], let them know that they will involve themselves in transgression and in no small danger. . ... You will afford us joy and gladness if being obedient to the things which we have written through the Holy Spirit, you will root out the wicked passion of jealousy"* (Letter to the Corinthians *1, 58–59, 63* [A.D. 80]).[7]

Bishop Ignatius: *"Ignatius . . . to the church also which holds the presidency, in the location of the country of the Romans, worthy of God, worthy of honor, worthy of blessing, worthy of praise, worthy of success, worthy of sanctification, and, because you hold the presidency in love, named after Christ and named after the Father"* (Letter to the Romans *1:1 [A.D. 110]).[8]*

"You [the church at Rome] have envied no one, but others you have taught. I desire only that what you have enjoined in your instructions may remain in force" (ibid 3:1)[7]

Origen: *"Look at [Peter], the great foundation of the Church, that most solid of rocks, upon whom Christ built the Church [Matt. 16:18]. And what does our Lord say to him? 'Oh, you of little faith,' he says, 'why do you doubt?' [Matt. 14:31]"* (Homilies on Exodus *5:4 [A.D. 248]).[9]*

On Bishops, Priests, and Deacons:

Bishop Ignatius: *"Take care to do all things in harmony with God, with the bishop presiding in the place of God, and with the presbyters in the place of the council of the apostles, and with the deacons, who are most dear to me, entrusted with the business of Jesus Christ, who was with the Father from the beginning and is, at last, made manifest"* (Letter to the Magnesians 2 [A.D. 110] *(ibid., 6:1).[10]*

Clement of Alexandria: *"Even here in the Church the gradations of bishops, presbyters, and deacons happen to be imitations, in my opinion, of the angelic glory and of that arrangement which, the scriptures say, awaits those who have followed in the footsteps of the apostles and who have lived in complete righteousness according to the gospel"* (Miscellanies *6:13:107:2 [A.D. 208]).[11]*

On Confession:

Bishop Ignatius: *"For as many as are of God and of Jesus Christ are also with the bishop. And like many, as shall, in the exercise of penance, return into the unity of the Church, these, too, shall belong to God, that they may live according to Jesus Christ"* (Letter to the Philadelphians *3 [A.D. 110]).[12]*

"For where there are division and wrath, God does not dwell. To all them that repent, the Lord grants forgiveness, if they turn in penitence to the unity of God, and to communion with the bishop" (ibid., 8).[12]

On Mary

Irenaeus: *"… Mary, betrothed to a man but nevertheless still a virgin, being obedient, was made the cause of salvation for herself and for the whole human race. . .. Thus, the knot of Eve's disobedience was loosed by the obedience of Mary. What the* **virgin Eve** *had bound in unbelief, the* **Virgin Mary** *loosed through faith"* (Against Heresies *3:22:24 [A.D. 189]).[13]*

"In this way, the **Virgin Mary** *might become the advocate of the* **virgin Eve.** *And*

189

thus, as the human race fell into bondage to death by means of a virgin, so it is rescued by a virgin. Virginal disobedience has been balanced in the opposite scale by virginal obedience. For, in the same way, the sin of the first created man received amendment by the correction of the First-Begotten" (ibid., 5:19:1 [A.D. 189]).[13]

Hippolytus: *"...At that time, the Savior coming from the Virgin, the Ark brought forth His own Body into the world from that Ark, which was gilded with pure gold within by the Word, and without by the Holy Ghost." (c. 170-236) (S. Hippolytus, In Dan.vi., Patr. Gr., Tom. 10, p. 648) (Blessed Virgin, p. 77) [14]*

St. Gregory: *"The Ark is verily the Holy Virgin, gilded within and without, who received the treasure of universal sanctification". (c.213-270) (Orat. in Deip. Annunciat. Int. Opp. S. Greg. Thaumaturg) (Blessed Virgin, p. 89). [15]*

Let us, therefore, forsake the vanity of the crowd and their false teachings, [the vanity of the world] and turn back to the word delivered to us from the beginning. [Once delivered]
Polycarp, Bishop of Smyrna

References

Chapter 1

1) *Glenn Beck*

2) *Habits of the Heart; Robert Bellah 1984*

3) *The Body; Ellen Vaughn & Charles Colson (1993)*

4) *The Social Contract; Jean-Jacques Rousseau's Du Contrat social (1762)*

5) *The Civil Religion in America; Robert Bellah (1967)*

6) *The Polity in Biblical Israel; Authority, Power and Leadership in the Jewish Polity: Cases and Issues - Chapter 1* Daniel J. Elazar

7) *Against the Protestant Gnostics; Phillip J Lee (1987)* large body of work about Calvin's views

8) *"Kinship and Consent in the Jewish Community: Patterns of Continuity in*

9) *Jewish Communal Life,"* Tradition, Vol. 14, No. 4 (Fall 1974), pp. 63-79; *"Covenant as the Basis of the Jewish Political Tradition,"* ,Kinship and Consent:

10) The Jewish Political Tradition and it's Contemporary Uses, Elazar, ed. (Ramat Gan: Turtledove, 1981); Elazar and Cohen, *The Jewish Polity: Jewish Political Organizations from Biblical Times to the Present* (Bloomington: Indiana University Press, 1985).

11) *The Three Crowns: Structures of Communal Politics in Early Rabbinic Jewry; Stuart A Cohen (1990)*

12) *"Intercession: Moving Mountains by Living Eucharistically,"* George Kosicki, Faith Publishing Company): p. 22.

Contemporary postmodern American society is highly narcissistic, and far beyond individualism.
Narcissism is post-Sheilaism

For further reading and information:

Robert Bellah, "The Protestant Structure of American Culture: Multiculture or Monoculture?", *Hedgehog Review* 4, no. 1 (spring 2002): 7-28. You can read more of Bellah's articles and lectures on his website.
Rebecca Arrington,"*Bellah urges search for the common good,*"*Inside UVA Online,*   November 17-30, 2000.
Robert Bellah, et al., *Habits of the Heart: Individualism and Commitment in American Life* (University of California Press, 1985).
Being the Body, an updated edition of *The Body* is published

Chapter 2

1) *www.beliefnet.com/faiths/catholic/2005/04/what-is-relativism.aspx*
2) *Dictatorship of Relativism, The: Pope Benedict XVI's Response;* Ratzinger (Society of Saint Paul/Alba House 2011)
3) *www.theologyofwork.org/old-testament/exodus-and-work/israel-in-egypt-exodus-111316/gods-work-of-redemption-for-israel-exodus-51-628*

Chapter 3

1) *The Polity in Biblical Israel; Authority, Power and Leadership in the Jewish Polity: Cases and Issues - Chapter 1*; Daniel Elazar
2) *The Three Crowns: Structures of Communal Politics in Early Rabbinic Jewry [Stuart A. Cohen]*
3) *Israel and Its Bible: A Political Analysis;(1996) By Ira Sharkansky*
4) *The Book of Joshua as a Political Classic; Daniel J. Elazar*
5) *Important works by political scientists dealing with the Bible in this way include:*
6) *Benedict Spinoza, Theologico-Political Tractate (1670).*
7) *John Locke, First Treatise on Government (1689).*
8) *Hans Kohn, The Idea of Nationalism (New York: Macmillan, 1961).*
9) *Eric Voegelin, Israel, and Revelation (Baton Rouge: Louisiana State University Press, 1957).*
10) *Michael Walzer, Exodus and Revolution (New York: Basic Books, 1985).*
11) *Dealing with Fundamental Regime Change: The Biblical Paradigm of the Transition from Tribal Federation to Federal Monarchy Under David; Elazar*

12) *Malamat, "Organs of Statecraft in the Israelite Monarchy" The Biblical Archeologist 28 (2), 19656, pp. 34-50; Roland de Vaux, "The Administration of the kingdom", in Ancient Israel (New York, 1965) vol. 1 pp. 133-142*

Chapter 4

1) *The Polity in Biblical Israel-Authority, Power and Leadership in the Jewish Polity: Cases and Issues - Chapter 1;* Daniel J. Elazar
2) On the era of the patriarchs, see A. Malamat, *"Origins and the Formative Period,"* in H.H. Ben Sasson, ed., *A History of the Jewish People* (Harvard University Press, 1976), pp. 3-87; B. Mazar, ed., *"The Patriarchs," The World History of the Jewish People, Vol. I* (New Brunswick, 1970); E.A. Speiser, ed., *"Genesis," The Anchor Bible, Vol. 1: Social Institutions* (New York, 1965), pp. 3-15.
3) *Chayei Sarah(Genesis 23:1-25:18); The Servant of Abraham; Mo'ray Ha'aish- Advanced Level Midrashic and Kabbalistic illustrations yhrweekly Parsha;* Rabbi Ari Kahn*(Midrash Rabbah. Genesis 60:15); Rabbi Eleazer*
4) *John Bright, A History of Israel, 3rd. ed. (Philadelphia: Westminster Press, 1982) G.E. Mendenhall, "Ancient Oriental and Biblical Law," Biblical Archeologist 17:2 (1954), pp. 26-46; M. Weinfeld, "Berit - Covenant vs. Obligation," Biblica 56:i (1975), pp. 109-128.*
5) *The Ancient Egyptian Culture Revealed;* Moustafa Gadalla
6) *From Atlantis to the Sphinx;* Colin Wilson (1996)
7) *Joseph in Egypt; Dr. Charles Aling (2003); Aling, Charles (1984) Egypt and Bible History. Grand Rapids MI: Baker.; Ward, William(1960) The Egyptian Office of Joseph Journal of Semitic Studies 5: 144-50.;*
8) *The Gods of the Egyptians; British Egyptologist, E. A. Wallis Budge,[1969]*

Chapter 5

1) *The Concept of the Three Ketarim;* Stuart A. Cohen, (Ramat Gan: Bar Ilan University, 1986); J. Mailenberg, "The 'Office' of the Prophet in

Ancient Israel" in J.P. Hyatt (ed), The Bible in Modern Scholarship (1966), pp. 79-97.

2) M. Weinfeld, *"Judge and Officer in Ancient Israel and in the Ancient Near East,"* Israel Oriental Studies 7 (1977), pp. 65-88; "Keter ve-Atarah," *Encyclopedia Mikra'it,* Vol. 4 (Jerusalem, 1962), clmns. 405-408; Stuart Cohen, *The Concept of the Three Ketarim: Its Place in Jewish Political Thought and Its Implications for a Study of Jewish Constitutional History,* Paper No. 18 (Jerusalem: Center for Jewish Community Studies, 1982), pp. 1-40, "Keter as a Jewish Political Symbol: Origins and Implications" in *Jewish Political Studies Review,* I:1-2 (Spring, 1989); C. Umhau Wolf, "Terminology of Israel's Tribal Organization," *Journal of Biblical Literature.*

3) *The Polity in Biblical Israel; Authority, Power and Leadership in the Jewish Polity: Cases and Issues* - Chapter 1; Daniel J. Elazar

4) (Ephesians 1:20, Hebrews 1:3, Hebrew 8:1, Hebrews 9:23-25, Acts 7:49, Revelation 4:1-2, Revelation 7:9 Revelation 19:1-4)

5) (Matthew 3:2, 4:17, 6:10, 6:33, 9:35, Matthew 18:3, Mark 10:14-15, Luke 12:32, Luke 17:21, John 3:5, 18:36, Romans 14:17, 1 Corinthians 4:20, Colossians 1:12-22).

6) *The Book of Joshua as a Political Classic;* Daniel J. Elazar

7) John Bright, *A History of Israel,* 3rd. ed. (Philadelphia: Westminster Press, 1982); G.E. Mendenhall, "Ancient Oriental and Biblical Law" *Biblical Archeologist* 17:2 (1954), pp. 26-46; M. Weinfeld, "Berit - Covenant vs. Obligation," *Biblica* 56:i (1975), pp. 109-128.

8) *The Concept of the Three Ketarim: Its Place in Jewish Political Thought and Its Implications for a Study of Jewish Constitutional History;* Stuart A. Cohen Volume 9, Issue 1 Spring 1984, pp. 27-54

Chapter 6

1) *Dealing with Fundamental Regime Change: The Biblical Paradigm of the Transition from Tribal Federation to Federal Monarchy Under David;* Daniel J. Elazar

2) *Covenant & Polity in Biblical Israel: Biblical Foundations & Jewish*

Expressions; Volume 1; (1998) Daniel Elazar (pg.238-240)(pg.298-302)

3) *The Concept of the Three Ketarim Stuart A Cohen (1986); "The 'Office' of the Prophet in Ancient Israel" in J.P. Hyatt (ed), J Mailenburg The Bible in Modern Scholarship (1966), pp. 79-97*

4) *B. Halpern, The Constitution of the Monarchy in Israel (Harvard Semitic Monographs No. 25, 1981). The idea that the Torah should be understood as the constitution of the Jewish people is an old and oft-recurring one, expressed by traditional and modern thinkers, as diverse as Spinoza, who understood the Torah as a political constitution first and foremost, and Mendelsohn, who viewed the political dimension as utterly dispensable. See Benedict Spinoza, Politico-Theologico Tractate; Moses Mendelsohn, Jerusalem, and Eliezer Schweid, "The Attitude Toward the State in Modern Jewish Thought Before Zionism" in Elazar, ed., op. cit.*

5) *A. Alt, "The Formation of the Israelite State," in Essays on Old Testament History and Religion (New York, 1966); Daniel J. Elazar, "Dealing with Fundamental Regime Change: The Biblical Paradigm of the Transition from Tribal Federation to Federal Monarchy of David," in Jacob Neusner, Ernest S. Frerichs, and Nahum M. Sarna, eds. From Ancient Israel to Modern Judaism (Atlanta: Scholars Press, 1989), Vol. I, pp. 97-129; Moshe Weinfeld, "From God's Edah to the Chosen Dynasty: The Transition from the Tribal Federation to the Monarchy," in Kinship and Consent, pp. 151-166; J. Levenson, "The Davidic Covenant and Its Modern Interpreters," Catholic Bible Quarterly 41 (ii) (1979); W.A. Irwin, "Saul and the Rise of the Monarchy," American Journal of Semitic Languages and Literature 58 (1941), pp. 113-138.*

6) *THE ANTIQUITIES OF THE JEWS; By Flavius Josephus; Translated by William Whiston*

7) *Covenant as the Basis of the Jewish Political Tradition; Kinship and Consent, Chapter One; Daniel J. Elazar; Martin A. Cohen, "The Role of the Shilonite Priesthood in the United Monarchy of Ancient Israel" in Hebrew Union College Annual (Cincinnati: Hebrew Union College, 1965), Vol. XXXVI; Josephus's Antiquities of the Jews; Abravanel's commentary Deuteronomy -Samuel; and Buber's Kingship of God (New York: Harper and Row, 1967). Elijah-traditionally been considered an anti-monarchist; the biblical portrayal is a more complex position, supporting Ahab as King but seeking to keep the*

*monarchy tied to the Torah as mediated through the prophets. The reference here
is to the tradition rather than to the more complex reality*

Chapter 7

1) *Birth of the Messiah*, Father Raymond Brown, New York: Doubleday, 1993.
2) *Ancient Israel,* Father R. De Vaux, New York: McGraw-Hill, 1961.
3) *"Tract Sanhedrin, Volume VIII, XVI, Part II (Haggada), Chapter XI"*, *The Babylonian Talmud* Boston: The Talmud Society, p. 376 Translated by Michael L. Rodkinson
4) A. Alt, *"The Monarchy in the Kingdoms of Israel and Judah,"* in *Essays on Old Testament History and Religion* (1951), English translation (Oxford: Basil Blackwell and Mott, 1966), pp. 239-259; A. Malamat, "Organs of Statecraft in the Israelite Monarchy," *Biblical Archeologist* 28 (2) (1956), pp. 34-50; Roland de Vaux, "The Administration of the Kingdom," in *Ancient Israel* (New York, 1965), Vol. 1, pp. 133-142; B. Halpern, *The Constitution of the Monarchy in Israel* (Harvard Semitic Monographs, 1981), No. 25; Y. Kaufman, "The Monarchy," *The Religion of Israel* (Chicago, 1960), pp. 262-270.
5) *"Organs of Statecraft in the Israelite Monarchy"*, A. Malamat; *The Biblical Archeologist* 28 (2), 19656, pp. 34-50; Roland de Vaux, "The Administration of the kingdom", in *Ancient Israel* (New York, 1965)
6) vol. 1 pp. 133-142.

Chapter 8

1) *Mary, the New Eve, freely obeyed God; Pope John Paul II, General Audience; Sept.18, 1996*
2) *Romans 5 12-21: 1Corinthians 15 45-49*
3) *[See: David Noel Freedman, ed-in-chief., The Anchor Bible Dictionary, vol 5 (New York: Doubleday, 1992) 629.]*

4) *Old Testament Types of Mary– Father Johann Roten, S.M/ udayton.edu/imri/mary/o/old-testament-types-of-mary.phd*
5) *Septuagint LLX Esther 15: 8-10 Esther 4:10-5:3*
6) *Esther: the queen Esther-Mary connection/TimStaples.com*
7) *Targum on Ruth 2:12/ Rabbi Ruth 5.5 at 2:13 Peskita of Rob. Kohaha 26. 1.*

Chapter 9

1) *Passover: A Summary of our Current Understanding* Norman S Edwards Mustard Seed News
2) *Qorbanot: Sacrifices and Offerings;* www.Jewishvirtuallibrary.com
3) *Qorbanot: Sacrifices and Offerings; Judaism101;* www.jewfaq.com
4) *Doctrine Concerning the Sacrifices of the Mass; Chapter 2;* The Canons and Decrees of the Council of Trent(1563)
5) *Passover; Catholic Encyclopedia;* New Advent; www.newadvent.org
6) OESTERLY, BOX, Religion and Worship of the synagogue (London, 1907); DEMBITZ, Jewish Services in the Synagogue and Home (Philadelphia, 1898); GINSBURG in KITTO, Cyclop. Of Bibl. Lit..; ABRAHAMS in HASTINGS, Dict. Of the Bible, s.v. Passover; SMITH, Bibl. Dict.; ZANGWILL, Dreamers of the Ghetto (London): JACOBS, Jewish Year Book (LONDON, annual); EDERSHEIM, Life and Times of Jesus the Messiah, II (London, 1900), 479.This article was transcribed for New Advent by John Looby. *Nihil Obstat.* February 1, 1911. Remy

Chapter 10

1) *Eucharisticum Mysterium (1967), Instruction on Eucharistic Worship, Sacred Congregation of Rites*
2) *Encyclical Letter, ECCLESIA DE EUCHARISTIA of his holiness Pope John Paul II*
3) *"Doctrine Concerning the sacrifice of the Mass", Chapter 2, The Canons and Decrees of the Council of Trent. Session XXII(1743)*

4) *Pius XII, Encyclical Letter Mediator Dei (20 November 1947): AAS 39 (1947), 548*

5) *Vat. II Const. on Lit., Sacrosanctum Concilium, n. 47-AAS 56(19646)*

6) *(Luther's Works, 37, 317)*

7) *Aufer a Nobis, The Latin Mass Society of Ireland; The Text of the Mass; Part 3; The Mass of the Catechumens*

Chapter 11

1) *Strongs Concordance;G1492 eido;G1097 ginosko*

2) *A somewhat different version that illustrates the connection between tradition and the constructs of society, appeared in the Jewish Journal of Sociology, Vol. XX No. 1 (June 1978):5-37*

3) *Birth of the Messiah, Father Raymond Brown, New York: Doubleday, 1993.*

4) *Ancient Israel, Father R. De Vaux, New York: McGraw-Hill, 1961.*

5) *Covenant & Polity in Biblical Israel: Biblical Foundations & Jewish Expressions By Daniel Elazar page 239; page 355*

6) *What's An Ebenezer? By: Dr. Gregory S. Neal*

7) *God's Federal Republic: Reconstructing Our Governing Symbol; William J Everett (New York 1988) pg 106*

8) *God and Globalization: Volume 3: Christ and the Dominions of Civilization; Max L Stackhouse; Continuum (2001); page 191*

Chapter 12

• There are summaries of the first eleven chapters in chapter twelve. The reference was cited in the chapter that it appeared, and not here. The Didache and the Church Fathers were all taken from the *New Advent.org, Catholic Encyclopedia/Churchfathers.*

1) George Kosicki, *"Intercession: Moving Mountains by Living Eucharistically,"* (Faith Publishing Company): p. 22.

2) *Didache, The Teaching of the Twelve Apostles* (c. 50-70 CE)

3) Ignatius *(Letter to the Smyrnaeans 6:2–7:1 [A.D. 110])*
4) Ignatius *(Letter to the Philadelphians 4 [A.D. 110])*
5) Justin Martyr *(First Apology 66 [A.D. 151])*
6) Hippolytus *(The Apostolic Tradition 21:16 [A.D. 215])*
7) Pope Clement *(Letter to the Corinthians 1, 58–59, 63 [A.D. 80])*
8) Ignatius *(Letter to the Romans 1:1 [A.D. 110])*
9) Origen *(Homilies on Exodus 5:4 [A.D. 248])*
10) Ignatius *(Letter to the Magnesians 2 [A.D. 110] (ibid., 6:1)*
11) Clement of Alexandria *(Miscellanies 6:13:107:2 [A.D. 208])*
12) Ignatius *(Letter to the Philadelphians 3 [A.D. 110])*
13) Irenaeus *(Against Heresies 3:22:24 [A.D. 189])*
14) Hippolytus *[c. 170-236](S. Hippolytus, In Dan.vi., Patr. Gr., Tom. 10, p. 648) (Blessed Virgin, p. 77)*
15) St. Gregory *[c. 213-270](Orat. in Deip. Annunciat. Int. Opp. S. Greg. Thaumaturg) (Blessed Virgin, p. 89).*

Index

A

Aaron, 60–62, 66–67, 82, 85, 87, 91, 97, 110, 119, 126, 172

Aaron's rod, 120–21

Aaron's sons, 82

Abraham, 28–30, 33, 37, 51–53, 60, 62–63, 65, 108, 130, 161, 163–64, 174, 176

Abrahamic Covenant, 40, 51, 53, 66, 174

everlasting, 54

… Household of God, 114

Abraham is our Father, 163

Abraham's death, transcended, 54

Abraham's household, 62, 101

Absalom's Monument, 162

abyss, 92, 142, 176

Acts, 3, 20–21, 42, 44, 60, 67, 74, 126, 149, 170–71, 176

Adam's disobedience, 107

Adat B'nai Yisrael, 43, 81-82, 88, 90, 143, 158, 169

administration, 41, 187, 190

administrative body complex, 175, 177

Adonijah, 99, 113–14

adultery, 41, 98

ages, patriarchal, 51–52

Agnostic, 23

agreement
 bilateral, 37
 covenantal, 95

agricultural festival, 132

Akhenaten, 56

altar, 124, 126, 138, 141–43, 148–49, 152, 155, 169, 172, 174, 176, 182
 local, 45, 152
 new, 44, 73, 141, 143–44, 148–50, 173, 178
 sin of stealing from the, 138

ambassadors, 31–32, 144, 148, 176

American civil religion, 12

anarchy, confederal, 16, 80

Ancient Israel, 13, 52, 55, 59, 187–90, 192

Ancient Israelite ratification ceremony, 92

anoint, 78, 95–96

Apostle James, 169

Apostle Matthew, 157

Apostle Paul, 3, 29, 145

Apostles, 3, 38, 142, 144–45, 147, 167–69, 172, 174, 177, 180–83, 192
 teachings of the twelve, 181

Apostolic age, 74, 180

Apostolic Church, 149, 164, 169

Apostolic Succession, 177, 180

Apostolic Tradition, 180, 182,

Ascension, 137, 166–68

Asherah, 115

assembly
 fledgling, 61
 national, 43

Athaliah, 116–17
atonement, 138–39
Augustine, 78, 134
authority
  central, 13
  civil, 67–69
  delegated, 68, 101
  divisions of, 51, 66, 68, 71, 75, 91, 100, 173
  handed down Apostolic, 177
  national, 44
  positions of, 52, 114
  tripartite divisions of, 74, 105

B
Babylon, 106, 112
Babylonian exile, 78, 122
baptism, 76, 136, 146, 166–67, 172, 182
Baptist, 103, 121–22, 158
Bathsheba, 98–100, 113–14
… Gebirah Queen Mother, 99
B'Chol dor vador, 129
Beersheba, 84–85, 117
Bellah, 9–10, 16–17, 186
Betrothal Cup, 130
Bishop Ignatius, Antioch 180 181–83
Bishop of Rome, 18
Bishop of Smyrna, 184
bishops, 73, 93–94, 144–45, 160, 177, 179–80, 182–83
  offices of, 72, 145
Blessed Virgin Mary, 109, 113, 119, 184
Blessed Virgin Mary's role, 120
blessing, Cup of, 127, 130

blood, 36, 73, 124–25, 127, 130, 133, 135, 138–39, 141–42, 145–46, 148–54, 170, 173–74, 178–79, 181–82
board, national Elder, 66
body, 10–11, 77, 138–39, 141, 143, 146, 148–50, 152, 154, 169–70, 174, 176, 178, 181, 185–86
body and blood, 73, 139, 145, 150–51, 153–54, 178
body politic, 40, 43, 45, 81, 85
bond, 125, 151, 153, 159, 166, 170
bondage, 15, 20, 30–31, 35, 48, 125–26, 129, 131, 135, 139, 171
Book of Obadiah, 103
booths, 133
Brazen Altar, 143
Brazen Laver, 152
bread, 73, 124, 127, 135, 137, 139, 144–48, 150, 170
  break, 181
  consecrated, 149
  daily, 133, 145–46, 150, 152, 177
  unleavened, 35, 37, 124, 130, 135, 144, 152
bread and wine, 65, 77, 141, 152, 178
Bread of Life discourse, 146
bride, 3, 31, 53–54, 107, 130, 133, 158, 164, 169–70, 174–75
bridegroom, 31, 144, 152, 172, 174, 179
Burnt Offering, 90, 137

C
cabinet, 73, 81, 94, 97, 114, 176
cairn, 41, 93

cairn guideposts, 150
cairn markers, 162
Calvary, 77, 107, 110, 173
Calvin, 11, 17–18, 74, 185
Cana, 110, 118, 146
Canaan, 32, 39–40, 55, 62
Canaan wilderness, 15
Cardinals work, 176
Catholic, 1, 5, 8, 12–13, 24, 28, 149, 169
Catholic Church, 5
Catholic doctrine, 61
Catholic Theologians, 11
ceremonies, 3, 29, 88, 92–94, 99, 152, 171
  marital, 133
  national, 90
  ratification, 36, 92, 94
chair, 159, 161–62, 180, 182
chief councilor, 114
chief overseer, 58
Chief Priests and teachers of the Law, 167
Chief Servant, 48, 53–54, 62–63, 101–3, 158–62, 169–70, 174–75
  recognized, 48
… Verses, 103
Chief Steward, 39–41, 53–54, 58–60, 66, 73, 81, 86, 101–3
children, baptize, 136
Christ
  ambassadors for, 144
  believing in, 146
  blood of, 127, 151
  body of, 16, 77, 127, 139, 143, 154, 170
  the bride of, 158, 164, 169–70

  confronted, 165
  new creatures in, 107
  in the person of, 152
Christianity, 1, 7–8, 10–11, 17–18, 20–21, 23, 26, 33, 48, 73, 75
  biblical, 18
  historic, 11
  modern, 63
  orthodox, 75
  post-denominational, 75
  separated Post-reformation, 74
Christian pantheon, contemporary, 21
Christians
  biblical, 26
  contemporary, 11
Christ's office of Chief Servant, 159
Christ's Passion, 158
Christ's Seventy, 163
Chuppah, 132–33
church
  apostate, 18, 24
  authentic, 53, 55, 63, 73, 181
  early, 9, 13, 16, 18, 32, 48, 75, 92, 145
  once-delivered, 13
  recognizable, 30
  seeker, 10
  true, 20, 28
  universal, 151
church councils, 150–51
Church Fathers, 2, 9, 171, 180, 192
Church Militant, 158
Church of Acts, 3
church of one, 21–22
church split, 62
Church's sacerdotal duties, 139

Church Triumphant, 158
City of Jerusalem, 97
city on a hill, 15, 66, 169
civilizations, 39, 43, 63, 192
civil servants, national, 45
clean oblation, 179
cleansing, final, 136
Clement, 180, 183
climax, 82, 129, 131
cloud, 21, 72, 119, 167
cognitive dissonance, 8, 27
Cohen, Stuart A., 15, 71, 185, 187–88
collectivism, 22
Colson, Charles, 10–11, 185
commandments, 41, 44, 120, 163
commissioner, high, 87–88, 96, 98, 104
common good, 13
common practices, 15
commonwealth
  balanced, 13
  good, 15, 40
communalism, 12–13
communion, 31, 47, 62, 78, 125, 127, 149–51, 154, 158, 183
  symbolic, 150
community, 10, 12–13, 16, 34, 137, 153
  political, 13
community leaders, 69
confession, 148, 154, 183
confirmations, 100, 132, 143
congregation, 14–15, 24, 26, 39, 45–46, 60, 62, 68, 82–83, 85, 88–89, 95, 174
  tabernacle of the, 43

Congregation of Israelites, 48
Connacht, 92–93, 99
constitution, 37, 44–45, 60–61, 69, 99–100, 104–5, 189–90
  covenantal, 14, 16, 66
constructs, 159–60, 163, 166, 192
consummation, 77, 137, 151, 153–54
Corinthians, 73, 139, 145, 149–50, 182, 188, 192
Council of seventy, 163, 172, 175
counselor, 113–14, 170, 176, 180
court, inner, 95, 112, 143
covenant, 13–15, 31, 40–48, 52, 60–61, 66–68, 78–79, 84, 87–88, 96–101, 104–5, 119, 122, 128–30, 159–60, 164, 171–72, 187–89
  first, 51, 53, 142, 161, 176
  multi-lateral, 74
  patriarchal, 55
  ratified, 130
  separate, 60, 66, 70, 96
Covenantal Law, 51
covenantal system, 104
covenant-making Lord, 168
Covenant-making Promise-keeping God, 30
Covenant-making Son, 136
Covenant Virgin Mary, 120
crowd, bible alone, 142
crowns, 15, 65, 67–68, 71, 74, 104, 106, 114, 123, 176, 185–86
  glorious, 106, 115
crucifixion, 143, 166
cult, 7, 22, 24
Cultural Relativism, 22
Cup of Deliverance, 129

Cup of Deliverance/Judgment, 128
Cup of Praise, 131
Cup of Redemption, 130
Cup of Redemption/Blessing, 128
Cup of Sanctification, 128–29
Cup of Thanksgiving, 130
cups
  first, 129
  fourth, 126–29, 131, 136
  second, 129
  spiritual, 148
  third, 4, 124–25, 127, 130–31, 135,
148, 156, 178

D
daily Provision, 145, 172
Damascus, 169
David, 87, 92, 95–102, 110, 113–15,
119, 121, 125, 156, 161–62, 180,
186, 188–89
David, King, 72, 96, 99–100, 121
Davidic Covenant, 170, 189
Davidic kingdoms, 63, 101, 107–8,
175
Davidic Monarchy, 62
Davidic Queen Mothers, 112
David's son Absalom, 116
deacons, 25, 144, 160, 177, 182–83
Deborah, 110
Deconstructionism, 22, 26–27
deliverance, 31, 35, 89, 109, 128–29,
131, 152
  great, 57, 63
  personal, 130
Deliverance/Judgment, 128
denominations, 10, 19, 33, 149
  first cousin-once-removed, 18

protestant, 6
descendants, 14, 37, 44, 46, 54, 63,
76, 82, 97–98, 110, 116
destination, eternal, 129, 131
Deuteronomy, 105, 120, 189
devotion, 110–11, 138, 151
Diabolical Disorientation, 21
Diakonia, 160
Didache, 181, 192
Diocesan Cathedrals, 179
disciples
  making, 170
  trusted, 74
disciples partook, 132
Divine, 68–70
Divine authorization, 69
Divine Providence, 110
divinity, 8, 56, 69, 77, 118, 122, 139,
152, 154, 174, 177–79
divisions, 10, 13, 17, 20, 66, 82, 173–
74, 183
  ketaric, 68
  tripartite, 66, 97
divorce, 33, 164
domains, 66, 68–72, 74, 80, 82, 85,
89–91, 97, 99, 103, 177
  civil, 85
domains of authority, 74–75, 81, 92,
162, 175
drinks judgment, 150
dynastic principle, 98
dynasties, 57, 91, 166, 189

E
Early Church Fathers, 181
Early Rabbinic Jewry, 15, 185–86
earthly king, 16, 34, 39, 47–48, 50,

69, 78, 85–86, 155–56, 171, 173

earthly throne, 41, 43, 48, 101

Easter Tridium, 135

ecumenism, 24, 26

Edah, 41–45, 60, 66–68, 70, 99, 143, 189

Egypt, 15, 20, 35–37, 48, 51, 54–58, 60, 62, 124–26, 128–30, 132–35, 164, 166

Egyptian captivity, 35, 67

Egyptian Hellenists, 171

Egyptian kingdom, 56

Egyptian pantheon, 56

Egyptian queen, 115

Egyptian's firstborn, 36

Egyptian Vizier, 58

Ekklesia, 174

Elazar, Daniel, 40, 52, 55, 59, 61, 64, 79, 166, 186, 188, 189

Elder/Priests, 144

elders, 46, 51, 55, 60, 66–67, 69, 80, 86, 96–97, 103, 175–76

Eli, 81–84, 87, 143

Eliakim, 101–2, 162

Eliezer, 53–54, 60, 63, 101

Elijah, 38, 103, 167, 189

Elijah's cup, 128

Eli's sin, 83, 92

Eli's sons, 83–84

Elizabeth, 110, 120–22

Emmaus, 168

enter in, 143–44, 152

Ephesians, 158, 188

era, 12, 15, 25, 39, 59, 63, 79, 84, 105
    monarchal, 105

establishment, 12, 15, 37, 44, 48, 52, 60, 87–88, 166

Esther, 112–13, 190

Eternal Father, 139, 179

Eucharist, 17, 135, 140–41, 149–51, 153, 170, 172, 174, 179, 181–82

Eucharistic Mass, 179

Eucharistic mystery, 178

Eucharistic Prayer, 152, 179

Eucharistic Sacrifice, 153

Eucharisticum Mysterium, 140, 191

evangelical, 1, 6, 10–11, 24–25, 28, 33

Evangelical Christianity, 26

evangelical denominations, 150

Eve, 107–8, 119

Eved Adonai, 16, 39–40, 42, 44, 46, 48, 50–51, 53, 59–61, 63, 66–69, 80–81, 104, 158–59, 175–76
    last recognized, 62
    office of, 51, 79, 81, 89, 91, 174
    term, 40
… Servant, 50

Eved Elohim, 161

Eved Neeman, 60, 63

Everlasting Father, 170, 180

Eve's disobedience, 183

Exodus, 28–30, 35, 38, 51, 55, 60–61, 120, 125–30, 132, 134, 138, 182, 186

Exodus journey, 129, 131

Ezekiel, 20, 40, 108, 118, 159, 166

Ezekiel's utopia, 40

F

faith
    deposit of, 2, 150
    source and summit of, 179

faithfulness, 31, 91, 103, 112, 166,

172
families, royal, 87, 94–96
father, calling priests, 101
Father Abraham, 163
Fatima, 21
feast, 37, 131, 133, 167, 172
Feast of Tabernacles, 36–38, 133, 166, 167, 172
Fellowship Offering, 137
festivals, 3, 37–38, 119, 129, 131, 133–35, 139
    spring, 37
First Temple, 72, 105
flesh, 54, 76, 120, 135, 147–48, 173, 178, 181–82
forefathers, 30, 52, 163
foreshadows, 3, 134, 151
forgiveness, 72, 90, 98, 168
Former Prophets, 76, 78
Four-Step Plan of Redemption, 28
fruit, first, 37, 131–32, 139
fruit harvest, 37
Full Gospel, 1
Fundamental Regime Change, 79, 186, 188–89

G
Gate of Mercy, 156
Gebirah, 106–8, 112–13, 115–16, 118, 136, 176
Gebirah Queen Mother, 99
Gehenna, 111, 119
Gentiles, 30, 75, 142, 156, 169, 179
Gethsemane, 118, 128
Gideon, 47, 87, 104
Gihon, 99–100
God

covenant-making, 36, 130
covenant   making-promise
keeping, 29
    making, 16, 34
    word of, 16, 120, 140, 182
Gods Sovereign leadership, 48
Golden Gate, 155–56
Good Friday, 136
Good Shepherd, 165
gospel, delivered, 162
governance, civil, 17, 68, 73–74, 78, 104, 125
government, 20, 41, 43, 59–60, 66, 74, 96–97, 104, 170, 180, 186
    civil, 67, 74
    federal, 13, 60
    portable seat of, 41
governor, 52, 88–89, 94, 102
grace, 30, 37, 76, 107, 109, 111–12, 120, 123, 141, 148, 153–54
Grain Offering, 137
grammatical genders, 160–61
Grand Vizier, 113
Great Commission, 168
Great Council, 175
Great Lady, 108, 176
    dignity of, 115
Great Sanhedrin, 175
group thinking, 22
Guilt Offering, 137–38

H
Haggadah, 125–26, 129
Hallel, 126, 128, 131
harvest, grain, 37
heaven
    kingdom of, 15, 156–57, 159

new, 32, 76
queen of, 115, 176
Heavenly Altar, 75
Heavenly Gift, 148, 154, 170
Heavenly Tabernacle, 77, 145, 150, 152
Hebrew Roots Movement, 8
Hebrews, 61, 63, 76–77, 120–21, 134, 137, 140–42, 149, 160, 164, 168, 188
hell, gates of, 159, 161
Hellenistic priests, 156
Hellenization, 171
Herod, 155–56
Hezekiah, 117
hierarchy, complex, 175
Hierateia, 160
High Priest, 41, 44–45, 66, 75, 77–78, 82, 99, 141, 143–45, 155, 178
  eternal, 121
  interim, 91
  legitimate, 121
High Steward, 93–94, 101–2
Hippolytus, 182–83, 192
Holy Commonwealth, 12–14, 17, 37, 40, 48, 52, 65, 68–69, 75, 78–79, 81, 91, 165–66
  great, 72
  new, 169
Holy Ghost, 144, 149, 163, 183
  promised, 169
Holy of Holies, 82, 119, 121, 139, 143, 149
Holy Saturday, 136
Holy Spirit, 2, 6–9, 17–18, 27, 34, 109, 119–20, 122, 140–41, 168, 182
Holy Thursday, 136

Holy Trinity, 170
Holy Virgin, 184
Hosanna, 156
household, 51, 53–54, 58–59, 62, 66, 93–94, 101, 103, 108, 158, 161
household of god, 53, 62, 76
house of Judah, 96, 101, 164, 166
humility, 53–54, 103, 111
Hymns, unending, 151, 179

I
idolatry, 39, 41, 46–47, 79–80, 90, 105, 174
Ignatius, 180, 182, 192
inauguration, 93
incident, golden calf, 70, 143
individualism, 12–13, 61, 185–86
  radical, 10, 22
Ingathering, 38
inheritance, 90–91, 166
institutions, traditional, 67, 97
intercedes, 84, 99, 113, 164, 170, 176
intercession, 85, 112–13, 185, 192
Irenaeus, 180, 183
Isaac, 28–29, 53–54, 124, 130, 163
Isaiah, 101–2, 108, 161–62, 170, 180
isms, 21–22
Israel, 12–16, 28–29, 32–37, 39–42, 44–49, 66–69, 72–73, 78–89, 95–97, 99, 108–17, 131, 133, 135–37, 152, 157, 161–66, 173–74, 176–77, 186–90
Israelite Commonwealth, 37, 71
Israelite Monarchy, 187, 190
Israelite nation, 2, 45, 47, 55, 59, 76, 96, 99, 104, 132, 134
Israel's Matriarch, 108

Israel's Ministry of Reconciliation, 137

Israel's sin, 41

Ithamar, 82

J

Jacob, 14–15, 28–29, 54–55, 109, 130, 163

James, 166, 169, 172, 177

Jeremiah, 72, 106, 115–16, 164

Jericho, 42

Jerusalem, 97, 101, 115–16, 121, 156, 163, 168–69, 173, 175, 177, 188–89

Jerusalem Council, 16, 73, 150

Jerusalem Temple, 70

Jesus, 9–11, 34, 68–69, 73, 76–77, 102, 104–5, 118, 120, 146–48, 155–56, 158–59, 161–68, 170–71, 175

Jesus and me mentality, 142

Jewish kingdom, 165

Jewish Passover, 163

Jewish Queen Mother, 112

Jewish Tradition, 53, 110, 125, 130, 163

Jezebel, 103, 106, 117

Jochebed, 110

John, 76–77, 103, 106, 121–22, 124, 146, 148–49, 152, 155, 157–58, 164, 166, 178, 180, 188

Jordan, 29, 36, 41–42, 44–45, 131, 133, 136–37, 172

Joseph, 35, 46, 51, 54–55, 57–60, 62–63, 72, 109, 164, 187

Joseph's assent, 57

Joseph's ordination ceremony, 57

Joshua, 38–46, 48, 50, 59–60, 62–63, 69, 71, 78–79, 81–82, 84, 88, 186, 188

Joshua's Farewell, 45

Joshua-styled regime, 81

Josiah, King, 105

Judah, 96–97, 99, 101, 105–6, 110, 114–16, 118, 155, 164–66, 190

hill country of, 119–20

the house of, 96

province of, 158, 165

tribe of, 46, 165

Judah's Queen Mothers, 113

Judea, 2–3, 13, 21, 28, 30, 105, 120, 155, 163, 165, 174–75

Judges, 32–33, 35, 38–39, 45–47, 50, 61–63, 67, 69, 78–81, 83–87, 91, 110, 175

charismatic, 46

era of, 38, 66, 102

period of, 16, 35, 43, 78, 82, 91

judgment, 41, 98, 126–27, 129, 132, 170, 180

justice, 12–14, 75, 166, 170, 180

K

Kairos, 157, 173

Ketaric authority, 97

Ketaric branches, 99

Ketaric domains matter, 16

ketaric terminology, 68

ketarim, 65, 67–68, 70–71, 74, 78, 90–91, 99, 104, 177, 187–88

Keter Kehunah, 16, 65, 68, 70, 75, 80, 85, 94, 97, 100, 104, 144

Keter Malkhut, 50, 65, 68–70, 75,.80, 81, 85, 94, 97, 104

Keter Torah, 48, 50, 65, 68–70, 75,

80–81, 84, 88, 94, 98, 104, 110
keys, 101–2, 157, 159, 162, 175
Kiddush, Cup 128–29
kingdom
  ideal, 76
  identifiable, 165
  southern, 106, 164
Kingdom of Earth, Church, 166-67
Kingdom of God, 16, 31, 34, 76, 134–35, 143, 155, 157–60, 167, 170
Kingdom of Judah, 106, 155
kingdom perspective, 173
kingdoms keys, 102
Kingdoms Queen Mothers, 108
kingdom terminology, 157–58
King of Righteousness, 65
King's chief Counselor, 106
King's court, 161
kingship, hereditary, 47
kingship of God, 157–58, 189
knowledge of God, 124, 132
kohanim, 70–71, 138
Kohen Gadol, 70, 90

L
laity, 6, 70, 143, 151–52, 177
lamb, 35–36, 124–25, 137–38, 153
land of Egypt, 57–58, 133, 159, 164, 166
Larson, Sheila, 9
Last Supper, 127-28, 130, 134, 153, 179
leaders, 12, 15–16, 40, 44–45, 47, 51, 69, 73, 84, 86, 90, 174, 176
  national, 47, 67, 80, 85, 90, 95
leadership, sovereign, 31
leadership structure, ideal, 81

Leah, 110–11
Leah tribes, 110
Leitourgia, 160
Leitourgos, 160
lesser courts, appointed, 175
Levite priests, 143
Levites, 70, 85, 110, 125, 141, 177
Levitical law, 83
Levitical rites, 144
Leviticus, 82, 143
Litany, 126, 129
Lord God, 14, 100, 159, 166
Lord of all the Earth, 41
Lord's day, 136
Lord's death, 151
Lord's Supper, 151
loving-kindness, 14–15, 113, 133
Luke, 119–23, 128, 130, 134–35, 141, 151, 155, 157, 165, 168, 188
Luther, 11, 17–18, 74

M
Maacah, 114, 116
Maccabees, 68, 155
Magdalene, Mary, 168
Maggid, Cup 126, 128–29
Magisterium, 81
Malachi, 178–79
… prophesy, 179
Malamat, 187, 190
manna, 31, 36, 48, 119–20, 136, 145–48, 152, 172
  supernatural, 36, 38
marital Covenant, 31, 36–37, 133
marriage ceremony, 132–33
marriage feast, 118
Marty, Martin, 12

Martyr, Justin, 180, 182, 192
Marxism, 22
Mary, 107–11, 119–22, 176, 183, 190
Mary intercedes, 118
Mass, 138–40, 144–45, 150–54, 170, 179, 187, 191
  8-to-9,000, 179
  morning New, 179
Matriarchs, 107–10
  great, 108, 111
Matthew, 68–69, 74, 76, 133, 157–61, 164–65, 169, 188
Matthew's gender-izing, 161
meal, 37, 124, 126, 130, 132
Melchizedek, 65–66, 71, 141, 178
Melchizedekian Rite, 144, 152, 178
Melchizedek king, 65
melekh, 71, 87–88, 91, 96
Messiah, 108–10, 128, 155–56, 165, 169, 190–92
Midianites, 47
Midrash, 53, 130
Midrash Rabbah, 53–54, 187
milestones, 35, 37, 95, 126, 166
ministerial priest consecrates, 145
ministerial priesthood, 143
  ordained, 143
ministers, consecrated, 153
miraculous Matriarch, 176
Miriam, 61, 110
Mishnah, 128
Mishnah Pirkei Avot, 65
Modernism, 22, 24–26
Mosaic constitution, 15, 61, 79
Mosaic Covenant, 62, 66
Mosaic Law, 48, 61, 114, 130, 132–

33
Mosaic office, 16, 50–51
Moses, 29, 35–38, 50–52, 55, 59–60, 62–63, 66–69, 78, 82–83, 91–92, 110–11, 132–33, 162–63, 167–68, 175
Moses' authority, 50, 61
Moses' office, 50, 63
Moses our Teacher, 163
Moses' seat, 50–51, 68
Moses' sons, 87
Mother, Queen, 100, 103, 106, 108, 112–18, 170, 172, 176
Mother of God, 122
mother of those who truly live, 108
Mothers of Israel, 110–11, 119
Moustafa Gadalla, 55–56, 187
musical chairs, 158, 173
musical thrones, 92, 156–58, 173
mystery, 140, 173

N
nagid/melekh, 80, 87-88, 96, 161
Nasi, 163, 175
Nathan, 98–100
nation
  fledgling, 51
  foreign, 69
  set-apart, 15
  theocratic, 69
national historical marker, 42
nationalism, 81, 186
  renewed, 158
national patriotism, 12
national self-worship, 17
nation-building, 38
Navi, 71, 80

Nebuchadnezzar, 106
negidim, 98, 104
nesiim, 69, 80
New Adam, 107, 118
New Ark, 120
New Covenant, 119–20, 131, 135, 137, 139, 142–43, 149, 151, 157–59, 163–64, 171, 176, 178
New Covenant Creed, 151
New Covenant Gospel, 152
New Covenant Melchizedekian, 178
New Eve, 106–7, 118, 190
New Pentecost, 169
New Tabernacle, 143, 150, 177
New Testament, 6, 30, 75–76, 78, 107, 109, 136–37, 141, 164, 172, 180
Nicodemus, 146
Noah, 55
non-denominational, 6, 18, 33
Northern Kingdom, 102, 105, 113, 164–65

O
Obadiah, 102–3
obedience, 31, 111, 118–19, 174, 183
offerings
  perpetual, 142
  varied, 151
officeholder, 71, 161
offices, 50–51, 53, 58–60, 62–63, 65–66, 68–69, 71–73, 78–79, 97–99, 101–3, 111–12, 114–15, 144–45, 159–62, 175–77
  highest, 40, 91, 95, 175
  perpetual, 159, 161, 175
offices of Christ, 16, 65, 75

Old Ark, 120, 137
Old Covenant, 119–20, 157, 163, 170, 176
Old Law, 135
Old Manna, 147–48
Old Tabernacle Sacrifices, 137, 142
Old Temple, 156
Old Testament, 14, 16, 33–34, 48, 76–77, 81, 104–8, 125, 128, 137, 139, 143, 152–53
Old Testament Matriarchs, 108
Old Testament Queen Mother, 112
Omer, 36, 132, 136, 145
  counting of, 124, 167, 169
Oral Torah, 128
oral tradition, 17, 70, 74, 142, 163
ordained presbytery, 73
ordination, 68, 71–72, 144, 161, 175, 177
  ancient, 92
Ordination Ceremony, 71
Origen, 182, 192
our father Abraham, 163
overshadow, 109, 119
Overton's Window-Imagine, 23

P
pagans, 100, 112, 115
Paschal Lamb, 174
Paschal Sacrifice, 151
Passion, 136, 163
Passover, 3, 29, 31, 36–37, 124–29, 131–32, 134–37, 139, 153, 156, 191
  first, 36, 70, 124, 126
Passover lambs, 124, 135, 139
Passover Seder, 28–29, 124–26, 129, 131–32, 139, 150, 156

Passover vigil, 124, 136, 139

patriarchs, 52, 54–55, 60, 158, 163–64, 187

Paul, 71, 73, 135, 140–42, 144, 146, 148–49, 169, 172, 177, 180–81

peace, 3, 20, 34, 55, 65, 67, 154, 164, 170, 180

Peace Offering, 138

peg, 102, 160–61

Pentecost, 31, 36–37, 127, 131–32, 134, 136, 151, 167, 171–72, 175
  day of, 73, 132–33
  personal, 172

perfection, 108, 119, 137, 151, 153

period, anarchical Judges, 48

perpetual, 142, 153

Persona Christi, 145

personal interpretation, 75, 79

personal Jordan, 136

personal relationship, 11

Peter, 73, 96, 134, 136, 148, 159–62, 166–67, 169, 172, 175, 180–82

Petras, 159–60

Pharisees, 50, 52, 68–69, 77, 146, 149, 155–56, 163–64, 169, 175

Pilgrimage Festivals, 29, 37–38, 48, 127, 129

plan, redemptive, 2, 28–31, 126, 129

Plan of Salvation, 107–9, 111–12, 120, 136

pluralism, 22–24

polity, 40, 52, 55, 66, 73, 105, 185–86, 188

Polycarp, 180, 184

Pope, 6, 18, 80, 179

Pope Clement, 182, 192

Post-Reformation world, 39, 149

power, separation of, 40, 50, 61, 68, 75

presbyters, 72, 144, 177, 183

Presbytery, 144

presidency, 160, 182

president, 160, 163, 175

priesthood, 59, 65–66, 68, 70–71, 73–74, 78–79, 83, 89–91, 96–97, 140–41, 143–44, 160, 177
  common, 143, 152
  hereditary, 61, 80, 143
  royal, 143

priests
  chief, 58, 70, 75, 82, 90
  church of, 143, 177
  local ordained, 145
  ministerial, 151
  ordained, 143, 177
  trained, 143

priests eat, 138

Prime Minister, 40, 53, 59, 61, 63, 175

Prime Minister of Egypt, 58

prince, 96, 161, 164, 170, 180

Promised Land, 29, 31, 35–36, 38, 60, 126, 129, 133–34, 136, 174

prophetic, 16–17, 63, 66–68, 70, 74–75, 85, 89, 91–92, 99, 103, 105, 110

prophetic domain, 63, 69, 74, 92, 161, 177

prophetic responsibilities, 66–67

prophetic roles, 17, 68

prophetic theocracy, 60, 63

prophet Isaiah, 101

prophet Jeremiah, 164

prophets, 38, 62, 65–66, 68, 70–71, 73, 75–76, 78–82, 84–85, 90–91, 94,

96–100, 103–5, 167–70, 189

Protestant, 5–6, 8, 11, 142, 150

Protestant Christianity, post-, 11

Protestantism, 18, 33

Providence, 23, 25, 75, 159–60
  faithful, 31

Psalms, 91, 126, 131, 156, 168, 179

Purgatory, 136–37

purpose, redemptive, 28–29

Q

Qorbanot, 191

queen, 106, 113, 115, 176

Queen Mother Gebirah, 106

R

Rachel, 109–11

ratify, 68, 99, 105

Rebekah, 109, 111

reconciliation, 32, 70, 74, 77, 137, 153, 176
  ministry of, 31–32, 36, 71, 73, 119, 144–45, 148, 154, 170

redemption, 20–21, 28, 30–31, 107–8, 111, 126, 130–31, 136, 142
  work of, 29–30

Redemption/Blessing, 128

Redemption Plan of God, 21, 30, 108, 111, 126, 127,135–36

Red Sea, 36, 42, 124, 129, 136

regime, ideal, 40, 48

reign, 39, 76, 78, 86, 104, 115, 157–58, 160, 162

relationship, 3, 10–11, 14, 30–31, 124, 126, 129–32, 134, 137–39, 147, 150, 152–54, 158, 172–74, 177

Relativism, 21–22, 24–25, 186

dictatorship of, 22, 186

religion, civil, 12, 16–17

Religious Deconstructionism, 26–27

remembrance, 42, 70, 135, 139

repentance, 140–41

restoration, 16, 78, 131, 157, 160, 165, 175

Resurrection Sunday, 136, 167

Revelation, 122, 186, 188

Rite of Melchizedek, 178

rituals, 15, 29, 60–61, 66, 70–71, 80, 105, 124, 144, 152, 171

rock, 36, 41, 56, 85, 159–62, 182
  large, 46, 84
  large immovable, 160

role, 17, 50, 55–56, 69–70, 85, 90–91, 100, 104, 118, 122, 143, 145, 161
  prophetic domain's, 69

Roman Catholic Church, 5

Romans, 135, 155, 182, 188, 190, 192

Rome, 18, 30, 135, 171, 182

royal court, 73, 94, 97–99, 106, 114, 158

ruler over my people Israel, 88

Ruth, 111, 190

S

Sabbath, 134, 145
  great, 136

Sacramentarian-ism, 149–50

sacraments, 31, 149, 153, 170, 172

Sacred Scripture, 54, 76, 115, 140

Sacred Tridium, 139

sacrifices, 43–44, 70, 72, 89–90, 109, 111, 124–26, 136–44, 151–55, 172–

73, 177–79, 181–82, 191
  clean, 179
  continual burnt, 138
  evening, 124, 138, 140
  many and varied, 137
  morning's, 138
  perpetual, 173, 176
  pure, 180–81
  tabernacle, 31
  true, 178
  unending, 179
  varied, 137, 139, 145, 151, 178
Sadducees, 156, 163, 175
salvation, 2–3, 24, 28, 108–9, 111–12, 120–21, 134, 136, 140, 182–83
salvation history, 14, 29, 47, 136, 160
sanctification, 126, 128–29, 182
sanctuary, 87, 120–21, 138, 143–44, 151–52, 178
  true, 138, 141
Sanhedrin, 51, 155, 162–63,171, 175
Sarah, 108–9, 111, 176
Saul, 72, 87–90, 92, 95–97, 100, 175, 189
Saul's missteps and David's sidesteps, 96
scribes, 50, 52, 56, 68–69, 102, 146, 163, 171
scriptural calisthenics, 3
Seat, Moses, 68–69
Second Commonwealth, 68
Second Temple Period, 68, 72
secularism, 17, 75, 82
Seder, 125, 128–29
Seder meal, evening Passover, 37
Seder service, 126, 129

semikhah, 71
Servant of the Lord, 40, 51, 59, 86, 101, 159–60
servants, 16, 34, 41, 44, 46, 51, 53–54, 59, 61, 63, 66–67, 86–87, 99, 101–2, 174–75
  faithful, 60, 63
set order, 125–26, 144, 152
seventy elders, 175
shadow of things to come, 2–3, 28, 111, 125
Shavuot festival, 132
Shebna, 101–2, 162
sheep, lost, 165, 169
Sheila, 9, 11–12, 22, 28
Sheila-ism, 9-11, 21
Shekinah, 72, 119, 152, 173
Shemesh, Beth, 84
shepherd, 21, 76, 145, 161, 180
Shiloh, 43, 45, 82–85, 90, 131
shotrim, 55, 67, 69, 80
Side Note, 23, 52, 146, 160, 176
Simon, 155, 160
Sinai, 15, 30–31, 36–37, 51, 53, 63, 67, 70, 129, 131–33, 151
Sinai covenant, 16
Sin Offering, 137
sins
  confessing, 143
  remission of, 72, 149, 182
Skepticism, 22–23
Socialism, 12
social programs, large national, 13
Sofer, Moses, 71
Sole Mediator, 141–42
solidarity, 12–13, 16, 60
Solomon, King, 113–14

Solomon's sins and idolatry, 105
Son of God, 76, 109, 119–20, 141, 151, 164
Sorrowful Mother, 110
soul, body blood, 177
Southern tribes, 97
Sovereign, 48, 60, 67, 81, 89, 92, 105, 157, 165, 173
Sovereign Lord, 62, 158, 160
Sovereignty, 59, 67, 157–58, 173, 175
Sovereignty of God, 75, 174
spiritual cleansing, final, 36
stallion, white, 69, 155, 173
St. Gregory, 120, 184
St. Irenaeus, 107
stone, large, 82, 161
stone cairn, 42
stone monuments, 162
Stone of Scone, 93–94
Subjective truth, 22
Subsidiarity, 12–13, 16, 61
supplication, 71, 151–52, 178–79

T
Tabernacles, 36–38, 60, 77–78, 82–83, 119, 124–27, 131, 133–38, 140–43, 145, 149, 151–52, 166–67, 172, 177
    earthly, 141
    temporary, 167
    time of, 167, 172
Tabernacles' Time, 172
Talmudic homilies, 74
taxation, 58–59
teaching, false, 184
teaching authority, 74, 160, 177

teaching domain, 103
teachings of Moses, 69–70, 78
Temple Court, 156
temporary structures, 36, 38, 133
Tent of Meeting, 41, 43, 45, 46, 61, 80, 82–83, 119
Tertullian, 180
thankfulness, 36, 70, 138
thanksgiving, 31, 119, 126, 128, 130–31, 154–55, 172
    festival of, 38, 133
time
    appointed, 108, 157, 172–73
    linear, 173
time God, 90, 104
Timothy, 21, 72, 142, 144
Titus, 72, 144
tomb, empty, 57, 136, 167
Torah, 36, 41, 52–54, 60, 65–66, 69–70, 100, 104, 126, 132–33, 189
Torah constitution, 41
tradition, 2, 6, 8, 43, 60–61, 70–71, 85, 88, 159–60, 163, 166, 176–77, 180–81
    appropriated, 142
    constitutional, 69
    homiletic, 74
traditionalism, 55
tradition of the covenant, 162
Transfiguration, 38, 166–67
Transfiguration verses, 166
Trans-Jordan, 40
transnational, 169
Transubstantiation, 145
    mystical, 178
Trent, 137, 153
tribal federation, 40, 43, 45, 59, 80,

105, 186, 188–89
Triumphal Entry, 156
True Manna, 136, 146, 148, 172, 178
True Tabernacle, 141–42, 156, 173, 177–79
truth, objective, 22–23

U
unbelief, 138, 183
unblemished Pascal lamb, 125, 130
union, 61–62, 170, 181
United Monarchy, 189
unity, 18, 24, 28, 34, 39, 43–44, 49, 74, 78, 149, 153–54, 174, 183
Universalism, 24
Upper Room, 136, 163, 167, 169, 172, 175

V
Vatican, 24
Vaughn, Ellen, 10, 185
Very Truly, 146–47
virgin Eve, 107, 183
Virgin Mary, 107–8, 110, 119, 122, 164, 183
Virgin's obedience, 107
Vizier, 52, 58, 60

W
Way of the Cross, 167
wedding, 110, 118, 146
Wilderness Tabernacle, 48, 70, 100, 134, 141, 174

Z
Zadok, 99–100
zeal, 6, 18, 27–28, 170, 180

zekenim, 55, 61, 67, 69, 80
Zwingli, 11, 18, 74
Zwinglians, 150

Made in the USA
Monee, IL
13 September 2021

77962599R00134